SAYINGS OF THE FATHERS

PIRKE ABOTH

פרקי אבות

The Ethics of the Talmud:

SAYINGS OF THE FATHERS

EDITED WITH INTRODUCTION, TRANSLATION AND COMMENTARY

BY R. TRAVERS HERFORD

PREFACE BY JOHN J. TEPFER

Schocken Books   NEW YORK

15 14 13 12 11   82 83

This edition, originally published under the auspices
of the Alexander Kohut Memorial Foundation, is re-
printed by arrangement with Hebrew Union College/
Jewish Institute of Religion

Library of Congress Catalog Card No. 62-13138

Manufactured in the United States of America

ISBN 0–8052–0023–1

על ישראל ועל רבנן ועל תלמידיהון ועל כל תלמידי תלמידיהון ועל כל מן
די עסקין באורייתא די באתרא הדן ודי בכל אתר ואתר יהא להון ולכון שלמא
רבא חנא וחסדא ורחמין וחיין אריכין ומזונא רויחא ופרקנא מן קדם אבוהון
די בשמיא ואמרו אמן:

(קדיש דרבנן.)

Upon Israel and upon the Rabbis, and upon their disciples and
upon all the disciples of their disciples, and upon all who engage
in the study of the Torah in this place and in every place, unto
them and unto you be abundant peace, grace, lovingkindness,
mercy, long life, ample sustenance and salvation, from their Father
who is in Heaven. And say ye Amen.

(Kaddish de Rabbanan.)

PREFACE BY JOHN J. TEPFER

Travers Herford's edition of Pirke Aboth, with his commentary, has been in continuous demand since its first publication in 1925. The third and last edition of 1945 has gradually disappeared from the market, and a new edition is called for to satisfy the needs of an ever growing number of readers.

This work of Herford's is especially noted for its systematic treatment, lucid exposition, and historical notes, making it a veritable godsend for the teacher introducing the student to Rabbinic literature and ethics. Through its portals the general reader as well will find himself pleasantly conveyed to the Jewish world of thought and consciousness. Although there have appeared in the past a number of other English works dealing with this tractate, to mention only Taylor's *Sayings of the Fathers* and Oesterley's article in Charles' *Apocrypha,* none have been as successful in catching the spirit of Jewish piety. Herford seems to have constantly borne in mind the fact that Pirke Aboth came to be prized by the synagogue as a source of religious and moral instruction, and that it was actually incorporated into the liturgy. His commentary, then, is not merely a work of scholarship examining the text philologically and historically from the outside. He was able to penetrate its spirit and analyze the contents from within, a remarkable feat for a non-Jewish scholar. Indeed, no Jewish scholar could have written the commentary with deeper understanding or sympathy.

Over the centuries the many-tomed Talmud, and kindred products of the early Rabbinic mind such as the Midrash, have been subjected to keen scrutiny by numerous learned Christians, mainly, however, with an eye to their value for Christian faith and dogma. The aims of these men being largely apologetic, they drew invidious comparisons between the two faiths, pointing up what they considered to be the absurdities of Rabbinic law and lore, and demonstrating the superior spiritual worth of the authoritative writings of the Church. Within the tradition-bound prejudices of these scholars, a purely impartial examination of Rabbinic thought and expression was hardly to be expected. It was truly a distinctive and courageous achievement on the part of certain outstanding scholars of the 19th century—Strack in Germany, Renan in France, Taylor, Danby and

Herford in England—that they were able to break through this mist to
the clearer light of critical but genuine scholarship and impartial ap-
praisal. It was Herford's purpose, as he stated in his preface to the first
edition, "to give to Jewish readers an English edition of Aboth in which
they will not be met by frequent comparisons with Christian ideas and
Christian doctrines, especially when the comparison is not meant to be
favourable to the Jewish side. Christianity has its own ground and its own
significance, both for Christians and for the world at large. But a
reference to Christianity is not necessary for the understanding of Aboth,
or for any other work of Jewish teachers."

Never was the emphasis on the purely pious aspects of Rabbinic
literature, even if slightly exaggerated in Herford's work, more needed in
order to counteract the oft-repeated charges of legalism hurled against it.
Without actually arriving at the surer insight—that even the so-called
legalisms of the Talmud reflect the spirit of man at its finest—these
scholars, and Herford most signally, drew attention to the multifarious
strata of Rabbinic literature which treat purely of the moral and spiritual
in terms as lofty as those found anywhere. This explains Herford's particular interest in that classic of ethical thought, the Chapters or Sayings of
the Fathers.

But this was not his sole interest. Like other non-Jewish scholars in
this field, Herford took up the study of Rabbinics as an inquiry into
Christian origins. The patent fact was borne in on the scholars of the
19th century that the life, activity, and teachings of the founder of
Christianity and of the Church itself, with its doctrines and practices, cannot be fully understood without a thorough knowledge of the society and
culture from which both Jesus and the Church arose. Moreover, they were
forced to recognize that this society and culture were Jewish, and lay
enshrined within the Talmud and the various books of the Midrash. In
writing their monumental commentary on New Testament thought,
Strack and Billerbeck marshalled all the parallels to New Testament
thought, expression, and style which they could find in this literature—
and their number was legion. Herford followed in their path with works
like *Christianity in Talmud and Midrash,* and like *The Pharisees,* described
by that great Cambridge scholar, Israel Abrahams, as "this brilliant and
successful attempt to do justice both to Jesus and the Pharisees." Between
the years 1903 and 1925, when he delivered to the students of the Jewish
Institute of Religion the lectures on Pirke Aboth which form the basis
of the work now reissued, a stream of articles, scholarly studies and
lectures flowed forth, fructifying the halls of learning and gradually

breaking down the prejudices of both the learned and cultured laity. In 1928 another important volume of a more popular nature appeared, *Judaism in the New Testament Period,* published for the General Assembly of Unitarian and Free Christian Churches. Herford continued to contribute to periodicals and encyclopedias almost to his death at the ripe age of ninety.

As this work is being reissued just after the 100th anniversary of Herford's birth in 1860, a few further details of his life would be a deserved tribute to his memory.

He came from a long line of Lancastrian gentry and yeomen, some of whom in the century immediately preceding his birth had turned to the Dissenting ministry. Taking up Semitics at an early age, he attended the Universities of London and Leyden where he worked under the Dutch scholar Kuenen in Old Testament studies. In 1885 he began a successful ministry of nearly thirty years at Stand Unitarian Chapel in Manchester. During the years of his ministry he published many works, among them, *Prophecies of the Captivity* (1890), in which he opposed Kuenen and argued for the historicity of "The Great Synagogue" and the Ezra tradition.

In 1886 Herford's first effort in Talmudics appeared in an article on "The Jerusalem Talmud" contributed to *The Christian Reformer.* From 1914 to 1925 he lived in London, having been appointed to the charge of Dr. Williams' Library, a noted center of theological research. In addition he was Honorary Professor of Semitics at the Presbyterian College in Wales, and remained active in the Unitarian ministry, preaching regularly from Unitarian pulpits and serving as a member of the General Assembly of Unitarian and Free Christian Churches. He was a public-spirited citizen and a figure in his church, and many are the institutions which are proud to honor the names of the Herfords, man and wife, as their founders or benefactors.

It will be mainly to his dedication to Jewish learning that Travers Herford will owe his lasting fame, and the reissuing of his Pirke Aboth will help perpetuate the memory of a fine scholar and gentleman.

January 1962

CONTENTS.

ABBREVIATIONS

(not including titles of books of the Bible or tractates of the Talmud).

A. d. T.	Bacher, Agada der Tannaiten.
A. R. N.	Aboth di Rabbi Nathan; (A). (B) two recensions edited by Schechter.
Antiq.	Josephus, Antiquities.
Bell. Jud.	— Bellum Judaicum. (Wars).
Caph. w. Pher.	Parḥi Estori, Caphtor wa-Pheraḥ.
Cod. Mon.	Codex Monacensis. The Munich MS. of the Talmud.
D. ha. M.	Frankel, Darkē ha-Mishnah.
Dik. Soph.	Rabbinowicz. Dikduke Sopherim.
Dor, dor.	Weiss, Dor, dor vedoreshau.
Ent. Jud.	Eisenmenger, Entdecktes Judentum.
Gesch. d. V. I.	Geschichte des Volkes Israel.
Gesch. d. J.	Geschichte der Juden.
Hor. Heb.	Schoettgen, Horæ Hebraicæ.
J. Q. R.	Jewish Quarterly Review.
J. Enc.	Jewish Encyclopedia.
N. T.	New Testament.
R. E. J.	Révue des Études Juives.
Tac. Hist.	Tacitus, Histories.
Tanḥ.	Tanḥuma.
Tos.	Tosaphoth.
b.	after a personal name, denotes 'ben', son of.
b.	before title of tractate, denotes Babylonian Talmud.
j.	before title of tractate, denotes Jerusalem Talmud.
M.	before title of tractate, denotes Mishnah.
R.	before personal name, denotes Rabbi.
R.	after title of Biblical book, denotes Rabbah (i. e. Midrash Rabbah).
T.	before title of tractate, denotes Tosephta.

INTRODUCTION

The short tractate of the Mishnah known as Aboth, or Pirke Aboth, holds a unique place in Jewish literature, and possesses an importance out of all proportion to its size. It has never been a rival of the Talmud, of which indeed, as a portion of the Mishnah, it forms a part; but it has from the first exerted an influence distinct from that of the whole Talmud. It is not, like the Talmud, intended to develop the Halachah, the rule of right conduct by which the life and action of the Jew were to be regulated. Neither is it specifically a devotional work, although for many centuries it has been incorporated in the Liturgy. Whatever may have been the intention with which Aboth was compiled (a question which will be discussed below), that intention was fulfilled by collecting together a number of sayings, some by named teachers, others anonymous, with no strict adherence, as it would seem, to any one method or any single point of view, and then leaving them to make their own impression. That impression, upon Jewish readers, has been very deep and lasting, as is shown by the number of commentaries and editions of Aboth which have been published from time to time, and which still continue to appear. Aboth takes rank as a classic in Jewish literature, yet it has never been regarded by Jews as mere literature, as if its readers had no personal concern with what it said, and were only pleased with the manner of saying it. Aboth speaks to the heart of the Jew in a manner and with a force seldom realized by non-Jewish readers, and attempts to expound its teaching and significance fail insofar as that fact is not understood. The commentary, which accompanies the translation here offered to the reader, will show whether the present attempt to expound the teaching of Aboth is a failure or not. If it is, that failure will not be due to a want of sympathy on the part of the writer with those whose words are enshrined in Aboth, nor with those who through the centuries have pondered over and loved its pages. It will be due to the fact that the present writer is not himself a Jew, and may perhaps be deaf to melodies which sing divinely in a Jewish ear.

In this Introduction some points will be noted and discussed which are of importance for the right understanding of the true nature of the book; and, more especially, a new view of the intention and significance of Aboth will be offered in place of the explanation given in the second edition. It is, of course, incorrect to apply the word "book" to such a compilation as Aboth, just as it is incorrect to apply the word "book" to the Mishnah or the Talmud, or, for that matter, to the Bible. It is only used for convenience to denote such-and-such a collection of written or printed matter grouped together for some specific purpose. In the case of Aboth, the varied contents were, no doubt, arranged by some one editor or compiler in the order in which they are now read; but they are not the work of any one author producing them all from his own mind. The original Aboth was, in form, a constituent part of the Mishnah, along with all the other sixty-two tractates; and the Mishnah in its turn was not the work of any one author. It represents the classification of the traditional Halachic material as it recommended itself to the discriminating judgment of the final editor, Judah the Holy, usually known as Rabbi. In what he did, he made use of the experience and completed the labours of Akiba and Meir, and more or less of all the Tannaim. The date of the completion of the Mishnah by Rabbi cannot be exactly determined; but it was approximately about the end of the second century of the Common Era. The question of the origin and date of Aboth is therefore, in some respects, only one part of the larger question of the origin and date of the Mishnah, with no independent significance; and the answer to the larger question, so far as the very scanty evidence supplies an answer, can be found in the books which deal with the history of the life and work of the religious teachers of Israel during the first two centuries.

But for Aboth such a reference is by no means sufficient. Not only because, in the history books, there is not, so far as I know, any treatment of the origin and date of Aboth apart from the rest of the Mishnah, but because Aboth demands such separate treatment by reason of its own peculiar character which marks it off from all other products of the Jewish mind. It is the main purpose of this Introduction to describe and make clear the peculiar character of Aboth, in a series of discussions of particular points. I only remark, before proceeding to these discussions, that there is no need to spend much time upon the manuscript authority for the text of Aboth. The MSS which contain it usually contain much else as well, either the whole Talmud, as in the case of the Munich MS, or else the Mishnah, or else the Liturgy. Moreover, the critical work in regard to the text has been done once for all by Taylor, in his "Sayings of the Jewish Fathers," to which the reader who wishes to pursue this line of study is referred. For the present edition (as for the previous ones) the Munich MS, in Strack's facsimile edition, has been collated, and its readings are given in the critical notes. I proceed now to the discussion of several questions which are of importance in bringing out the peculiar character of Aboth. I shall deal first with the title, which deserves much more attention than has usually been given to it; then I shall give an analysis of the contents of the book. Next, on the basis of this survey, I shall discuss the question of the significance of the work and the intention of Rabbi in introducing this collection of sayings into the structure of the Mishnah. I shall withdraw the partial explanation put forward in the previous editions, and replace it by a new answer to the questions raised, on the basis of my subsequent studies of Aboth. Then I shall describe the use which has been made of Aboth, and finally estimate its significance as a document of Pharisaism.

A. The title of the tractate.

The portion of the Mishnah under present consideration was originally entitled Aboth. That was the name which was used by those who had occasion to refer to it or to quote some passage of its contents. It is quite incorrect to say with Oesterley (p. ix of his edition) that Aboth is a shortened form of Pirke Aboth. Each of the tractates of the Mishnah had its own distinctive name, as Berachoth, Joma, Gittin &c. Aboth was just one of these distinctive names, and although the name means "Fathers," it is primarily the title of the tractate, and does not specify any particular persons as being the "fathers" referred to. In a similar way a reference to a passage in "Judges" would at once be understood to refer to the Biblical book so called, and not immediately to the persons whose history formed the subject matter of the book.

Now if it were desired to set apart some tractate of the Mishnah by itself, e. g. for detailed commentary and exposition, the natural way to do so would be to separate the several chapters of the tractate and present them as an independent group. Each chapter of any tractate was called a "perek," and the group of perakim forming a tractate was known as the "chapters" of that tractate, in the present instance "chapters of Aboth," i.e. Pirke Aboth. Pirke does not refer to the sayings of the individual teachers contained in the book, even supposing that they were the Fathers designated in the title. It only denotes the five chapters, afterwards enlarged to six, which together make up the tractate. The frequent rendering of "Pirke Aboth" by "Sayings of the Fathers" is quite incorrect; while "Ethics of the Fathers" is not a translation at all and gives a wrong impression of the intention of the work.

Aboth then was the title originally given, or the earliest given, to this particular portion of the Mishnah. Whether the several tractates had each its own title when the Mishnah was finished, it is impossible to say. No such title appears in the actual text of any tractate, and it would seem natural to suppose that the titles were given only from time to time as the Mishnah was made the subject of detailed study by the teachers who came after the Tannaim. In the case of Aboth, the title must have come into use not very long after the Mishnah was completed; for there is at least one reference to Aboth in the Gemara, the detailed commentary on the Mishnah elaborated in the schools of Babylonia and Palestine. In B. Kam. 30^a is found the often quoted statement:

אמר ר' יהודה מאן דבעי למהוי חסידא לקיים מילי דנזיקין רבא אמר מילי דאבות:

R. Jehudah said, "He who would become a saint (pious) should fulfill the words of 'Nezikin;'" Raba said, "The words of Aboth." Nezikin* is the name of that one of the six main divisions of the Mishnah which contains the tractate Aboth. No doubt the reference, both by R. Jehudah and Raba is to the same collection of "words," though R. Jehudah (d. 299 C. E.) used only the wider designation presumably because the title Aboth had not come into general use, as it would seem to have done by the time of Raba (d. 352 C.E.).

The name Aboth was thenceforth in constant and regular use as the name by which this tractate of the Mishnah was referred to. Bahja (circa 1050) and Maimonides (1135-1204) may be cited as writers who used the term Aboth. They might well be expected to have known, and perhaps to have used, the title Pirke Aboth, if it had been current in their time. It occurs, however, in the Mahzor Vitry (circa 1100). So far as I know, the first instance in print of the title Pirke Aboth occurs in a Christian not a Jewish work. The treatise De Arcanis Catholicae Veritatis, by Petrus Galatinus, was published (according to the preface) in 1516. Now Galatinus, as is well known, plagiarised a great deal of what he published as his own from the Pugio Fidei of Raymund Martini (circa 1278) which was still only in manuscript. The plagiarism was exposed when the Pugio Fidei was edited and published by De Voisin in 1651. From this edition it is clear that Raymund himself used the title "Pirke Aboth." On page 297 of this edition he states that certain matters are related "in Tract. Talmudico qui dicitur Pirke

---

* Nezikin is more strictly the collective title for the first three tractates of the fourth Seder, or main division; and presumably the Seder was called Nezikin because it led off with this group of tractates. But the reference to מילי דנזיקין must surely be to the Seder as a whole, as including the one specially ethical tractate, rather than to the Threefold tractate which is purely juridical and in no way calculated to promote "Hasiduth". In b Taan. 24ab (see below p. 9) "Nezikin" clearly denotes the Seder as distinguished from the threefold tractate.

Aboth." Raymund evidently knew the title from previous usage, and
he must have found it in one or other of his Jewish authors. The need
of a particular title, whether Aboth or Pirke Aboth, would be felt especially when there was occasion to treat the book apart from the Mishnah,
as was the case when Christian writers took notice of it, being attracted
by its contents, so different from the mainly halachic tractates composing the rest of the Mishnah. Galatinus then was the writer responsible
for the first appearance in print of the title Pirke Aboth, and at the
same time he introduced what has been generally accepted as its Latin
equivalent. In the *De Arcanis* (edition of 1612, col. 5) he says, speaking of the succession of teachers who carried on the tradition, "ordo
hactenus deductus ex patrum capitulis פרקי אבות nuncupatis elicitus est."
"Capitula patrum" is clearly incorrect; the title ought to have been
"Capitula Patres" (nuncupata), that is, "the chapters of (the tractate
which is entitled) Fathers." The form Capitula Patrum, however, became the regular Latin name in use among scholars. Thus Paul Fagius
included in his book published in 1541, "Sententiae vere eleganter . . .
utiles, veterum Sapientum Hebraeorum, quas פרקי אבות id est Capitula
Patrum nominant, in latinam versae &c." The two titles Aboth and
Pirke Aboth occur in printed books for a considerable time after the
first appearance of the longer form in the work of Galatinus. Thus, in
the preface to the *Midrash Shemuel,* 1579, the tractate is called Massecheth Aboth. A later edition has Pirke Aboth on the title page but
Aboth in the preface. The *Jüdische Theriack* of Salman Zebi, 1615
(quoted by Eisenmenger, Ent. Jud. I. 231) has Pirke Aboth. It was,
however, chiefly Christian scholars who popularized the name Pirke
Aboth. Leusden and Buxtorf both have it. The latter says *De Opere
Talmudico,* p. 254, "Aboth . . . vulgo vocatur Pirke Aboth." From
that time the longer form is well established and more frequently used.

B. Analysis of the contents of Aboth.

The tractate as Rabbi left it contains five chapters (perakim) being
the same which are still read there. The sixth chapter, which is usually
added, was compiled after the closing of the Talmud, and forms no
part of the original Aboth. It is included in the present edition in
accordance with long usage in order that the reader may have all the
"Aboth" to which he has been accustomed.

The whole of Ch. I is taken up with the succession of those who
handed down the Tradition, beginning with the giving of the Torah
to Moses on Sinai and coming down to the fall of Jerusalem. The
earlier stages are merely named,—Moses, Joshua, the Elders, the

Prophets—because they were so to speak the common property of all Israel, acknowledged by Sadducees no less than by Pharisees. The more detailed development begins with the men of the Great Synagogue, meaning Ezra and the early Sopherim. These were the real spiritual ancestors of the Pharisees and therefore presumably designated "Fathers," Aboth, in the title. By their handing on of the tradition, especially as the embodiment of the Unwritten Torah, they guaranteed the validity of that tradition. From the time of Simeon the Just, who is said to have been one of the last members of the Great Synagogue, down to the time of Hillel the names are given of successive eminent teachers, first two singly then ten in pairs, ending with Hillel and Shammai. After Hillel are mentioned Gamliel his grandson, a certain Simeon whose identity is disputed, and Simeon ben Gamliel, son of the Gamliel just mentioned. This is the Simeon who was a leader in Jerusalem during the siege, and the conclusion lies ready to hand that the list of names in this chapter was intended to trace the transmission of the Tradition from Moses down to the fall of Jerusalem without interruption.

While the form of this chapter is that of a list of teachers, the substance of it is made up of a number of ethical maxims or sentences, of which one or more is attributed to each teacher mentioned by name. The continuity of the chapter is not in the sayings but in the succession of those who uttered them.

Ch. II begins with Rabbi and his son (vv. 1-4) but in v. 5 goes back to Hillel. The greater part of the chapter, however, vv. 5-19, is concerned with one group of teachers, of whom the central figure is R. Johanan b. Zaccai. The intention would seem to be to connect the great Rabbi, who rescued the spiritual treasure of Israel after the fall of Jerusalem, with the line of the earlier teachers, and thus to continue the valid tradition past the great dislocation caused by the loss of Jerusalem and the dispersal of the teachers. It is therefore shown how Johanan b. Zaccai "received from" Hillel and Shammai, and how in his turn he raised up disciples. The passage, vv. 5-19, is, as it were, a historical note accounting for the place of Johanan b. Zaccai in the succession of teachers, and for the importance of what he did; and while in its present form it is clearly discontinuous with Ch. I it may have been intended to supplement that chapter, by some one who knew that there had been some opposition to Johanan b. Zaccai when he was establishing his authority in the assembly at Jabneh, after the siege. The sayings of Rabbi and his son (vv. 1-4) have no relation to the historical passage, and were presumably editorial additions, the former possibly the latter certainly, after the completion of the Mishnah. The sayings of R. Tarphon (vv. 20, 21) have no relation to the preceding passage, and may have been added merely to round off the chapter. For further discussion see the commentary.

Ch. III and Ch. IV contain maxims of various characters ascribed to one or other of some forty named teachers. There is no attempt at chronological sequence, nor is any obvious rule followed in the choice of the teachers to be included. They are arranged in what I should now call studied disorder.

Ch. V contains for the most part not the maxims of named teachers but reflexions of an ethical character, arranged on a numerical basis, probably for convenience as a help to memory. The remainder of the chapter (vv. 19-26) contains miscellaneous sayings which might apparently have found a place anywhere else in the book, some being added in order to make a fitting conclusion to it.

It will be seen from the above analysis of the contents of Aboth that the division into five chapters is a purely artificial arrangement, not corresponding to or required by anything in the text. If the tractate had been read as a continuous whole there would have been nothing to mark the omission of the separation into chapters. It is quite possible, and indeed seems to me probable, that originally Aboth was so read, and that the division into chapters was only made when that which now forms the sixth chapter was added for liturgical purposes (see below p. 13). If this suggestion be adopted, it becomes somewhat easier to understand the relation of Aboth to the Mishnah. It is now seen to be a unity not a patchwork; the contents are a collection made for some purpose (whatever that purpose may have been), and the arrangement of the several items collected depended on the judgment of the collector, not on the relation of one item to the next, before or after it. Except for the chronological sequence in Ch. I and Ch. II, 5-19, all the rest of the contents of Aboth might have been arranged in any order, with no injury to the effect of the whole. If I am right, then Rabbi the compiler or editor of the Mishnah, dealt with Aboth as a single work, having a unique character of its own, sufficient to distinguish it not only from the Mishnah but from all other Jewish works of religious importance. There is nothing to prevent the supposition that Rabbi himself collected together the several items which make up Aboth; and, until the contrary be shown, I shall assume that he did, and so added to the grounds of his fame the merit of having bestowed on Israel the special benefits which Aboth has brought. More will be said on this below p. 10).

C. The purpose and significance of Aboth.

After what has been said it will be possible to gain some further light upon Rabbi's intention in giving Aboth the place in the Mishnah which it has held from the beginning. There is no occasion to disintegrate it into several documents afterwards pieced together, least of all to adopt the suggestion of Neubauer (Med Jew. Chron. preface, p. 6) that all the ethical matter should be stripped off in order to reach the real core in the chronological matter of the first two chapters. Rabbi dealt with it as a whole, and perhaps himself compiled and arranged it, so as to give it a peculiar character of its own. It at once suggests comparison with the biblical books of Proverbs and Koheleth, and with the extra-biblical book of Ben Sira, all three of which were purely ethical in their contents. Yet the maxims contained in the books named were for the most part anonymous, while in Aboth the names of those who uttered the various sayings are given in all but a few cases. No other Jewish work within the knowledge of Rabbi was at all like Aboth in this respect. Moreover, although the Mishnah was entirely made up of Halachah and Haggadah, the former in greater abundance, there is neither Halachah nor Haggadah in Aboth, and therefore no apparent justification for combining Aboth and Mishnah together, as in fact Rabbi did combine them.

Before going on to what I hold to be the true explanation of this surprising fact, it may be well to dispose of two criticisms of Aboth which are sometimes made. It is evident that Aboth makes no claim to be a systematic ethical treatise, and such a claim could not be made good if it were advanced. "Ethical" it certainly is, but "systematic" is far from truly describing its contents. It is therefore unfair to judge Aboth by the standard of a systematic treatise of ethics, and then to disparage it because it does not conform to that standard. The time for a systematic treatment of ethics was far distant in the days of Rabbi, and he was not thinking of any such thing.

So too, if Aboth is not an ethical treatise and ought not to be judged as such, still less is it a devotional treatise, or even to any great extent, devotional at all. There is no devotional literature of the talmudic period, except (and it is a very important exception) what is imbedded in the liturgy. The private prayers of the pious "Hasid" were not written down, or, if they were, have not been preserved. It is therefore unfair, and a sign of mere ignorance, to say that Aboth is a witness to prove the spiritual poverty and devotional aridity produced by the halachic discipline. Rabbi did not set out to make a devotional book at all, or a book of theology, let alone systematic theology. He had in mind a wholly different purpose, and the contents of Aboth which he gathered together and arranged, were admirably suited to his real purpose.

To the explanation of what I believe to have been that purpose I now proceed. A suggestive hint as to what that purpose was is supplied by the consideration of the place which Aboth occupies in the text of the Mishnah, viz: at the end, or almost at the end, of Seder Nezikin, the fourth main division of the Mishnah. Commentators have sought to trace some connexion between the contents of Aboth and those of the adjacent tractates, and they have not altogether failed. But if Aboth had been placed anywhere else in the Mishnah it would have been no less possible to trace some plausible connexion with neighboring tractates than in the present arrangement. I do not think that Aboth was placed where it is now found on the ground of any suitability of its subject matter. As noted above, it is placed at the end, or nearly at the end, of Seder Nezikin. Now it is a remarkable fact that in the editions of the Talmud the group of post-Talmudic tractates, *Massich-toth Qetannoth.* is always printed after Nezikin, instead of following on after the end of the sixth and last Seder. It is hard to see why this should be done unless it were thought that the end of Nezikin had been, at some time and for some purpose, the terminus of the Mishnah, so far as ordinary study was concerned. That this was actually the case is shown by a remark in the Talmud (b. Taan. 24. a.b.) "In the days of R. Jehudah the whole study (of the Mishnah) was confined to Nezikin, whereas we (i.e. Raba and Abaji) extend our study over all the six Sedarim." I do not know why there was this limitation, but of the fact of it there can be doubt. Both Weiss, Dor, dor III. 187, and Bacher, Terminologie II. 240. n. 1, hold that the reference is to the four Sedarim ending with Nezikin, and not to Nezikin alone. If, therefore, the end of Nezikin was regarded as in some way the terminus of the Mishnah, so that the minor tractates should be placed just there, may not Aboth have been placed at the end, or almost the end of Nezikin for the same reason? It is true that the final tractate of Nezikin in the Mishnah is now Horaioth. but the order of the tractates is known to have varied to some extent. Be that as it may, Aboth is sufficiently near to the end of Nezikin for it to be regarded as in some sense the conclusion of the Mishnah. And this I believe to be its true significance.

To define it more precisely, I now hold that Aboth was compiled by Rabbi and placed where it is now found in order to serve as an *Epilogue to the Mishnah,* an elaborate composition whose contents, and even whose form, were deliberately chosen because in various ways they served his purpose. On this view Aboth gains greatly in importance, because, while its contents judged on their own account are no less valuable than before, it is now seen to be structurally and organically a part of the Mishnah, not, as I formerly thought, just the contents of a commonplace book emptied out to form a sort of appendix, such that if it had not been there its absence would never have been noticed. It is a deliberate and grave conclusion to the Mishnah. In a sense, it expresses the judgment of Rabbi upon the great work now brought to completion, his view of the ethical worth and not merely of the halachic value of the *corpus juris* upon which the thought and labour of at least two centuries had been expended. I frankly admit that I cannot prove the truth of what is here suggested. But I hold not only that it is in accordance with the known facts about Aboth, but that it accounts for the peculiar features of the tractate more fully than any other theory. To bring out its meaning I will examine it in detail.

In the first place, it entirely removes the difficulty of explaining why this tractate, containing neither halachah nor haggadah, was made part of a great work containing both halachah and haggadah and nothing besides. It was certainly combined with the Mishnah, but its contents stood, so to speak, on a different footing from the other tractates making up the Mishnah. A dedicatory inscription upon the facade of a great Law Court would not be expressed in terms of the laws administered within.

On the lines of the theory that Aboth is an Epilogue to the Mishnah there is an obvious fitness in beginning it with the present first chapter, which traces the succession of the teachers of Torah from Moses to the fall of Jerusalem. By placing this particular piece in the very beginning of his Epilogue, Rabbi gave it a far greater importance than it would have had if it had stood by itself, a mere detached fragment of historical reminiscence. Presumably, Rabbi himself composed it as being exactly what he wanted for his Epilogue. For, by so treating it, he brought it into the closest connexion with the whole Mishnah and not merely with its adjacent tractates. The declaration that "Moses received Torah from Sinai, &c." was the warrant for the validity of all that was contained in the Mishnah; it was the declaration that all the halachahs, whose authenticity it was the object of the Mishnah to set forth, were organically part of the Torah as given on Sinai. And unless Rabbi had thought fit to place this chapter at the very beginning of the Mishnah, by way of a prologue, there was no better place for it than in the Epilogue of which it should form the opening sentences.

Chapter II follows naturally on Chapter I, especially if, as suggested above, there was originally no division of Aboth into chapters. In that case the mention of Rabbi and his son would be an editorial addition, put where it now stands perhaps when the division into chapters was made. The main purpose of what is now Ch. II is, as explained above (see p. 6) to establish the connexion between the teachers of tradition who came before the fall of Jerusalem and those who came after, so that the unbroken line of succession is shown to extend from Moses to all the teachers whose collective work produced the Mishnah.

The contents of these two chapters, however, are not merely historical records, but consist largely of ethical sayings ascribed one or other of the persons named in the line of tradition. Together with the historical matter, they strike the keynote for all the rest of Aboth by suggesting an ethical anthology fit to be placed as an Epilogue to the whole Mishnah. Looked at from this point of view, the contents and arrangement of what are now the third, fourth and fifth chapters become intelligible in a new way, and are seen to be no mere haphazard jumble of names. The teachers whose names occur in these chapters are some 40 or so in number, out of a total of more than 200 in the whole Mishnah. These 40 include not only men of the first rank but also men whose names are hardly at all mentioned elsewhere. Moreover, the 40 include at least two men who were excommunicated, and one who became an apostate, the notorious Elisha ben Abujah. Rabbi certainly knew what he was about when he included these men.

Not only the names included but the names omitted cause some surprise. Of course, when only 66 for the whole of Aboth are included, there must have been a large number omitted of the 200 or more in the Mishnah. But even Gamliel II of Jabneh, Rabbi's grandfather, was left out, as also was Simeon b. Gamliel, Rabbi's father. Both these men were of outstanding importance in the succession of teachers; and there were others hardly less eminent who were also left out. It is clear that Rabbi did not make his selection on the ground of eminence. Moreover, in the case of those whom he did include, the eminence of the men is not always shown by the amount of the sayings ascribed to them. In two cases, Levitas and Samuel ha-Katan, the sayings attributed to them are not even their own. What is the explanation of this apparently arbitrary selection and arrangement? On the Epilogue theory, the suggestion lies ready to hand that Rabbi intended Aboth to illustrate the fact that the Mishnah was the outcome of the labours of a great number of teachers through two centuries, some of them eminent, some obscure; that their combined work was a great act of service of God, and that all who took part were equal in that service. The apparent want of arrangement, what I have called above "a studied disorder," shows that Rabbi meant to avoid any distinction of eminence or priority in time between those whom he included, and thus his choice of names serves all the better to illustrate the collective as opposed to the individual character of the Mishnah, while no disrespect is implied towards those who names were left out. And perhaps even in the case of Elisha b. Abujah, apostate though he became, there was the remembrance in Rabbi's mind that he had been a notable man in his time, honoured till he fell away, and that even after he had fallen his devoted disciple Meir had clung to him to the last. It may have been a kindly thought on the part of Rabbi to find a place in his Epilogue for that "Other"— Aher. This is a mere speculation, as it is also a mere speculation to find in the inclusion of anonymous sayings in Chapter V the thought of those who in their time had helped to build up the fabric of Judaism and had left no name. They too should be commemorated in the Epilogue in the only way possible. Such appears to be the character and significance of Aboth when regarded as an Epilogue to the Mishnah. The theory cannot, indeed, be proved, for there is no evidence one way or another. It is conceivable that Rabbi may have intended something quite different. But I hold that if Aboth be regarded as an Epilogue to the Mishnah, deliberately planned and carefully constructed, then all its contents fall into place, even its apparent want of arrangement is accounted for, and an intelligible and consistent answer is supplied to all the questions which present themselves to the critical student of Aboth. The theory set forth above leads to a deeper understanding of the real significance of Aboth as one of the ancient and venerable treasures which Israel has carried with him down through the ages.

D. The use made of Aboth.

The concluding sentence of the foregoing section leads to the consideration of the question: What has been the use actually made of Aboth? How did it come to be made the object of special study so as to gain the unique place which it holds in Jewish literature? Aboth is now, and for many centuries has been, included in the Jewish prayerbook, and it is placed there in order to provide matter for edification in connexion with worship. The prayer-book contains, besides prayers and hymns (piyutim), passages from the Talmud for memorial purposes. But no other tractate or complete work of any kind shares with Aboth the distinction of being included in the prayer-book.

The custom of reading it otherwise than in the regular course of study of the Mishnah began at Sura, where it was read or recited on Sabbaths after the Minhah service. This was done at first only in the colleges, but the practice was adopted in the synagogues, and was already established there by the eleventh century of the common era. There was much diversity in the local usage in regard to the time of year at which Aboth was read. The details, so far as they are known, are given in Zunz, *Ritus,* pp. 85-86.

It was probably the liturgical use of Aboth, which led to the compilation of the Perek Rabbi Meir, and its addition to the existing Aboth as a sixth chapter. If it were desired to spread the reading over six Sabbaths, the division of the tractate, thus enlarged, into six chapters would offer the obvious means of doing so. The Perek Rabbi Meir, also known by the title of Perek Kinjan Torah, is found in two other ethical works, and it is not clear in which of them its first appearance was made. It is found in the post-Talmudic tractate Kallah Rabbathi, of which it forms Ch. VIII, and in the Tanna de Be Elijahu Zuṭa, where it appears as Ch. XVII. These two versions agree very closely with each other and with that in Aboth; but they do not contain the passage (Ab. VI. 9) beginning "R. Jose b. Kisma." There is no reference to Perek Rabbi Meir in the Aboth de Rabbi Nathan, nor in the tractate Kallah, of which Kallah Rabbathi is, as it were, the Gemara. A different version of Perek Rabbi Meir was discovered by Margoliouth in a Yemenite MS. (Brit. Mus. Or. 2390), and published by him in the J. Q. R. (old series) XVII., p. 700. Of the origin of this sixth chapter nothing is definitely known. Its form is that of a collection of sentences, somewhat after the manner of the original tractate but with a much greater abundance of proof-texts. Its subject is almost exclusively the praise of Torah, and no doubt this was what guided the compilers in their choice of material.

To the liturgical use of Aboth is also to be ascribed the practice. commonly adopted in the prayer-book, of prefixing to each chapter the words taken from the Mishnah (Sanh. X. 1.), "All Israel have part in the world to come." For the like reason it became usual to add, at the close of each chapter, the saying of R. Hananiah b. Akashja (Mishnah-Macc. III. 16) "The Holy One, blessed be He, was pleased to make

Israel acquire merit." These form no part of Aboth, and are only included in the translation and commentary in order that the reader may have what has long been associated with the reading of the book.

E. Aboth as a document of Pharisaism.

The famous saying already quoted (b. B. Kam. 30ª) "He who would become 'Hasid' should fulfill the words of Aboth" shows that from at least the middle of the fourth century of the common era the special character of Aboth was recognized, as containing the essential teaching of true piety. It was not that there was anything in the theology or ethics implied in the "sayings" which was not to be found elsewhere. On the contrary, the teachers whose words are there recorded were among the men who had built up the Mishnah, and developed the system of Halachah and Haggadah in which the whole mental life of Pharisaic Judaism found expression. It was only because they were already known and revered as teachers that a collection of their sayings became interesting and important. It would therefore be a waste of time to set forth the theology and ethics of Aboth as if these differed in any way from those of Pharisaism in general. But it will not be useless to remind the reader of what constituted the real essence of Pharisaism, because that is the fundamental thought upon which everything in Aboth really rests, the centre round which it all turns. The real significance of Aboth, the probable reason why it was recommended for special study in the remark quoted above, was that it did contain this essential principle, not indeed unfolded in detail but illuminated by personal utterances of men who had founded their lives upon it.

The central conception of Pharisaism* is Torah, the divine Teaching, the full and inexhaustible revelation which God had made. The knowledge of what was revealed was to be sought, and would be found, in the first instance in the written text of the Pentateuch; but the revelation, the real Torah, was the meaning of what was there written, the meaning as interpreted by all the recognized and accepted methods of the schools, and unfolded in ever greater fullness of detail by successive generations of devoted teachers. The written text of the Pentateuch might be compared to the mouth of a well; the Torah was the water which was drawn from it. He who wished to draw the water must needs go to the well, but there was no limit to the water which was there for him to draw. The Talmud and the Midrash represent the Torah as it was interpreted, its contents made known, its teaching made

---

* For a full exposition of the Pharisaic theory see my "The Pharisees," 1924, and "Talmud and Apocrypha," 1933.

explicit instead of implicit. In terms of the figure just used, the Torah as set forth in the Talmud and the Midrash was the body of water which had been drawn from the well up to the time defined by that literature. In volume it exceeds enormously the actual capacity of the well, but the well nevertheless being ever replenished was the source from which it had all been drawn. If there had been no well there would have been no water.

The study of Torah—Talmud Torah, as the Pharisees called it—means therefore much more than the study of the Pentateuch, or even of the whole of Scripture, regarded as mere literature, written documents. It means the study of the revelation made through those documents, the divine teaching therein imparted, the divine thought therein disclosed. Apart from the direct intercourse of prayer, the study of Torah was the way of closest approach to God; it might be called the Pharisaic form of the Beatific Vision. To study Torah was, to the devout Pharisee, to "think God's thoughts after him," as Kepler said. The student might be dull or indolent, might let his study become a mere perfunctory routine, might in various ways fall short of his ideal; but none the less, the Torah which he studied was the divine revelation set open before him.

Now Aboth is full of this thought of Torah and the study of it, and Aboth is wholly misunderstood unless this conception of Torah be constantly kept in mind. Non-Jewish readers seldom have the least comprehension of this, and in consequence they point out that Aboth rarely refers directly to God. This is true but it is beside the mark. Wherever Torah is mentioned, there God is implied. He is behind the Torah, the Revealer of what is revealed. It was the deep consciousness of this which found utterance in that passionate devotion to Torah which marks the Talmud in general and Aboth in particular. This is the explanation of the undying hold which Aboth has had upon Jewish minds, and of the immense influence it has exerted in all ages since it first appeared. Even Jewish readers may possibly find help in this reminder of the inner meaning of Aboth. They at least will know that the men whose words they read there were both saints and sages, men deeply in earnest in their service of God, and intent to learn whatever he vouchsafed to teach; men who sought him in the way which he had appointed for them, and found him because they "sought him with their whole heart." Aboth is the monument of these men, and it is a noble one; but on it is inscribed "Not unto us, not unto us, but unto the Lord give glory."

HEBREW TEXT

OF

PIRKE ABOTH

WITH TRANSLATION
AND COMMENTARY

כָּל־יִשְׂרָאֵל יֵשׁ לָהֶם חֵלֶק לְעוֹלָם הַבָּא שֶׁנֶּאֱמַר וְעַמֵּךְ כֻּלָּם צַדִּיקִים לְעוֹלָב
יִירְשׁוּ אָרֶץ נֵצֶר מַטָּעַי מַעֲשֵׂה יָדַי לְהִתְפָּאֵר׃

M. SANHEDRIN. X. 1.

All Israel have part in the world to come, as it is said 'and thy people shall be all righteous; they shall inherit the land for ever, the branch of my planting, the work of my hands that I may be glorified'. (Isa. LX. 21.)

פרק ראשון

١. מֹשֶׁה קִבֵּל תּוֹרָה מִסִּינַי וּמְסָרָהּ לִיהוֹשֻׁעַ וִיהוֹשֻׁעַ לִזְקֵנִים וּזְקֵנִים לִנְבִיאִים וּנְבִיאִים מְסָרוּהָ לְאַנְשֵׁי כְנֶסֶת הַגְּדוֹלָה׃ הֵם אָמְרוּ שְׁלֹשָׁה דְבָרִים הֱווּ מְתוּנִים בַּדִּין וְהַעֲמִידוּ תַלְמִידִים הַרְבֵּה וַעֲשׂוּ סְיָג לַתּוֹרָה׃

THE TRACTATE 'FATHERS'.
CHAP. I.

1. Moses received Torah from Sinai and delivered it to Joshua, and Joshua to the Elders, and the Elders to the Prophets, and the Prophets delivered it to the Men of the Great Synagogue. These said three things; Be deliberate in judging, and raise up many disciples, and make a hedge for the Torah.

COMMENTARY.

1. It is a fundamental axiom of Rabbinical Judaism that the tradition, of which the subject matter was the Torah, began with Moses to whom it was committed on Sinai. The compiler of Aboth, however, had no need to dwell upon the earlier stages in the history of the tradition, where in a sense all was common ground. The Elders and the Prophets belonged to all Israel. But the Great Synagogue, as that term was used in the Rabbinical literature, marked the beginning of a new development; for it was historically the ancestor of Pharisaism, and the Pharisees could not claim the undivided support of their nation. The real interest of the com-

piler would be to trace the succession of the teachers in the Pharisaic line, and he indicated the special importance of this line by citing ethical or religious maxims attributed to the teachers whom he named, beginning with the Men of the Great Synagogue. These teachers, down to Hillel or possibly Johanan ben Zaccai, may be supposed to be the persons referred to in the name Aboth; these are preeminently the 'Fathers' of the tradition.

The Great Synagogue, for historical purposes, may be taken to represent those who followed the lead of Ezra in developing the religion of Torah. The idea of an assembly is based on the statement in Neh. IX and X, as was long ago shown by Kuenen. The evidence is not sufficient to afford a definite answer to the question of the constitution or even the existence of a specific body called the Great Synagogue. But it is reasonable to suppose that there must have been some kind of teaching body, whose authority would be exercised on the lines of the school of Ezra and would be accepted by members of that school. The Sanhedrin, if by that term be understood the council which exercised supreme political authority, would in no way suffice for such a purpose. It was not a teaching body, and was during most of its existence by no means in sympathy with Pharisaic ideas. The Zūgoth, or Pairs of teachers who are named in this first chapter of Aboth, and who are elsewhere (M. Ḥag. II. 2) said to have held the offices respectively of *Nasi* and *Ab Beth Din* of the Sanhedrin, certainly did not hold these offices in the political Sanhedrin; but it is not impossible that they may have held the presidency in some assembly constituted on Pharisaic lines.

The chronology of the period is very obscure. The date of Ezra is 444 B. C. or thereabouts. Simeon the Just is one of two men of whom the older was High Priest from B. C. 310 to 291 (or 300—270), and the younger (grandson of the elder) was High Priest from B. C. 219 to 199. Josephus mentions both, Antiqq. XII. 2. 5 and XII. 4. 10; but he only applies the epithet "the Just" in connexion with the older Simeon. The High Priest in Ecclus. ch. L is probably the younger Simeon, and it is significant that he is not called "The Just". If then the elder Simeon be the one referred to as being of the remnants of the Great Synagogue, there is an interval of 110 years between his death in 270 (taking the later date) and the death of José ben Joezer in B. C. 160. Antigonos of Socho must be placed somewhere within this period, and there is approximately a period of eighty years to be accounted for. The teacher or teachers during those eighty years, if there were any, may have been men of too slight importance for their names to be remembered.

The maxims here ascribed to the Men of the Great Synagogue were intended as it would seem for the guidance of teachers and expounders of the Torah, and the spirit of the sayings passed completely into Rabbinism. Deliberation in judgment originally as here, the judgment of a judge, but later 'argument', is the key to the casuistry of the Talmud, and in the main justifies that casuistry. For deliberation expresses the desire to study a question from every point of view, and to take account of every possible even though improbable contingency. To make disciples, in the sense of imparting knowledge of Torah, has always been both the aim and the practice of Rabbinism, as the Talmud bears ample witness. In the larger relation the minor one of discipleship to a particular teacher held but a small place. The Rabbi was enjoined not to make followers of himself, but to impart to all whom he could influence such knowledge as he possessed of divine truth. To make a hedge for the Torah is a famous phrase, which, like many another Rabbinic saying, has been much misunderstood. It certainly does not imply any intention to make a rigid system of precept, in which all the spiritual freedom enjoyed by the enlightened soul in communion with the divine should be lost. The Rabbis never had that intention, and never supposed that they suffered any such loss. That is an idea which exists only in the minds of Christians, misreading an experience which as Christians they have never known. The Rabbis always intended by 'the hedge for the Torah', and always understood the term to mean, the precaution taken to keep the divine revelation from harm, so that the sacred enclosure, so to speak, might always be free and open for the human to contemplate the divine. So far as the Torah consisted of precepts positive and negative, the 'hedge' consisted of warnings whereby a man was saved before it was too late from transgression.

The Rabbis, following the counsel of the Men of the Great Synagogue, did make a 'hedge' for the Torah, and did their work so well that whatever else was torn from Israel in the course of cruel centuries the Torah remained and still remains the peculiar treasure of the Jewish people.

That these maxims actually originated with the Men of the Great Synagogue, even in the interpretation of that phrase suggested above, cannot be proved. But they are certainly ancient, and the tradition which places them in the earliest stage of the development of Rabbinical Judaism has this in its favour that their logical place is there. Either they date from a time not remote from Ezra, or they express the opinion of some later teacher as to the aims and methods of the early Sopherim. The latter interpretation is possible; but the form in which the maxims are given shows that the Rabbis had no suspicion that they were the utterance of a later teacher. If there had been such a thought, the statement would have taken the form "Rabbi A. said that the Men of the Great Synagogue said, &c". The maxims are clearly regarded as old tradition[1]; the fact that these three and no more are ascribed to the Men of the Great Synagogue indicates, by its very moderation, some reason for so ascribing them. A capricious inventor would have attributed much more to so ancient an authority in order to obtain for his inventions the

---

[1] The saying היו מתונים is found in b. Sanh. 7ᵇ. There it is quoted by Bar Qappara as מלתא דאמרו רבנן. There is no mention of Aboth, nor of the Men of the Great Synagogue.

sanction of high antiquity. There is really nothing impossible in the transmission, even from the time of Ezra, of these bare fragments of ancient teaching. Their contents are in keeping with their presumed origin; and, even if they be a later invention, they accurately define what the teachers of Ezra's time must chiefly have had at heart.

2. שִׁמְעוֹן הַצַּדִּיק הָיָה מִשְׁיָרֵי כְנֶסֶת הַגְּדוֹלָה, הוּא הָיָה אוֹמֵר עַל שְׁלֹשָׁה דְבָרִים הָעוֹלָם עוֹמֵד עַל הַתּוֹרָה וְעַל הָעֲבוֹדָה וְעַל גְּמִילוּת חֲסָדִים:

2. Simeon the Just was of the survivors of the Great Synagogue. He used to say: — Upon three things the world standeth; upon Torah, upon Worship and upon the showing of kindness.

2. Torah signifies divine revelation; either the fact of communion between God and man, or the wisdom so imparted. Though to Israel alone the Torah was given, yet Israel in this was representative of humanity. Intercourse between God and man is fundamental, and without it human life above the merely animal stage would be impossible. The service; this is the service in the temple, regarded as the worship of God in the manner appointed by him. If one special element in the service be intended, that may be the sacrifices, as a symbol of obedience to the divine commands, or the priesthood as the appointed agency for performing the service. Maimonides interprets the word in the former sense, and this lends itself better to generalisation. 'Deeds of kindness', denote unselfish beneficence in the fullest measure, to cover any good that one person can do to another. The 'three things' which are declared to be fundamental in human life are thus found to be Revelation, obedience to God, and brotherly love. It is possible however that the second term 'the service' was intended to symbolise worship as a fundamental in human life, including in its meaning both obedience to divine precepts, and the functions of consecrated ministers. The saying is only true when thus generalised; but it would be hard to say how much of that more general meaning was present to the mind of Simeon when he uttered it.

3. אַנְטִיגְנוֹס אִישׁ סוֹכוֹ קִבֵּל מִשִּׁמְעוֹן הַצַּדִּיק. הוּא הָיָה אוֹמֵר אַל־תִּהְיוּ כַּעֲבָדִים הַמְשַׁמְּשִׁין אֶת־הָרַב עַל מְנָת לְקַבֵּל פְּרָס אֶלָּא הֱווּ כַעֲבָדִים הַמְשַׁמְּשִׁין אֶת־הָרַב שֶׁלֹּא עַל מְנָת לְקַבֵּל פְּרָס וִיהִי מוֹרָא שָׁמַיִם עֲלֵיכֶם:

3. Antigonos of Socho received from Simeon the Just. He used to say: — Be not like servants who serve the master for condition of receiving a gift, but be like servants, who serve the master not on condition of receiving a gift. And let the fear of Heaven be upon you.

3. Man's service of God ought to be disinterested, without thought of gain or advantage to accrue from such service. The word used is explained to mean a gift or present which a man may make to his servant or any one else although he is not obliged to do so. It differs from reward, the payment which one who serves may rightly expect to receive from his master. It is a common-place of Rabbinical teaching that there is a reward for the righteous, and that they may and ought to look forward to it.[1] Not however in this world, but in the world to come. The term 'reward' which is frequently used in this connexion, both in Jewish and Christian writings, does not in either case refer to any thing which can be the object of selfish desire. It refers to the divine approval, God's "well done, good and faithful servant". For that 'reward' a man may well serve God; and such service is rendered for love, and not for gain, nor for the expectation of the fulfilment of any bargain, as if there could be any bargain between God and man. Service of God for love was always the ideal service in the Rabbinical teaching. The dictum of Antigonos does not deal with this service or this reward, it is the austere demand for a service of God without the thought of any gain which could be expressed in terms of .this world. **And let the fear** of Heaven be upon you. This is added in order to remind us that if we serve God from love, we must also serve him from fear. He is the Father in Heaven, but he is also Lord of the worlds, Sovereign and Judge.

Antigonos of Socho. The name is Greek, and may possibly represent some Hebrew name; the teacher himself was of course a Jew, but the period in which he lived, was one in which Hellenism had become strong as an influence in Jewish life and thought. סרם is said to represent the Greek Φόρος, but this is not certain. A Hebrew derivation is possible, yet a Greek word is not unlikely to have been used. The meaning, however derived, is an unconditional gift, to which there can be no claim. In A. d. R. N^A. ch. V. it is said that Antigonos had two disciples, Zadok and Boethos and that these rejected his teaching and lapsed into heresy. What, if any, historical basis underlies this legend has not been ascertained. See Herzfeld, Gesch. d. V. Israel II. 382. 'Fear of Heaven', means the fear of God. Except in

---

[1] For the Pharisaic conception of Reward see my "Pharisees" ch. v. § B.

Biblical quotations the word God is rather avoided in the Rabbinical literature. It is more usual to speak of "the Holy one blessed be He", or "Lord
of the Worlds" (when addressing the Deity), or "King of the Kings of the
Kings", or "The Name", or "The Place", meaning the "All Present". The
term "Our Father who is in Heaven" is well authenticated in Jewish usage, but
does not occur very frequently. It is of Jewish not Christian origin. All these
expressions are found in Aboth.

4. יוֹסֵי בֶּן־יוֹעֶזֶר אִישׁ צְרֵדָה וְיוֹסֵי בֶּן־יוֹחָנָן אִישׁ יְרוּשָׁלַיִם קִבְּלוּ מֵהֶם.
יוֹסֵי בֶּן־יוֹעֶזֶר אִישׁ צְרֵדָה אוֹמֵר יְהִי בֵיתְךָ בֵּית וַעַד לַחֲכָמִים וֶהֱוֵי
מִתְאַבֵּק בַּעֲפַר רַגְלֵיהֶם וֶהֱוֵי שׁוֹתֶה בַצָּמָא אֶת־דִּבְרֵיהֶם:

4. מהם. A.B.C.D.M. ממנו S.; ושותה. M. ויהוי שותה.

4. Josē ben Joēzer, of Zeredah, and Josē ben Johanan of Jerusalem
received from them.

Josē ben Joēzer, of Zeredah, said:— Let thy house be a place of
meeting for the Wise, and dust thyself with the dust of their feet,
and drink their words with thirst.

4. As the Torah was the full and perfect revelation from God,
those who were duly appointed to expound the Torah were entitled
to be treated with the greatest deference and their teaching received as being virtually inspired. For the disciple to wait on the
teacher is amongst the highest earthly duties, and he would feel
it an honour if the teachers used his house as a place of meeting.

5. יוֹסֵי בֶּן־יוֹחָנָן אִישׁ יְרוּשָׁלַיִם אוֹמֵר יְהִי בֵיתְךָ פָּתוּחַ לָרְוָחָה וְיִהְיוּ
עֲנִיִּים בְּנֵי בֵיתֶךָ וְאַל תַּרְבֶּה שִׂיחָה עִם הָאִשָּׁה בְּאִשְׁתּוֹ אָמְרוּ קַל וָחֹמֶר
בְּאֵשֶׁת חֲבֵרוֹ מִכַּאן אָמְרוּ חֲכָמִים כָּל־הַמַּרְבֶּה שִׂיחָה עִם הָאִשָּׁה גּוֹרֵם
רָעָה לְעַצְמוֹ וּבוֹטֵל מִדִּבְרֵי תוֹרָה וְסוֹפוֹ יוֹרֵשׁ גֵּיהִנֹּם:

5. איש ירושלם. M. om.

5. Josē ben Johanan of Jerusalem said:— Let thy house be opened
wide, and let the poor be thy household, and talk not much with
a woman.

He said it: in the case of his own wife, much more in the case
of his companion's wife.

Hence the Wise have said:— Everyone that talketh much with
a woman causes evil to himself, and desists from words of Torah,
and his end is he inherits Gehinnom.

5. The second group of maxims carries on the thought expressed
in the first, that of the house as a meeting place for the teachers
of Torah. It adds the thought of hospitality to the poor. "Talk
not much with a woman" expresses one of the austerities of the
Pharisaic system. The ground of the maxim is explained to be that
if a man talks much with a woman his thoughts will be turned away
from words of Torah to things of no importance. But he may talk
with her on the necessary affairs of the household, and upon serious
subjects. The maxim belongs to an ethic which modern thought
has outgrown, as it takes for granted the inferiority of the woman to
the man. Upon these lines the relation between the sexes never
attains to perfect companionship; and is the more exposed to de-
gradation, in so far as the woman is looked down upon as foolish
or shunned as a source of temptation.

Josē ben Joēzer and Josē ben Johanan were the first of the Zūgōth or
Pairs; their date may be put at 200—160 B. C. The first Josē died in B. C.
162, if he were one of the sixty who were put to death by the renegade
High Priest Alkimus, (1. Macc. VII. 16). Zeredah has not been identified
with certainty. 'Received from them'; the weight of evidence is in favour
of מהם 'from them', and against ממנו 'from him'. 'Them' is explained to
refer to both Simeon v. 2 and Antigonos v. 3. But this is against the plain
sense of the passage which traces *successive* and not collateral stages in the
tradition. 'From them' is the harder reading and to be preferred. I take it
to refer to other teachers intermediate between Antigonos and the two Josēs,
or more probably between Simeon the Just and Antigonos, whose names were
not preserved.[1] The saying about hospitality to the poor is cited by Raba,
b. Mez 60ᵇ. The clause explaining the reference of the maxim 'Talk not
much with a woman' is evidently an addition, probably later than the Gemara,
for it is not found in A. R. N. The word אמרו is here rendered 'He said it',
as in my translation of Aboth in the Oxford Apocrypha (Ed. Charles). This
rendering has been pronounced untenable, on the ground that אמרו is a
technical term and refers to 'The Wise', the right rendering being 'They
said'. No doubt אמרו is a technical term in many instances; but it is no
less certain that other passages occur in which the only possible translation
of אמרו is '(he) said it'. Thus, b. Jeb. 16ᵇ שר זה פסוק יונתן רבי אמר
העולם אמרו, R. Jonathan said 'This verse, the Prince of the World *said it*'.
Also, b. Hull. 60ᵃ the same word occurs in a similar connexion. Other instances are Tanhuma, Toldoth. XIII. (Ed. Buber p. 67ᵃ), הזה הפסוק אמר מי
וגו׳ עצמו על אמרו אירוב and Tanh. Vajetze XVII, XXIII, Vaera VI. Ahare XI,

---

[1] Lauterbach, Midrash and Mishnah, p. 42 fol. has an admirable discussion of
this passage, and uses it to support his view that after Simeon the Just there were
no teachers for about eighty years.

and elsewhere.[1] (See Bacher, Ælteste Terminologie. II. 159. s. v. פסוק). This use of the word does not make it a technical term, but it does conclusively show that the rendering 'He said it' is often not only tenable but necessary. In the passage in Aboth the word occurs in a comment upon the maxim of Josē b. Johanan, intended to explain why *he said it*. There is no point in rendering 'They said', because they, (the Wise) did not say it, except in the same sense as that in which they said every thing in the Mishnah. In this sense the saying is quoted,—חכמים אמרו b. Erub. 53[b]. It should be noted also that the word is immediately followed by אמרו חכמים which would not have been required if אמרו by itself necessarily referred to 'the Wise'. There can be no question but that 'He said it' is the right rendering here, and that 'He' is Jose b. Johanan, and 'it' is his maxim about speaking to a woman. The author of this explanatory addition is presumably the editor.

6. יְהוֹשֻׁעַ בֶּן־פְּרַחְיָה וְנִתַּאי הָאַרְבֵּלִי קִבְּלוּ מֵהֶם יְהוֹשֻׁעַ בֶּן־פְּרַחְיָה אוֹמֵר עֲשֵׂה לְךָ רַב וּקְנֵה לְךָ חָבֵר וֶהֱוֵי דָן אֶת־כָּל־הָאָדָם לְכַף זְכוּת:

6. Jehoshua ben Perahjah and Nittai the Arbelite received from them.

Jehoshua ben Perahjah said:— Make thee a Master and get thee a companion, and judge every man by the scale of merit.

6. The maxims of Jehoshua b. Perahjah are treated in the commentaries as of general application, advice to students how they may study to best advantage, and an injunction to give every person the benefit of the doubt if he is under suspicion. If they had a more particular reference originally it was not known to, or not emphasised by, the compiler of Aboth. To learn what must be learned in the study of Torah was scarcely possible without a teacher, if only to save the solitary student from blunders that might have serious consequences. For the same purpose companionship was a great help and encouragement, when both were at the same stage in their studies, and could spur each other on to further progress. The counsel to judge every man by the scale of merit teaches a lesson of which there are several illustrations in the Talmud, where

---

[1] A good parallel from the literature contemporary with the Mishnah is T. Sot. XIII. 5 where after the dying words of Samuel Hakaton this remark follows:— ובלשון ארמית אמרן, 'and he said them in the Aramaic tongue'. This illustration meets the case, yet is scarcely necessary; for if the clause is later than the Mishnah, and even than the Talmud, as is shown by its absence from A. R. N., the use of אמרי is sufficiently illustrated by the examples given from the Gemara and Tanhuma. Schœttgen, Hor. Heb. p. 350, renders אמרי by 'dixit'.

stories are told of eminent Rabbis to the effect that they found
themselves accidentally open to grave suspicion, and their disciples
refused to judge by appearances and put the best construction on
the conduct of their master.

Jehoshua b. Peraḥjah was involved in the persecution of the Pharisees by
John Hyrcanus, and it is quite conceivable that his maxims originated in some
phase of the controversy now no longer to be traced. Jost claims that they
illustrate the efforts of Pharisaism to develop its principle of the oral Tradition, while Grätz III. 89 says that they throw no light on the history of the
time. What is certain is that very little was known to the Talmudic Rabbis
concerning Jehoshua b. Peraḥjah and his colleague. A saying of his is quoted
in b. Men. 109[b], in a baraitha. In Talmudic tradition he is associated with
Jesus, as having been his teacher, although in fact he lived a full century
earlier. The story is given in b. Sanh. 107[b], b. Sot. 47[a], and is referred to in
j. Ḥag. II. 2, j. Sanh. VI. 9. What gave rise to this extraordinary anachronism
has not been satisfactorily explained, and there does not appear to be the
material with which to construct an explanation. If there were a similarity
of name between some disciple of Jehoshua b. Peraḥjah and the later Jesus,
it is intelligible that the story of how the former incurred the censure of his
master should have been attached to the latter. The point is dealt with in
my "Christianity in Talmud and Midrash", p. 52 fol., where however the
attempted explanation is given with more confidence than I could express
now. The saying "Judge every man ... merit" is referred to b. Shabb. 127[b]
and is illustrated by a מעשה and by several stories of unjust suspicion rejected. It is also found b. Shebu. 30[a] with no mark of quotation.

7. נִתַּאי הָאַרְבֵּלִי אוֹמֵר הַרְחֵק מִשָּׁכֵן רָע וְאַל תִּתְחַבֵּר לְרָשָׁע וְאַל
תִּתְיָאֵשׁ מִן הַפּוּרְעָנוּת:

7. נתאי so M. and most. A. מתאי.

7. Nittai the Arbelite said: Keep far from the evil neighbour,
and consort not with the wicked, and be not doubtful of retribution.

7. The maxims of Nittai are negative in form, though positive in
intention. They illustrate that side of Pharisaism which consisted
in protest against the evil of the world. The extreme form of this
was the austere discipline of the Essenes, which the Pharisees as
a body never adopted. The Pharisees remained in the society of
their fellow men; but they drew very definite lines between themselves and their Gentile neighbours[1], in regard to subjects where

---

[1] It is true that the "evil neighbour" was not necessarily a Gentile; and, if he
was, that the fact of his being a Gentile did not make him evil. Yet there was
much more ground for fear of moral danger in the society of Gentiles than in
that of Jews.

temptation was felt to be most dangerous. The heathen world, in
the time when Pharisaism arose and developed its principles, was
morally neither sweet nor clean; and while opinions may differ
upon the question whether the Pharisaic line is the best to take
in regard to the world's evil, certainly no better line was taken
then. If it had not been taken it is doubtful whether Judaism would
ever have survived. On the general question whether the Pharisaic
line is the best, it may be observed that on any ethical theory the
soul's protest against evil must be made at some point, and the
fact that it is made does not imply of necessity any want of sympathy with human nature either in its failures or its sins. The saint
who seeks to save that which was lost is not indifferent towards
the evil in which the sinner is involved. Negative precepts like
those under consideration have always, in Jewish thought, been felt
to be capable of a divine interpretation, as expressing the will of
God in regard to the character he desires in his children.

'Be not doubtful of retribution'. This may be taken as referring
to retribution in general as an element in the divine moral order,
or as referring to the consequence of disregarding the precepts already given. There is no need to seek for any occasion for the
injunction in the history of the times in which it was given. The
warning has always been needed that "God is not mocked; but
whatsoever a man soweth that shall he also reap".

The form 'Nittai', which is better attested than the alternative 'Matthai',
is a shortened form of Nethanjah. Nothing is known of him. It is noteworthy
in regard to all the Zūgōth that one of each pair is chiefly known through
his association with the other. Of Hillel and Shammai, the last pair, it is
indeed true that both were known on their own account, yet Hillel was by
far the more important of the two. It was not claimed for Shammai that when
the Torah was forgotten he restored it; b. Succ. 20ᵃ.

8. יְהוּדָה בֶּן־טַבַּאי וְשִׁמְעוֹן בֶּן־שָׁטַח קִבְּלוּ מֵהֶם יְהוּדָה בֶּן־טַבַּאי
אוֹמֵר אַל־תַּעַשׂ עַצְמְךָ כְּעוֹרְכֵי הַדַּיָּנִין וּכְשֶׁיִּהְיוּ בַּעֲלֵי הַדִּין עוֹמְדִים לְפָנֶיךָ
יִהְיוּ בְעֵינֶיךָ כִּרְשָׁעִים וּכְשֶׁנִּפְטָרִים מִלְּפָנֶיךָ יִהְיוּ בְעֵינֶיךָ כְּזַכָּאִין כְּשֶׁקִּבְּלוּ
עֲלֵיהֶם אֶת־הַדִּין:

8. Jehudah ben Tabbai and Simeon ben Shetah received from
them.

Jehudah ben Tabbai said:— Make not thyself as they that prepare the judges; and when the suitors are before thee let them be

as wrongdoers in thy sight; and when they have departed from before thee let them be in thy sight as innocent men, seeing they
have accepted the sentence upon themselves.

9. שִׁמְעוֹן בֶּן־שָׁטַח אוֹמֵר הֱוֵי מַרְבֶּה אֶת־הָעֵדִים וֶהֱוֵי זָהִיר
בִּדְבָרֶיךָ שֶׁמָּא מִתּוֹכָם יִלְמְדוּ לְשַׁקֵּר:

9. צורכי דיינין, Charles, Pseudepigr. II. p. 692, suggests דיינין. The suggestion
had been made long before (Büchler). There is no authority for this reading and
no occasion for this interpretation; צדיקים B. (מ)זכאין C.D.S.M.

9. Simeon ben Shetaḥ said:—Examine thoroughly the witnesses,
and be careful in thy words; perchance through them they may
learn to lie.

8. 9. The maxims of both teachers in this pair are legal rather than
ethical, and to that extent special rather than general. The intention
of them is to foster the most scrupulous sense of justice, the most
strict impartiality. They are addressed to such as were called upon
to administer the Torah in its application to civil or criminal offences, and they have no immediate bearing upon matters outside
the courts. To 'prepare the judges' means to get at them before
the trial so that they may come to the case with minds biassed
in favour of the suitor who has so prepared them. The precept is
addressed to those who were themselves to be judges, and it means
that they are not to prejudice their colleagues by using their influence for or against one of the parties to the suit.

The strictly impartial judge should not presume the innocence
of either litigant, but must regard both alike until the case is decided. When the sentence has been given, on the other hand, the
judge must not presume guilt beyond what has been proved; for
the sentence of the court, if just, is adequate to the case and clears
the score against both litigants. They are to be considered innocent inasmuch as there is now no ground for condemning either.

Jehudah ben Tabbai is mentioned in j. Sanh. VI. 9 as having fled to Alexandria on the occasion of the persecution of the Pharisees by Alexander Jannaeus:
evidently the same occasion as that mentioned in b. Sanh. 107[b], (see above
p. 27) where the story is told of Jehoshua b. Perahjah. It is not probable
that both went to Alexandria. The tradition is uncertain whether Jehudah
b. Tabbai or Simeon b. Shetaḥ was the nasi or chief of the pair; but the
priority of Jehudah is certified at least by the place assigned to him here
in the Mishnah. Simeon b. Shetaḥ is however the prominent figure in history,
partly owing to the fact that he was brother-in-law to the king. What is

recorded of him goes to show that he was a masterful man, and while he was technically second to Jehudah b. Tabbai, he was probably the leading spirit of the two.

10. שְׁמַעְיָה וְאַבְטַלְיוֹן קִבְּלוּ מֵהֶם שְׁמַעְיָה אוֹמֵר אֱהַב אֶת־הַמְּלָאכָה וּשְׂנָא אֶת־הָרַבָּנוּת וְאַל תִּתְוַדַּע לָרָשׁוּת:

10. Shemaiah and Abtalion[1] received from them.

Shemaiah said:—Love work and hate mastery, and make not thyself known to the government.

10. The maxims of the fourth Pair are not legal, but general. 'Love work and hate mastery.' The word translated mastery, רבנות, is that which denoted the office of a Rabbi, but it can hardly have that meaning here. The commentators explain it by illustrations of persons who have domineered over their fellows. Presumably the word, in what may be called its official meaning, was not in use in the time of Shemaiah. The intention of the maxim is to enjoin humility.

'Make not thyself known to the government.' A counsel of prudence when the government is not sympathetic towards the ideals and ideas of the person concerned.

Shemaiah had to do with Herod the Great, who was not inclined to favour the Pharisees either by training or temperament. Josephus, Antiq. XV. 10. 4, relates that Herod imposed on his subjects an oath of fidelity towards himself, and that he tried to persuade Pollio the Pharisee and Sameas and the greatest part of their followers to take the oath, but they refused. It may perhaps have been this demand on the part of Herod which prompted Shemaiah to give the advice to his friends not to make themselves known to the government. The commentators explain generally that the government will only take notice of a man in order to use him for its own purposes. Maimonides points out that the maxims of Shemaiah are warnings against three sources of injury to a man's faith. To neglect work leads to dishonesty. To acquire high rank exposes a man to the temptations of power. To be intimate with rulers encourages ambition.

11. אַבְטַלְיוֹן אוֹמֵר חֲכָמִים הִזָּהֲרוּ בְדִבְרֵיכֶם שֶׁמָּא תָחוּבוּ חוֹבַת גָּלוּת וְתִגְלוּ לִמְקוֹם מַיִם הָרָעִים וְיִשְׁתּוּ הַתַּלְמִידִים הַבָּאִים אַחֲרֵיכֶם וְיָמוּתוּ וְנִמְצָא שֵׁם שָׁמַיִם מִתְחַלֵּל:

11. Abtalion said:—Ye Wise, take heed to your words, lest ye incur the guilt *that deserves* exile, and ye be exiled to a place of

---
[1] Note that Shem. and Abt. are not called בן אבֹ. Neither are Hillel and Shammai.

evil waters, and the disciples that come after you drink and die
and the name of Heaven be found profaned.

11. Abtalion's precept is a warning to teachers of their responsibility towards those who learn from them. The exact reference
of each clause is not free from difficulty. The meaning seems to
be that a teacher must be careful in what he says, lest in controversy with heretics or unbelievers his words should be misrepresented,
and should be the means of leading the unwary into error. The
exile mentioned is not literal but figurative, and denotes the position
of one beset by false teachers, unable to receive the sound doctrine.
The 'evil waters' are the pernicious teaching of the unbelievers.
Incautious arguments may be used by opponents so as to persuade
'the disciples who come after' that the master whom they revere
taught what is nevertheless false doctrine. By this means error is
increased and the name of God profaned.

Abtalion is doubtless the Pollio mentioned by Josephus. In fact, the form
אבטליון represents Πτολλίων (Πολλίων) as אבטליות Bechor. 55ª represents
πτόλεις (πόλεις). This would seem to show that his real name was Pollio,
and that this was merely hebraized into Abtalion. Shemaiah closely resembles
Sameas, but so also does Shammai, the colleague of Hillel in the next Pair.
It is probable that Josephus confused Shemaiah and Shammai in his sources,
and that in Antiq. XIV. 9. 4 Sameas represents Shemaiah, while in Antiq.
XV. 1. 1, 10. 4, the same name represents Shammai. This would explain
why Sameas was called a disciple of Pollio, in the second passage. Shammai
may very probably have been a disciple of Abtalion; Shemaiah certainly
was not. Shemaiah and Abtalion are said to have been proselytes; but Grätz
maintains that they were Jews of Alexandria (Gesch. d. J. III. n. 17). The
question cannot be decided; for, if it be thought unlikely that proselytes
should attain to such eminence as teachers that they could be called גדולי
הדור (Pes. 70ᵇ), the obscure origin of Aqiba and Meir must not be forgotten.
The date of Shemaiah and Abtalion may be put B.C. 50. As for the dictum
of Abtalion, it is possible that it refers to a sojourn in Egypt on his part,
during the persecution of the Pharisees by Alexander Jannaeus when Jehudah
b. Tabbai fled thither. This is suggested by Ginzberg, (Jew. Encyc. s. v. Abtalion). But the allusion if any is too slight and general to afford any certainty.

12. הִלֵּל וְשַׁמַּי קִבְּלוּ מֵהֶם הִלֵּל אוֹמֵר הֱוֵי מִתַּלְמִידָיו שֶׁל אַהֲרֹן אוֹהֵב
שָׁלוֹם וְרוֹדֵף שָׁלוֹם אוֹהֵב אֶת־הַבְּרִיּוֹת וּמְקָרְבָן לַתּוֹרָה:

12. שֶׁל אַהֲרֹן. M. omit.

12. Hillel and Shammai received from them. Hillel said:—Be or
the disciples of Aaron, one that loves peace, that loves mankind
and brings them nigh to Torah.

12. All that is told about Hillel shows him to have been a lover of peace. It is possible that he was the first to see in Aaron the type of the man of peace and the peacemaker; it may have been suggested by Mal. II. 6. 'Loves mankind,' בריות denotes all created beings, although usually human beings are thought of. But love is to have no narrower limit than the human race. There is to be no national or sectarian barrier to universal good will. The natural desire of one who feels thus towards his fellow men is to 'bring them nigh to the Torah', for this means to make them sharers in the fuller knowledge of God and more conscious of his blessings. It is, in Rabbinical terms, the aim of every missionary; and it expresses the true intention of what was denounced as "compassing sea and land to make one proselyte". (Matt. XXIII. 15.) Yet why not, seeing that the Torah was the greatest blessing bestowed on man?

Hillel and Shammai are the fifth and last Pair. Their date may be put at 30 B. C. and after. Hillel is said to have lived to the age of 120 years, but this is more on the lines of haggadah than of history. More reliable is the famous Baraitha (b. Shabb. 15[a]) which says that the lives of Hillel, Simeon, Gamliel and Simeon together filled a hundred years up to the fall of Jerusalem, 70 C. E. But no certain dates can be given for the birth or death of Hillel or of Shammai. In place of succeeding Pairs, there is frequent mention of the Bēth Hillel and the Bēth Shammai, in the period which followed. Acute controversy is said to have existed between them, the exact nature of which is obscure. But the supremacy, or at least the last word, remained with the Beth Hillel. The result was expressed, as only the Rabbis could have expressed it, by saying that "the words of both are the words of the living God; but the halachah is according to the Bēth Hillel" (j. Ber. 3[b]). The descendants of Hillel, with the one exception of Johanan b. Zaccai, held the chief official place amongst Rabbinical teachers down to the year 415 C. E. No successors of Shammai in any official sense are recorded; and very few individual disciples. Baba b. Buta is mentioned as such, and it is commonly held that R. Eliezer b. Horkenos was also one, though the epithet applied to him שמותי (j. Bez. I. 60[c]) is not the natural way of expressing "disciple of Shammai", it is however so explained by the commentators. For the representation of Aaron as the type of the peacemaker see b. Sanh. 6[b] and A. R. N.[A] c. XII. The verse Mal. II. 6 mentions Levi, not Aaron; but the commentators agree in connecting this text with Hillel's dictum.

13. הוּא הָיָה אוֹמֵר נְגִיד שְׁמָא אֲבַד שְׁמֵהּ וּדְלָא מוֹסִיף יָסִיף וּדְלָא

יַלִּיף קְטָלָא חַיָּב וּדְאִשְׁתַּמַּשׁ בְּתָגָא חֲלָף׃

13. קטלא חייב.   M. add. וּדְלָא יסבר קטלא קוסמין.

13. He used to say:—Whoso makes great his name loses his name, and whoso adds not makes to cease, and he who does not learn deserves killing, and one who serves himself with the crown passes away.

13. The lesson is that of humility, as contrasted with boastfulness. Hillel's own name, i. e. fame, is amongst the very great of the "Masters in Israel", but not by his own selfseeking. 'Whoso adds not.' The point of the maxim is left undefined; but it may be taken to mean that he who imparts to another teaching or other benefit must contribute to it something of his own, must make some personal effort and not be merely a channel between the source of the benefit and its ultimate object. Without personal service a good deed loses its divine power. 'Who will not learn,' he who refuses to listen to the words of Torah which would impart spiritual life to him, 'is guilty ... killing,' in other words commits spiritual suicide, becomes dead in respect of his higher life. 'Serves ... crown,' uses for his own advantage whatever noble gift he possesses. This may refer only to the honourable practice of the Rabbis that no teacher should take pay for teaching. But it is capable of a wider and in some respects higher interpretation, in the sense that the free gift of God's grace to his servants must not by them be turned to earthly gain.

The dicta in this verse are in Aramaic, while those that precede and follow are in Hebrew. The only other Aramaic dicta in Aboth are those of Hillel II. 7, and Ben He He, V. 26. No argument for an early date can be founded on this occasional use of Aramaic. Both languages were familiar to the Rabbis; and the compiler of Aboth chose to include two or three dicta which happened to have been uttered in Aramaic. The saying 'serves ... passes away' occurs b. Meg 28ᵇ. The Munich MS contains a striking variant in this verse, in adding before the last clause the words דלא יסבר קטלא קוסמין. These are not noticed by most of the commentators nor included in the usual texts. They are mentioned in the Maḥzor Vitry, (edit. Hurwitz p. 474) as being contained in "some Mishnaioth". The meaning is explained thus:—"If a man does not think out his 'Talmud', the whole is magic spells, and they foretell concerning him that death is near to him." In other words, if he does not understand what he learns, the various propositions are to him unintelligible formulae pronounced for their effect like Abracadabra or Shabriri. A piece of sound advice, yet hardly needing to be expressed in a form so far fetched and obscure. None of Taylor's MSS appears to contain it. The words may have been originally a marginal gloss by some unknown reader.

14. הוּא הָיָה אוֹמֵר אִם אֵין אֲנִי לִי מִי לִי וּכְשֶׁאֲנִי לְעַצְמִי מָה אֲנִי
וְאִם לֹא עַכְשָׁו אֵימָתָי:

14. He used to say:—If I am not for myself who is for me? and when I am for myself what am I? and if not now, when?

14. The phrases are so terse that they are capable of many inter-pretations, and there is nothing to determine what exactly Hillel had in mind. The clue is lost, and interpretations are either mere conjecture or moral lessons which may be made to fit the words. The general sense seems to be that a man should rely on himself and not on others for what shall justify him, and that he must do so now without waiting for a future which he may not live to see. The words are applicable as a counsel, either of mere worldly prudence or of concern for the here and hereafter of the higher life. Hillel perhaps left it for his hearer to take to heart according to his character and view of life.

15. שַׁמַּי אוֹמֵר עֲשֵׂה תוֹרָתְךָ קֶבַע אֱמוֹר מְעַט וַעֲשֵׂה הַרְבֵּה וֶהֱוֵי מְקַבֵּל אֶת־כָּל־הָאָדָם בְּסֵבֶר פָּנִים יָפוֹת:

15. Shammai said:—Make thy Torah a fixed *duty*. Say little and do much; and receive every man with a cheerful expression of face.

15. Make ... fixed (duty). The word 'duty' is added to complete the sense, but 'duty' may not be the right word to add. The meaning may be that a fixed 'time' shall be set apart for and devoted to Torah, or that it shall be fixed and not allowed to be forgotten through negligence. In either case the claim of Torah must come before those of the transient affairs of the day. Torah must be 'fixed' and not give place to other things. 'receive ... cheerful ... face.' One would expect this to have been said by Hillel rather than by Shammai.

The precept "make thy Torah fixed" suggests a comparison with that of R. Simeon, II. 15 'make not thy prayer fixed'. Torah and prayer are both sacred, and both involve duty. Why is one to be fixed and the other not? Torah is the word of God to man, to be received with reverence and ac-cepted without question. It is 'fixed' and not to be modified to suit human convenience. Prayer is the word of man to God, it arises from within the soul; it must not be 'fixed' as a mere formal recital of words, but must be the varied utterance of the emotions of the devout heart. There is, however, nothing to show that R. Simeon was thinking of Shammai's dictum when he gave to his own the similar but negative form.

16. רַבָּן גַּמְלִיאֵל הָיָה אוֹמֵר עֲשֵׂה לְךָ רַב וְהִסְתַּלֵּק מִן הַסָּפֵק וְאַל תַּרְבֶּה לְעַשֵּׂר אֲמָדוֹת:

16. Rabban Gamliel used to say:—Make thee a master and re-move thyself from what is doubtful, and do not often tithe by con-jecture.

16. The dicta of R. Gamliel are purely practical and seem to refer to the duty of a judge. The general sense is:—Do not take sole responsibility more than you can help. Learn from someone who can teach you; keep clear of doubtful cases, when the decision will have to be made by you; and in the estimation of the amount of tithes do not rely on your own judgment. Sensible advice and useful, but not of any general ethical value.

Rabban Gamliel was the grandson of Hillel. He is the first to be distin-guished by the title of Rabban, or indeed by any title; for 'Rabbi' only ap-pears as a customary epithet in the next generation. The title Rabban did not become invariable for the head of the House of Hillel. Johanan b. Zaccai bore it, and after him Gamliel II and his son Simeon. Jehudah ha-Nasi was known as 'Rabbi' *par excellence*, never as Rabban Jehudah. His son Gamliel III is called Rabban Ab. II. 2, but no later members of the family. Gamliel I is the one mentioned in the N. T. Acts V. 34 as being 'held in honour of all the people', and was one of the leading men in Jerusalem in his time. The king Agrippa I and Cypros the queen are said to have depended much on his counsel (b. Pes. 88[b]). He was dead before the outbreak of the war in 68 C.E. His life therefore included the first half century of the common era. He was the teacher of the apostle Paul, and one would like to know his opinion of the disciple who left him and "went far hence to the Gentiles". The name Gamliel was borne by one person in the O.T. (Num. I. 10 and elsewhere), but otherwise only occurs, as it would seem, among the descendants of Hillel. The relation of R. Hanina b. Gamliel to the house of Hillel is pro-bable, but the nature of it is uncertain.

17. שִׁמְעוֹן בְּנוֹ אוֹמֵר כָּל־יָמַי גָּדַלְתִּי בֵּין הַחֲכָמִים וְלֹא מָצָאתִי לַגּוּף טוֹב מִשְּׁתִיקָה וְלֹא הַמִּדְרָשׁ עִקָּר אֶלָּא הַמַּעֲשֶׂה וְכָל־הַמַּרְבֶּה דְבָרִים מֵבִיא חֵטְא:

17. Simeon his son said:—All my days I have grown up among the Wise, and I have not found anything better for one than silence; and not study is the chief thing but action; and whoso multiplies words occasions sin.

17. This dictum hardly calls for any comment; as an ethical maxim it is scarcely of universal application, while, coming from one who says that he grew up among the Wise, it conveys a some-what severe criticism of them. It may be regarded, however, as the speaker's own apology for his modest retirement from the pro-

minent position which he could have claimed. Whoever he was, he could hardly have held the foremost place as being for the time the head of the house of Hillel. Ethically of no importance, the saying is psychologically interesting, as a disclosure of the character and disposition of the speaker.

Simeon his son. Who is this Simeon? The commentators all say that he was the son of Gamliel I of the preceding verse. But there are serious difficulties in the way of this explanation. The succession of the house of Hillel was as follows, and the pedigree will be useful for reference hereafter.

1   Hillel
             |
2   Simeon
             |
3   Rabban Gamliel I
             |
4   Rabban Simeon I b. Gamliel I
             |
5   Rabban Gamliel II
             |
6   Rabban Simeon II b. Gamliel II
             |
7   Rabbi (Jehudah ha Nasi)
             |
8   Rabban Gamliel III
             |
9   Jehudah Nesiah
             |
10   Gamliel IV
             |
11   Jehudah III
             |
12   Hillel II
             |
13   Gamliel V
             :
14   Gamliel VI.

The Simeon of v. 17 is either n° 4 or n° 2. In favour of the former is the fact that v. 17 follows on v. 16, and 'his son' would naturally refer to the Gamliel of v. 16.[1] Against this identification must be set the fact that Simeon of v. 17 is not called Rabban, whereas the son of Gamliel I was always so called. Moreover, Rabban Simeon b. Gamliel was a prominent figure amongst the men of his time, both as a teacher and as a leader. He was the Simeon mentioned by Josephus as one of the chief men just before the siege of Je-

---

[1] The same order is found in Ad. R. N^A XXII. id. ^B XXXII, which shows that the transposition here assumed must have been made in the original text of Aboth.

rusalem. (Bell. Jud. IV. 3. 9.) The words in v. 17 are quite inappropriate to
a man who played so distinguished a part. and are the last thing he would
be likely to say of himself. The words contained in v. 18, and there ascribed to Rabban Simeon b. Gamliel, would be naturally ascribed to the
man just referred to, i. e. n° 4 in the pedigree. And he would then close the
series given in the first chapter of Aboth, by bringing it down to the *terminus*
of the fall of Jerusalem. If, however, the Simeon of v. 17 is identified with
n° 4, then the man quoted in v. 18 must be n° 6, and would be placed here
by a violent break in chronological sequence. This would be no argument
if the case occurred in the later chapters, for there chronological sequence
is hardly regarded. But in the first chapter the argument from chronological
sequence has considerable weight, and it points strongly to the identification
of the speaker in v. 18 with n° 4, leaving the Simeon of v. 17 to be otherwise explained. This would account for the otherwise very surprising omission of Gamliel II, n° 5 of the pedigree, from this list of teachers cited in
Aboth. The explanation founded on the above arguments merely requires
that v. 16 and v. 17 should be transposed, so that "Simeon his son" comes
after v. 14, and denotes Simeon the son of Hillel, i. e. n° 2 in the pedigree.
Then would follow, in right order, (after Shammai) Rabban Gamliel I (n° 3),
and Rabban Simeon b. Gamliel (n° 4), with whom the series would close.
Simeon the son of Hillel is almost unknown; but the fact of his existence
is proved by the note in the Talmud (b. Shabb. 15ᵃ) which gives the succession: — 'Hillel, Simeon, Gamliel, Simeon' as filling the century which
ended with the siege of Jerusalem. The words in v. 17 are entirely in
keeping with the character of a man so little prominent as the retiring son
of Hillel. I hold ,therefore, in spite of the commentators, that the Simeon
in v. 17 was the son of Hillel, and that the words in this verse are to be
added to the very scanty information concerning him to be found in the
Rabbinical literature.[1]

18. רַבָּן שִׁמְעוֹן בֶּן־גַּמְלִיאֵל אוֹמֵר עַל־שְׁלֹשָׁה דְבָרִים הָעוֹלָם קַיָּם עַל־
הָאֱמֶת וְעַל־הַדִּין וְעַל־הַשָּׁלוֹם שֶׁנֶּאֱמַר אֱמֶת וּמִשְׁפַּט שָׁלוֹם שִׁפְטוּ בְּשַׁעֲרֵיכֶם:

18. Rabban Shimon ben Gamliel said: — Upon three things the
world stands, on Truth, on Judgment and on Peace. As it is said: —
Truth and judgment of peace judge ye in your gates (Zech. VIII. 16).

18. This dictum is a variant of that in v. 2, though the similarity
of form may be accidental. It is another attempt to indicate the
fundamentals of human life in its higher aspect. Simeon the Just

---

[1] Since writing the above I have found that this identification of Simeon with
the son of Hillel instead of the son of Gamaliel was proposed, with some hesitation,
by Hadr. Reland in his notes (anonymous) to Otho, Historia Doctorum Misnicorum,
1699, p. 95.

had summed them up in Torah, worship and brotherly love. Simeon
b. Gamliel defined them as judgment, truth and peace.[1] There is
no need to set up a comparison between the two series, as if one
were more true than the other; each expresses the opinion of a
wise and good man upon the essentials of right living. Judgment,
truth and peace belong chiefly to the sphere of human intercourse.
Torah, worship and brotherly love imply the divine as well as the
human relations.

Simeon b. Gamliel, n° 4 of the pedigree. See above, on v. 17. He appears
to have died before the siege, at least he is not mentioned during the course
of it; and, if he had survived, he and not Johanan b. Zaccai would have
taken the lead in reorganising the national life. His dates may therefore be
put at about 1—66 C. E.

His dictum is the first in Aboth to be accompanied by a text (Zech.
VIII. 16), either as proof or illustration. The addition of such texts becomes
much more frequent in the later chapters especially in Ch. VI. It is a question
which cannot be definitely answered whether the proof-texts were added by
the editor or compiler of Aboth, or were included in the dictum of the
original teacher. In the present instance we may perhaps say that Simeon
b. Gamliel pointed to Zech. VIII. 16 as a good summary of the essentials
of human life, and framed his dictum accordingly. But the formula "As it
is said" rather indicates an editorial addition, for that phrase is the usual
introduction to a quotation all through the Rabbinical literature.

With Simeon b. Gamliel the first chapter ends. For the bearing of this
upon the composition of Aboth, see the Introduction § B.

CHAP. II. פרק שני

א. רַבִּי אוֹמֵר אֵיזוֹ הִיא דֶּרֶךְ יְשָׁרָה שֶׁיָּבוֹר לוֹ הָאָדָם כָּל־שֶׁהִיא תִפְאֶרֶת
לְעֹשֶׂהָ וְתִפְאֶרֶת לוֹ מִן הָאָדָם, וֶהֱוֵי זָהִיר בְּמִצְוָה קַלָּה כְּבַחֲמוּרָה שֶׁאֵין
אַתָּה יוֹדֵעַ מַתַּן שְׂכָרָן שֶׁל מִצְוֹת, וֶהֱוֵי מְחַשֵּׁב הֶפְסֵד מִצְוָה כְּנֶגֶד שְׂכָרָהּ
וּשְׂכַר עֲבֵרָה כְּנֶגֶד הֶפְסֵדָהּ. הִסְתַּכֵּל בִּשְׁלֹשָׁה דְבָרִים וְאֵין אַתָּה בָא לִידֵי
עֲבֵרָה דַּע מַה־לְּמַעְלָה מִמְּךָ עַיִן רוֹאָה וְאֹזֶן שׁוֹמַעַת וְכָל־מַעֲשֶׂיךָ בַּסֵּפֶר
נִכְתָּבִים:

CHAP. II.

1. Rabbi said: — Which is that right way which a man should
choose for himself? Any that is an honour to him that does it and

---

[1] Cp. Debar. R. V. I. where S. b. G. gives a striking comment on this saying.

an honour to him in the sight of men. And be careful in the case of a light precept as in that of a weighty one, for thou knowest not how the rewards of the precepts are given. And count the loss by a precept against its reward, and the reward of a sin against its loss. Keep in view three things and that wilt not come into the power of sin; know what is above thee, — a seeing eye, a hearing ear and all thy deeds written in a book.

1. The comparison of life to a way, or path, or road, or course, is one of the great commonplaces of Jewish ethics, and has passed thence into Christian teaching. It is now so hackneyed that the force of it is almost lost. But how fundamental it is in Jewish ethics is shown by the fact that the term for the rule of right conduct in life is 'halachah', from the ordinary verb meaning to walk or to go. Without halachah Jewish ethics would be reduced to almost nothing. Halachah, in all its elaboration, is simply directions for finding the 'right way'. Life, the life which God would have his children live, is thus shown to imply active exertion, conscious obedience, moral determination, and not merely religious emotion, or even devout meditation. These were provided for in the haggadah; but it is beyond question that the strongest and most characteristic feature of Rabbinical Judaism was halachah.

To the question "which is the right way?", Rabbi gives the answer whatever is an honour to him that does it and an honour in the sight of men. The answer seems to fall below the level of the question. There must surely be some nobler standard of conduct than the approbation either of oneself or ones fellowmen, or the fact that an action does credit to the one or the others. It should be observed, however, that the question refers to men in general and not to Jews in particular. A Jew would find his "right way" in the directions of Torah and the doing of the precepts and good works. One who was not a Jew had not that guidance, yet ought, as a moral and rational being, to seek for some "right way" in which to live his life. Rabbi seems to mean that he will find what he seeks if he does such things as are an honour to himself and are applauded by his fellowmen, or (keeping more closely to the literal sense) are an ornament to human nature alike in himself and in them.

The remaining clauses of this dictum are addressed to those who follow the guidance of the Torah. The lightest precept is to be fulfilled with the same care as the gravest, because each expresses the divine will. It is not a question of reward, "thou knowest not how the rewards are given". Reward in connexion with conduct means an expression of divine approval, it does not mean a concrete benefit which could be claimed and earned by the fulfilment of a precept.[1] Whatever be said by way of criticism of Jewish ethical teaching in regard to rewards applies with precisely the same force to the teaching of Jesus on the same subject, as in Matt. V. 12; VI. 1. 6 and elsewhere. The fulfilment of a precept involves "loss" through selfdenial, as well as "reward" through the divine approval. The transgression of a precept involves gain of present advantage and loss through future retribution. The divine justice measures out both, treats the righteous and the sinner alike with strict fairness. So it becomes possible to speak of the "reward" of a sin, where there can certainly be no "divine approval" of a sin. The safeguard against falling into sin is to remember God who sees and hears and remembers.

Rabbi. This is Jehudah, n° 7 of the pedigree (see I. 17), otherwise known as J. ha-Kadosh, or J. ha-Nasi. He is said to have been born in 135 C. E. when R. Akiba died, and he died in 219 C. E. The traditional date of his birth may be correct, and can hardly be far wrong. He was the final editor of the Mishnah, completing what had been begun by R. Akiba and continued by R. Meir. The Mishnah now extant is substantially as Rabbi left it, though it has received additions and alterations to some small extent. Rabbi was probably not intellectually the equal of R. Akiba; but, by the skill and learning which he applied to the task of codifying the halachah, he acquired an immense reputation, and deserved the high honour in which he was held.

The fact that Ch. II of Aboth begins with Rabbi shows that there is no chronological continuity between this chapter and the first. Yet the dicta of Rabbi and his son are followed by more sayings of Hillel, thus reverting to the line of Ch. I see Introd. § C. p. 10. The inclusion of these two, Rabbi and his son, goes to show that additions were made to the text of Aboth after the time of Rabbi.

The exposition given above of his dicta is based on the received text, but that text is not free from difficulty. The question as to the right *way* is not logically answered by a statement concerning him who *does* it. עשה is not the verb which one would naturally expect, in connection with דרך. Moreover, the association "him who does it" and "in the sight of men", is weak and commonplace. Both difficulties would be met by adopting the conjecture of R. Israel of Toledo, (12th—13 cent., quoted by Taylor, II p. 139) לעושהו in place of לעושה ו, i. e. "to his Maker" instead of "to him that

---

[1] On the Rabbinical conception of 'Merit', see my 'Pharisees' Ch. V. § B and Marmorstein "The Doctrine of Merit in old Rabbinical Literature". 1920.

does it". The suggested reading is not found in any text or MS, and R. Israel says frankly that it came into his mind to read the words so.[1] But his interpretation is so much better than the ordinary ones and so much simpler that if conjecture be ever allowed it should be accepted here. The remaining clauses do not present any difficulty; but it may be noted that there is scarcely any connexion of thought between them such as would imply that they were originally spoken at the same time. They are a group of sayings which might have been arranged in any order, and might also have been distributed in separate verses introduced by "He used to say". Perhaps they seemed to the compiler hardly sufficient to stand alone. There is no other quite similar group of disconnected sayings in Aboth under the name of one teacher. With the possible exception of IV. 27, Rabbi does not occur again amongst the teachers whose words are quoted. The saying "Which ... way" occurs b. Nedar. 22[b]. That about the light precept, in b. Nedar. 39[b], and "count the loss" &c. in b. B. Bath. 78[b].

2. רַבָּן גַּמְלִיאֵל בְּנוֹ שֶׁל רַבִּי יְהוּדָה הַנָּשִׂיא אוֹמֵר יָפֶה תַלְמוּד תּוֹרָה
עִם דֶּרֶךְ אֶרֶץ שֶׁיְּגִיעַת שְׁנֵיהֶם מַשְׁכַּחַת עָוֹן וְכָל־תּוֹרָה שֶׁאֵין עִמָּהּ מְלָאכָה
סוֹפָהּ בְּטֵלָה וְגוֹרֶרֶת עָוֹן וְכָל־הָעוֹסְקִים עִם הַצִּבּוּר יִהְיוּ עוֹסְקִים עִמָּהֶם
לְשֵׁם שָׁמַיִם שֶׁזְּכוּת אֲבוֹתָם מְסַיְּעָתָם וְצִדְקָתָם עוֹמֶדֶת לָעַד וְאַתֶּם מַעֲלֶה
אֲנִי עֲלֵיכֶם שָׂכָר הַרְבֵּה כְּאִלּוּ עֲשִׂיתֶם׃

II 2. סופה, usual reading; D.M. לסוף; עוסקים. M. עמלים.
מעלה אני. usual reading. A.M. מעלין; הרבה מעלין A.B.C.M. om.

2. Rabban Gamliel son of Rabbi Jehudah the Prince said: — Study of Torah along with worldly occupation is seemly; for labour in the two of them makes sin forgotten. And all Torah without work ends in failure and occasions sin. And let all who labour with the congregation labour with them for the name of Heaven. For the merit of their fathers is their support, and their righteousness standeth for ever. And ye — I confer upon you *saith God* [plenteous] reward, as if ye had wrought.

2. The study of Torah being taken for granted as essential, this verse lays stress on work as an adjunct to it. "Derech eretz" here translated "worldly occupation" means also, and very often, "good behaviour", the usages of polite society. Both meanings are examples of the "way of the earth", which is the literal rendering of the phrase. The first meaning is clearly required in the present instance. The insistence of Jewish teachers upon the duty of having a trade or occupation is well known, and is a mark of that prac-

---

[1] Cp. Isa XLV 18. LI 13.

tical sanity which is preeminent in Jewish ethics. Even the student who is supported that he may give his whole time to study, is bidden to study that he may teach others. None is to live for himself alone, or benefit by others without benefitting them in return. Every one therefore who "works with the congregation" is to do so with no selfish motive, but "for the name of heaven", as a service rendered to God. What he does, with or on behalf of the congregation, is their act not his individual act; but the unselfish service thus rendered meets with the divine approval as if it were his own act. The lesson is a fine one, though expressed less clearly than might be wished.

Rabban Gamliel. This is n° 8 of the pedigree given in the note to I. 17. His date may be put at 230 C. E. but it is not known when he was born or how long he lived. The heads of the house of Hillel retained the rank of official chief of the Jews in Palestine, and were recognised as such by the Roman government; but the primacy as teachers of Torah passed out of their hands into those of men more learned and more original. The real successor of Rabbi as a "Master in Israel" was R. Joḥanan, with whom the R. Gamliel here mentioned was contemporary.

For an extreme instance of the Rabbinical insistence on the duty of having a calling and thus being independent of the support of others, see the answer of Rab to R. Cahana, Pes. 113ᵃ. 'Merit of their fathers', on the subject of merit see my Pharisees, Ch. V. § B. There is here, however, no stress upon the merit of their fathers as distinguished from their own merit. The point is that one who works with and for the congregation must not think about any merit of his own either as accruing to himself or conferred on them. Merit there is, but it is in the inheritance of goodness and piety in which all share, not in the act of the individual. 'And ye ... I confer upon you' &c. The transition to this clause from the preceding is somewhat abrupt. The various counsels already given are those of R. Gamliel. The form of the last clause shows that the words are ascribed to God for only he bestows reward. The Munich MS however reads מעלין, "they confer", where "they" is merely a term for people in general. If this is the right reading, then the clause may be part of R. Gamliel's dictum. But the common reading is both better supported and more in accordance with Rabbinical teaching. Cp. Kidd. 40ᵃ. "The good thought is connected with [its] act, as it is said, Mal. III. 16. Then they that feared the Lord spake one with another &c. ... R. Asi said:— If a man is minded to perform a mitzvah and is prevented and does not do it, the Scripture counts it to him, מעלה עליו, as if he had done it;" Scripture being of course the utterance of God. The clause may be an editorial addition to the words of R. Gamliel, or may be an exclamation of his own, not syntactically connected with his preceding words. 'Plenteous reward'. The Munich MS omits plenteous, הרבה.

3. הֱווּ זְהִירִין בָּרָשׁוּת שֶׁאֵין מְקָרְבִין לוֹ לְאָדָם אֶלָּא לְצֹרֶךְ עַצְמָן נִרְאִין כְּאוֹהֲבִין בְּשְׁעַת הֲנָאָתָן וְאֵין עוֹמְדִין לוֹ לְאָדָם בְּשְׁעַת דָּחֳקוֹ:

3. Be cautious with the government, for they do not make advances to a man except for their own need. They seem like friends in the hour of their advantage, but they do not stand by a man in the hour of his adversity.

3. A warning against having dealings with the government. It can hardly be regarded as a general maxim, but is rather a bitter comment on the character of the Roman officials as the speaker, who ever he was, had had experience of them.

This verse has nothing to indicate its author. If it were by R. Gamliel, we should expect it to begin with the usual phrase "He used to say", as in the next verse. If however it were anonymous, it would be the sole instance of such a thing in the first four chapters. It may have formed part of v. 2, and have been separated by some accident of transcribing. It is not clear who the persons are to whom the advice is addressed. I have translated "do not make advances to a man", because I believe that this is what was intended, and it is grammatically justifiable as the verb is certainly transitive. The usual rendering is "do not cause a man to draw near to them". In the one case they make overtures to a man, but it is for their own gain; in the other, they send for him to come to court, but let him beware.

4. הוּא הָיָה אוֹמֵר עֲשֵׂה רְצוֹנוֹ כִּרְצוֹנֶךָ כְּדֵי שֶׁיַּעֲשֶׂה רְצוֹנְךָ כִּרְצוֹנוֹ בַּטֵּל רְצוֹנְךָ מִפְּנֵי רְצוֹנוֹ כְּדֵי שֶׁיְּבַטֵּל רְצוֹן אֲחֵרִים מִפְּנֵי רְצוֹנֶךָ:

4. M. places this after v. 6.

4. He used to say:— Make his will as thy will, so that he may make thy will as his will; make naught thy will before his will so that he may make naught the will of others before thy will.

4. A maxim of a very different order from the preceding. It teaches the lesson of conformity to the will of God, yet not to the extent of unconditional resignation. One might wish that the speaker had stopped short after "Make his will as thy will", i. e. will what he wills; "he" being of course God. This would be on the lines of "our wills are ours to make them Thine" (Tennyson). The commentator in Mahzor Vitry indeed takes it in this sense, as he finely says "Strive to do the will of God, with a perfect heart and a willing soul; and efface thy will, even if the will of God be a

burden (laid) upon thee". The meaning of the verse seems to be to teach that there should be complete harmony between the human will and the divine. If a man bends his will to the divine will, then he will only desire what is pleasing to God, and may rightly pray that God will grant what he desires. There is no thought of a bargain by which a man by yielding to God on one point may obtain what he wishes on another. So it follows that if a man desires only what is according to the will of God, he may rightly pray that God will make ineffectual the will of those who desire the opposite.

There is a striking passage in A.R.N.^{B} XXXII. p. 36^a, where the idea of R. Gamliel's saying is given (in words attributed to Rabbi) as follows: — He used to say "If thou hast done his [God's] will as thy will, thou hast not done his will as his will. If thou hast done his will against thine own will, thou hast done his will as his will. Is it thy will that thou shouldst not die? Die while yet thou diest not. Is it thy will that thou shouldst live? Live not while yet thou livest. It is better for thee to die the death of this world, which is against thy will than to die the death of the world to come. For if thou willest thou art not dead."

'He used to say'. Presumably this is still R. Gamliel; Rashi says that in some copies this verse is found in Ch. IV, "Perek B. Zoma". It is found there, in some MSS, (see Taylor, II. p. 111) after IV. 19. In that case the author would be R. Jannai. There is nothing to show which is right place; but the common text assigns it to Ch. II, and there is no sufficient reason for removing it. The Munich MS places it after v. 6. There was evidently some uncertainty as to its position, and perhaps it was originally anonymous, perhaps a later addition to the original series of sayings. There is no special resemblance of thought or style to connect it with R. Gamliel, nor with the sayings which immediately precede it. The fact that Rabbi and R. Gamliel are placed first in this chapter which then reverts to Hillel suggests the possibility that this series originally began with Hillel, and that for some unknown reason his two remote descendants were prefixed to him. It is curious that this chapter should contain a further set of sayings by Hillel, and the fact points to the conjecture that the compiler found Ch. I complete, and added to it another series beginning with Hillel, either found by him in some other source or put together by him. This second series is almost entirely concerned with a closely connected group viz: — Hillel, his chief disciple R. Johanan b. Zaccai, and his five chief disciples. R. Tarphon, vv. 20. 21 is the only exception, other than Rabbi and R. Gamliel already mentioned.

5. הַלֵּל אוֹמֵר אַל תִּפְרוֹשׁ מִן הַצִּבּוּר וְאַל תַּאֲמִין בְּעַצְמָךְ עַד יוֹם מוֹתָךְ
וְאַל תָּדִין אֶת־חֲבֵרָךְ עַד שֶׁתַּגִּיעַ לִמְקוֹמוֹ וְאַל תֹּאמַר דָּבָר שֶׁאִי אֶפְשָׁר
לִשְׁמוֹעַ שֶׁסוֹפוֹ לְהִשָּׁמֵעַ וְאַל תֹּאמַר לִכְשֶׁאֶפָּנֶה אֶשְׁנֶה שֶׁמָּא לֹא תִפָּנֶה:

דבר שאי אפשר לשמיע...יאל תאמר. M. om.

5. Hillel said: — Sever not thyself from the congregation and
be not sure of thyself till the day of thy death, and judge not
thy associate until thou comest to his place; and say not of a word
which is impossible to understand that it will be understood in the
end; and say not when I am at leisure I will study — perchance
thou wilt not be at leisure.

5. A set of sayings by Hillel, having little or no connexion with
each other. 'Separate ... congregation.' A general maxim applicable
in all periods of Jewish history, and tending to strengthen the general
principle laid down by Ezra and fundamental in Pharisaism, 'Separate
from the Gentile but not from Israel'. To separate from the community of Israel is, so far as it goes, to undermine the principle
which makes it a community. It is probable that Hillel had in mind
the Essenes, who felt drawn to a life of ascetic seclusion. Hillel's
own colleague Menahem had "withdrawn from the congregation",
probably to become an Essene; and the secession of so eminent a
man must have produced a deep impression upon those who had
been associated with him. (See below.) 'Be not sure ... day of thy
death.' Again a general maxim, but one which may have had the
same origin as the preceding. It is the natural warning to those
who should protest that they could never do what Menahem had
done. 'Judge not ... his place.' Continuation of the same thought.
Hillel would not judge Menahem, though he disapproved his action,
and would not have others condemn him. If this particular reference
be put aside as unwarranted (and it is pure conjecture) the wisdom
and charity of the counsels of Hillel remain unaffected. His lesson
is one which all need to learn and practise.

'Say not ... leisure.' A general counsel intended for learners whatever be the subject of their study, but especially for those who
learn from their Rabbi. In general terms it is the lesson of per-
severance and diligence; the difficulty must be faced and overcome,
not put off till a more convenient time. It is on the lines of Hillel's
saying, I. 14, "If not now when"? The meaning is plain without
further comment.

It seems to be accepted that the Menahem who was Hillel's colleague is
the one mentioned by Josephus Antiq. XV. 10. 5 as being in high favour

with Herod. It is said, (j. Hagg. 77ᵈ) that as colleague of Hillel he "went forth" and was succeeded by Shammai. Some said that he went ממידה למידה, i. e. from one opinion or school of thought to another, in other words became a heretic of some kind; others said that he entered the service of the court. The latter tradition is probably based on Herod's favour towards him. In any case he must have been a remarkable figure in his time (see Grätz, G. d. J. III. 17ᵇ. J. Enc. VIII. p. 467). The saying "Be not sure of thyself &c." is found b. Ber. 29ª.

The clause about study gives occasion for its own application, for it is difficult to determine the exact meaning of it. The MS readings vary between a subject which אפשר, 'is possible', to understand and one which אי אפשר, 'is not possible'. Also, some commentators supply על, 'of' or 'concerning', before דבר. The various possible interpretations are accordingly these: —

(a) Do not say a thing which it is possible to understand. This may be ruled out at once.

(b) Do not say a thing which it is not possible to understand, i. e. Make your teaching plain and intelligible.

(c) Do not say of a thing which can be understood "I will learn its meaning hereafter". Learn it now. If it can be learned now it ought to be.

(d) Do not say of a thing which you cannot understand "I will learn it later" &c. If you cannot understand it now, study it till you do.

(c) and (d) amount to much the same, and are confirmed by the reference to future study. But both require the addition of על which is not in the MS, though Rashi supplies it. This difficulty might be got over by making דבר part of what is 'said', thus: — Do not say "A thing impossible to understand! It will be understood hereafter", or "I will study it later". This I believe comes most closely to the meaning of the original, if the exclamatory clause be allowable grammatically. The Munich MS omits the words from דבר to תאמר ואל thus reading "Say not When I am at leisure &c.". This is convenient but not convincing. It evades the difficulty, and does not account for its presence in the text.

6. הוּא הָיָה אוֹמֵר אֵין בּוֹר יְרֵא חֵטְא וְלֹא עַם הָאָרֶץ חָסִיד וְלֹא הַבַּיְשָׁן לָמֵד וְלֹא הַקַּפְּדָן מְלַמֵּד וְלֹא כָּל־הַמַּרְבֶּה בִסְחוֹרָה מַחְכִּים וּבַמָּקוֹם שֶׁאֵין אֲנָשִׁים הִשְׁתַּדֵּל לִהְיוֹת אִישׁ:

6. He used to say: — A rude man is not one that fears sin nor is a man who knows not Torah a saint; nor does a shy person learn nor a passionate person teach, nor does one who engages much in business impart wisdom. And in a place where there are no men, strive to be a man.

6. A series of dicta intended to show the defects which disqualify the person who has them for the character which might

be, and by some presumably was, ascribed to him. They are not uncharitable judgment or vainglorious depreciation of others, but statements meant to express psychological truth. Hillel may have regarded the 'bōr' as a fellow-man and still have recognised that such a person could not be "one that feared sin", simply because he had not the essential qualities of a "sin fearer", which for Hillel were dependent on knowledge of Torah. So of the "vulgar person", the man who did not order his life in accordance with Torah. The shy person is one who is afraid to ask his teacher to explain what he does not understand, and so fails to learn. The passionate man becomes angry when he is interrupted by the questions of his students and so fails to teach them anything. The man who engages much in business has no leisure for that study which leads to wisdom. Ben Sira said the same thing Ecclus XXXVIII. 24. Against this, however, must be set the constant insistence of all Jewish teachers upon the duty of having a calling so as to support oneself (see above on II. 2). Hillel himself had been, if he did not continue to be, a day labourer for a very small wage. The last clause echoes the sturdy independence of Hillel's earlier saying I. 14. The author of Midrash Shemuel says, (ad. loc.) "I have heard from an aged Sage who said 'And in a place where there is no one but thyself in the innermost recesses and none sees thee and none knows thee; ... say not I will sin, for who sees me? ... thou must strive to be a man, righteous upright and trustworthy.'" Even it this be not what Hillel meant, his saying includes it, and the lesson he taught is enriched by this interpretation.

This saying is in Hebrew not Aramaic. The difference between 'bōr', בור, and 'am-ha-aretz' עם הארץ seems to be this, that 'bōr' is an uncultured person, of rude undeveloped mind, not specially with reference to religion but generally; 'am-ha-aretz' is one who disregards the Torah in the conduct of his life. The am-ha-aretz was not necessarily estranged from religion; the 'synagogues of the am-ha-aretz' are referred to in Ab. III. 14, with disapproval it is true, but with the admission that there were such places. 'Vulgar person' is not quite a satisfactory rendering, unless it be taken in its original meaning "one of the 'vulgus'" the 'common herd'. It should be noted that the 'bōr' and the 'am-ha-aretz' were recognised as belonging to Israel, however slight the connexion might be. Thus, in Bamm. R. III. 1, it is said "So of Israel; there are amongst them sons of Torah and 'amme-ha-aretz' and '...bōrīm'." The last clause, 'in a place &c.' is found b. Ber. 63ᵃ but in Aramaic, and anonymous. It is followed by a comment of Abaji showing that it does not always hold.

7. אַף הוּא רָאָה גֻּלְגֹּלֶת אַחַת שֶׁצָּפָה עַל־פְּנֵי הַמָּיִם אָמַר לָהּ עַל
דְּאַטֵּפְתְּ אַטְפוּךְ וְסוֹף מְטַיְפַיִךְ יְטוּפוּן:

7. Moreover, he saw a skull which floated on the face of the
water, and he said Because thou drownedst, they drowned thee;
and in the end they that drowned thee shall be drowned.

7. Another saying of Hillel, being a moral epigram on retribution.
The thought is quite familiar, 'as thou hast done so it is done to
thee'. Illustration is needless.

This saying is quoted b. Succ. 53ᵃ and is there referred to Hillel by name.
Two other sayings of Hillel are quoted in the same passage, which are worth
noting here. The passage is "If I am here, all is here; if I am not here who
is here? He used to say To the place I love thither my feet carry me. If
thou comest to my house I will go to thy house; if thou comest not to my
house I will not come to thy house". Then follows the epigram about the
skull. With the first of these two sayings cp. that given above, I. 14. The
likeness of style and thought is very marked.

The epigram about the skull suggests that Hillel knew the man whose
skull he saw. How else did he know that he was now treated as he in his
time had treated others? Rashi (Succ. 53ᵃ *ad loc*) explains that the skull had
been severed from the body, and thence Hillel concluded that the victim
had been a robber, לסטים, and had been murdered by other robbers; they
in their turn would pay the penalty of their crime. This is perhaps as near
as we can get to the immediate reference of the epigram. The saying is in
Aramaic, and terse even for Hillel, being expressed in only six words, where
seventeen are needed in English.

8. הוּא הָיָה אוֹמֵר מַרְבֶּה בָשָׂר מַרְבֶּה רִמָּה מַרְבֶּה נְכָסִים מַרְבֶּה
דְּאָגָה מַרְבֶּה נָשִׁים מַרְבֶּה כְשָׁפִים מַרְבֶּה שְׁפָחוֹת מַרְבֶּה זִמָּה מַרְבֶּה
עֲבָדִים מַרְבֶּה גָזֵל מַרְבֶּה תוֹרָה מַרְבֶּה חַיִּים מַרְבֶּה יְשִׁיבָה מַרְבֶּה חָכְמָה
מַרְבֶּה עֵצָה מַרְבֶּה תְבוּנָה מַרְבֶּה צְדָקָה מַרְבֶּה שָׁלוֹם קָנָה שֵׁם טוֹב
קָנָה לְעַצְמוֹ קָנָה לוֹ דִּבְרֵי תוֹרָה קָנָה לוֹ חַיֵּי הָעוֹלָם הַבָּא:

8. מרבה דאנה M. after מרבה נשים דג.

8. He used to say:—More flesh, more worms; more wealth more
care; more women more witchcraft; more maidservants more lewd-
ness; more menservants more thieving; more Torah more life; more
assiduity more wisdom; more counsel more understanding; more
charity more peace. He who has acquired a good name has acquired
it for himself. He who has acquired words of Torah has acquired
for himself the life of the world to come.

8. The last saying of Hillel to be quoted may be compared with those in v. 6, being a series of incisive comments on human nature as Hillel had observed it in certain types of person. The underlying contrast is between the life of 'the world' and the life of Torah. In the former, increased possession leads to trouble, in the latter it leads to good. There is no reason to charge Hillel with being cynical and uncharitable; he only did as all others have done who have distinguished between the way of the world and the way of the perfect life. The terms in which he stated the lesson were based on the social life of his own time, and in a style characteristic of him; the substance of it is not peculiar to him, being simply the assertion of the service of God against "the world the flesh and the devil".

The last two clauses differ in form from the preceding, the characteristic word being קנה instead of מרבה. They were presumably a separate group, placed here to be included with the other sayings of Hillel. There seems to be no close connexion of thought between this last group and the preceding one. "More class room" means more study in the class room, more study generally, the object of study being of course Torah.

9. רַבָּן יוֹחָנָן בֶּן־זַכַּי קִבֵּל מֵהִלֵּל וּמִשַּׁמַּאי הוּא הָיָה אוֹמֵר אִם לָמַדְתָּ
תּוֹרָה הַרְבֵּה אַל תַּחֲזִיק טוֹבָה לְעַצְמְךָ כִּי לְכָךְ נוֹצָרְתָּ׃

9. למדת, usual reading. A.C.D.M. and cp. S. עשית.

9. Rabban Johanan ben Zaccai received from Hillel and from Shammai.

He used to say: — If thou hast learned much Torah, take not credit to thyself, for thereunto wast thou created.

9. A warning against self righteousness. A man can indeed do nothing better than learn Torah and live in accordance therewith, but this is the whole purpose for which he was sent into the world. He deserves blame if he does not do it, but if he does do it he does only what he was meant to do. It is the austere lesson of absolutely disinterested service of God, and echoes the maxim of Antigonos of Socho, above, I. 3.

Johanan b. Zaccai is said to have been one of the disciples of Hillel. He survived, probably by several years, the fall of Jerusalem in 70 C. E. so that the date of his death may be put at about 80 C. E. He was certainly an old man when he died, and therefore must have been born near the beginning of the common era. He played an extremely important part in the time which succeeded the fall of Jerusalem, as it was he who reorganised the religious life of the remnant of the Jewish people and made the assembly at Jabneh the chief centre of learning and spiritual leadership. It is nowhere explained in the Rabbinical sources how it was that he, not being a descendant of Hillel, succeeded Simeon b. Gamliel, (see I. 17 and n° 4 of the pedigree there given). The natural successor of this Simeon would have been his son Gamliel II, (n° 5 of the pedigree); but he only followed after the death or retirement of Johanan b. Zaccai. It is also remarkable that a man so eminent in the religious affairs of his time, long before as well as after the fall of Jerusalem, should be known only through the Rabbinical sources. Josephus does not mention him, although like himself, Johanan received favour from Vespasian.[1] Those, however, with whom Johanan was most closely associated and who looked to him as their leader, were the least concerned with the war, and probably kept as quiet as they could amid the strife and confusion which filled Jerusalem during the war and the siege.

Aboth contains no other than this one short saying by Johanan b. Zaccai, a fact which goes to show that the compiler was not influenced in his selection by the eminence of the several teachers. Gamliel II is not represented by a single saying, and Rabbi himself only by the one group already given, II. 1, and the saying in IV. 27. Neither can the compiler have intended a complete collection of the sayings of the teachers whom he included in his list, for he could have found many other sayings by Johanan b. Zaccai, as well as by Gamliel II, Rabbi and others. This confirms the suggestion made above (Introd. § B. p. 7) that the compiler noted down various sayings which seemed to him worth preserving, and added the names of their authors whoever those might be.

The phrase "R. J. b. Zaccai received from Hillel and Shammai" is the last instance of the formula used so often in ch. I. In a sense he closed the line of tradition of which the successive stages are there given. For though the tradition was carried forward, it was under very different conditions. R. Johanan was the founder of a new order of things, but just on that account it was well to mark his connexion with the old order by noting that he "received from" Hillel and Shammai as they had done from their predecessors, and so back to Moses. The use of the formula "received from" does not necessarily imply the continuity of ch. II with ch. I or a common origin. It is compatible with the hypothesis that the compiler found the series ch. I complete down to the war; and that he linked on this second collection by using the formula of ch. I in the only case where it was applicable.

The MSS mostly read עשית, 'hast performed' instead of למדת 'hast learned', (see Taylor ad loc.) which is found in the modern printed texts. There is not much difference so far as the essential meaning of the saying

<hr />

[1] So the Rabbinical tradition. In b. Gitt. 56ᵇ however, where the interview between J. b. Z. and the Roman 'king', מלכא, is described, the name of the king is not mentioned. It must have been Titus, for Vespasian had left him to finish the siege, and was himself in Egypt. See Tac. Hist. II. 82.

is concerned. 'Learning' and 'doing' are the two coordinates of every point
in the line of Torah, cp. the wellknown contrasted pair of axioms, (j. Pes. 30ᵇ,
j. Hagg. 76ᶜ), תלמוד קודם למעשה and מעשה קודם לתלמוד. There was truth
whichever way the two terms were placed.

10. חֲמִשָּׁה תַלְמִידִים הָיוּ לוֹ לְרַבָּן יוֹחָנָן בֶּן־זַכַּי וְאֵלּוּ הֵן רַבִּי אֱלִיעֶזֶר
בֶּן־הוֹרְקָנוֹס רַבִּי יְהוֹשֻׁעַ בֶּן־חֲנַנְיָא רַבִּי יוֹסֵי הַכֹּהֵן רַבִּי שִׁמְעוֹן בֶּן־נְתַנְאֵל
וְרַבִּי אֶלְעָזָר בֶּן־עֲרָךְ:

10. Five disciples had Rabban Johanan ben Zaccai and these are
they: — Rabbi Eliezer ben Horkenos, Rabbi Jehoshua ben Hananjah,
Rabbi Josē the priest, Rabbi Simeon ben Nathanel, and Rabbi Eleazar
ben Arach.

11. הוּא הָיָה מוֹנֶה שְׁבָחָם (רַבִּי) אֱלִיעֶזֶר בֶּן־הוֹרְקָנוֹס בּוֹר סוּד שֶׁאֵינוֹ
מְאַבֵּד טִפָּה (רַבִּי) יְהוֹשֻׁעַ בֶּן־חֲנַנְיָא אַשְׁרֵי יוֹלַדְתּוֹ (רַבִּי) יוֹסֵי הַכֹּהֵן
חָסִיד (רַבִּי) שִׁמְעוֹן בֶּן־נְתַנְאֵל יְרֵא חֵטְא (וְרַבִּי) אֶלְעָזָר בֶּן־עֲרָךְ כְּמַעְיָן
הַמִּתְגַּבֵּר:

11. He used to sum up their praise: — Eliezer ben Horkenos is
a plastered cistern that loseth not a drop. Jehoshua ben Hananjah
happy is she who bore him. Josē the priest is a saint. Simeon
ben Nathanel is one that feareth sin. Eleazar ben Arach is as a
full flowing spring.

12. הוּא הָיָה אוֹמֵר אִם יִהְיוּ כָּל־חַכְמֵי יִשְׂרָאֵל בְּכַף מֹאזְנַיִם וֶאֱלִיעֶזֶר
בֶּן־הוֹרְקָנוֹס בְּכַף שְׁנִיָּה מַכְרִיעַ אֶת־כֻּלָּם. אַבָּא שָׁאוּל אוֹמֵר מִשְּׁמוֹ אִם
יִהְיוּ כָּל־חַכְמֵי יִשְׂרָאֵל בְּכַף מֹאזְנַיִם וֶאֱלִיעֶזֶר בֶּן הוֹרְקָנוֹס אַף עִמָּהֶם
וְאֶלְעָזָר בֶּן־עֲרָךְ בְּכַף שְׁנִיָּה מַכְרִיעַ אֶת־כֻּלָּם:

12. אַף. So B.C.S. A.M. om. מכריע. M. add. הוא.

12. He used to say: — If all the Wise of Israel were in one scale
of the balance and Eliezer ben Horkenos in the second scale, he
would weigh them all down.

Abba Shaul said, in his name: — If all the Wise of Israel were
in one scale of the balance, yea and Eliezer ben Horkenos with
them, and Eleazar ben Arach in the second scale, he would weigh
them all down.

10—12. These three verses are of historical not ethical interest. Aboth contains no other instance of a similar note explaining the relation of one teacher to another. The interest of the compiler was clearly not biographical; and just on that account the question is forced on the reader, why is an exception made in the case of these five men? There is always a danger in drawing conclusions from a single instance; it is quite possible that the compiler merely happened to note the connexion of these five men with their teacher, and that it did not occur to him to do so in any other case. Any special reason must be pure conjecture; but, that being admitted, it is permissible to inquire if any special reason could be plausibly alleged, which would account for this exceptional mention of the five teachers named. They were R. Eliezer b. Horkenos, R. Jehoshua b. Hananjah, R. Jose the Priest, R. Simeon b. Nathanel, and R. Eleazar b. Arach. Of these, the first two far exceeded the others in the eminence to which they afterwards attained. But they are here grouped together, and it is emphatically implied that R. Eleazar b. Arach was the greatest of them all. Yet he was the one who most completely disappeared, who counted for least in the development of Rabbinical Judaism. In fact he is said to have withdrawn from his former associates after the death of R. Johanan b. Zaccai (A. R. N^A XIV.). I am inclined to think that the compiler of Aboth did not himself add vv. 10—12 as a historical note, but rather that he took over vv. 3—14 from some source and incorporated it in his collection (vv. 15—19 would naturally follow). Omitting the sayings of Rabbi and his son (vv. 1. 2), and those of R. Tarphon (vv. 20. 21), the bulk of ch. II forms a connected whole of which the central figure is R. Johanan b. Zaccai. It begins with his teacher, Hillel, then mentions himself, then names his five disciples. It is not continuous with ch. I, being arranged on a different plan, and following a different line of thought: but it is sufficiently akin to that and the succeeding chapters, to be incorporated with them in the whole work. Moreover, the way in which the master speaks of the disciples and criticises their opinions, shows that the original piece, in vv. 9—14, refers to a time when they were still under his tuition, and had not become independent teachers[1]; a time therefore when he and they were still in Jerusalem, before the siege. The mention of Abba Shaul in v. 12 suggests a further thought. For Abba Shaul (the elder, for there were two, the second being contemporary with Rabbi, or his father, b. Pes. 34^a) had been a shopkeeper in Jerusalem; and the fact that he spoke "in the name of" R. Johanan may (since they were contemporary) be taken as evidence that he knew him, and presumably heard him. May not Abba Shaul be the authority for, if not himself the author of, this slight sketch of R. Johanan and his disciples? This, I fully admit, is pure conjecture; but in itself it seems not unreasonable or improbable.

The terms of praise bestowed by R. Johanan on his disciples call for no special remark, being simply what he chose to apply to them. It is quite

---

[1] Some MSS omit 'Rabbi' before their names; the printed texts all have 'Rabbi'.

clear that Eleazar b. Arach was his favourite disciple, or rather the one of
whom he held the highest opinion. All the more striking is the way in which
his opinion was contradicted by the complete failure of Eleazar subsequently
to justify it. Of the five, only Eliezer b. Horkenos and Jehoshua b. Hananiah
became famous. Josē the priest and Simeon b. Nathanel are hardly more
than names in the Talmudic tradition, certainly they were never of any importance. See below, under the several names.[1]

13. אָמַר לָהֶם צְאוּ וּרְאוּ אֵיזוֹ הִיא דֶּרֶךְ טוֹבָה שֶׁיִּדְבַּק בָּהּ הָאָדָם, רַבִּי
אֱלִיעֶזֶר אוֹמֵר עַיִן טוֹבָה רַבִּי יְהוֹשֻׁעַ אוֹמֵר חָבֵר טוֹב רַבִּי יוֹסֵי אוֹמֵר שָׁכֵן
טוֹב רַבִּי שִׁמְעוֹן אוֹמֵר הָרוֹאֶה אֶת הַנּוֹלָד רַבִּי אֶלְעָזָר אוֹמֵר לֵב טוֹב:
אָמַר לָהֶם רוֹאֶה אֲנִי אֶת־דִּבְרֵי אֶלְעָזָר בֶּן־עֲרָךְ מִדִּבְרֵיכֶם שֶׁבִּכְלָל דְּבָרָיו
דִּבְרֵיכֶם:

13. טובה M. add. ש ישרה.

13. He said to them: — Go and see which is that good way to
which a man should cleave? R. Eliezer said A good eye. R. Jehoshua
said A good associate. R. Josē said A good neighbour. R. Simeon
said One who sees the event. R. Eleazar said A good heart. He
said to them I approve the words of Eleazar ben Arach more than
your words, for in his words are included yours.

13. A test question of ethics proposed by the teacher to his disciples. The form of the question closely resembles that of Rabbi
in v. 1 of this chapter. The answers however do not logically correspond to the question, for none of the things specified is in any
sense a 'way'. The meaning of the question is, what is the fundamental of a right life? or, what is the clue to the right way of
life? The answers are therefore given in concrete form, but imply
abstract qualities. Thus, 'a good eye' denotes freedom from envy;
'a good associate' friendship; 'a good neighbour', sympathy; 'one
who sees the event', the virtue of learning by experience; 'a good
heart' unselfish love in thought feeling and act. This last is approved because it includes all the others, the heart being regarded

[1] R. Joh. b. Zaccai and another group of his disciples are mentioned in b. B. Bath. 10ᵇ.
There the disciples named are R. Eliezer, R. Jehoshua, R. Gamliel, R. Eleazar of
Modiin, and R. Nehunjah b. ha-Kanah. There is another version of this passage in
Pesik. d. R. K. 12ᵇ, see Bacher A. d. T. I. 38—39, where he shows that two debates
are confused into one. R. Gamliel and R. Eleazar of Modiin took part in the later
at Jabneh, while R. Eliezer and R. Jehoshua were concerned with the earlier one in
which R. Johanan b. Zaccai presided.

as the source and seat of all the higher life of man. The first answer and the last find the essential of a good life within; the second and third seek it without, in a relation with some other person; the fourth, (if the interpretation given be correct) gives an answer which is not so much ethical as philosophical. The answers which find the essential of a good life in relation to others are nevertheless true in so far as they supplement those which find it in the inner disposition. The love in the heart must seek and find its object in another than itself. Neither the love alone, nor the object alone (the good neighbour, or associate) is sufficient, but the union of the two. This is part of the meaning of "Thou shalt love the Lord thy God" and "Thou shalt love thy neighbour as thyself".

The interpretations given above are what seem to me most probable; but phrases so brief may obviously be taken in more than one sense. The good associate, חבר, may be the companion in study of Torah; and, if so, then the clue to the right life would be that study is made more effectual through the fellowship of kindred minds. The answer of Simeon b. Nathanel stands apart from the rest. His principle involves no relation with others, but is the act of an isolated mind. He was described by his teacher as one who feared sin, and his clue to a good life consisted in forecasting the result of his actions, in order to judge whether they would lead to sin or not. Simeon is a type of one aspect of Pharisaism which has perhaps done most to produce an unfavourable impression upon the non-Jewish mind. The opening phrase "Go and see", is a mere formula of the schools, and means no more than "I put to you this question".

14. אָמַר לָהֶם צְאוּ וּרְאוּ אֵיזוֹ הִיא דֶּרֶךְ רָעָה שֶׁיִּתְרַחֵק מִמֶּנָּה הָאָדָם, רַבִּי אֱלִיעֶזֶר אוֹמֵר עַיִן רָעָה רַבִּי יְהוֹשֻׁעַ אוֹמֵר חָבֵר רָע רַבִּי יוֹסֵי אוֹמֵר שָׁכֵן רָע רַבִּי שִׁמְעוֹן אוֹמֵר הַלֹּוֶה וְאֵינוֹ מְשַׁלֵּם, אֶחָד הַלֹּוֶה מִן הָאָדָם כְּלֹוֶה מִן הַמָּקוֹם שֶׁנֶּאֱמַר לֹוֶה רָשָׁע וְלֹא יְשַׁלֵּם וְצַדִּיק חוֹנֵן וְנוֹתֵן. רַבִּי אֶלְעָזָר אוֹמֵר לֵב רָע: אָמַר לָהֶם רוֹאֶה אֲנִי אֶת־דִּבְרֵי אֶלְעָזָר בֶּן־עֲרָךְ מִדִּבְרֵיכֶם שֶׁבִּכְלַל דְּבָרָיו דִּבְרֵיכֶם:

14. Before אמר M. add. ו הזר.

14. He said to them: — Go and see which is that evil way which a man should shun. R. Eliezer said An evil eye. R. Jehoshua said An evil associate. R. Josē said An evil neighbour. R. Simeon said He who borrows and does not pay. He that borrows from man is as he that borrows from the Omnipresent; as it is said

(Ps. XXXVII. 21). The wicked borroweth and payeth not, but the righteous showeth favour and giveth. R. Eleazar said An evil heart. He said to them I approve the words of Eleazar ben Arach more than your words; for in his words are included yours.

14. The negative of the question and respective answers given in the preceding verse. No further explanation is therefore necessary, except in regard to the answer of Simeon, which is on lines different from those of the others. The reference is hardly to actual borrowing of money, for in this case the statement though it might be well founded would be irrelevant. Taken in the light of Simeon's previous answer, it would seem to mean that he found the essential of wrong life in presuming on the future without considering the consequences, acting without reflecting whether his act would lead to sin. In non-religious terms, but keeping to Simeon's metaphor, it means giving pledges to fortune, taking risks and being unable to meet them.

The clause which amplifies Simeon's answer, "He that borrows from man &c.", together with the proof-text from Ps. XXXVII. 21, are probably an editorial addition. They break the symmetry of the several answers, and give a meaning to Simeon's answer which makes it irrelevant to the question. It is found however in all the sources, both MSS and printed texts, and must therefore be very ancient.

15. הֵם אָמְרוּ שְׁלֹשָׁה דְבָרִים רַבִּי אֱלִיעֶזֶר אוֹמֵר יְהִי כְבוֹד חֲבֵרָךְ חָבִיב
עָלֶיךָ כְּשֶׁלָּךְ וְאַל תְּהִי נוֹחַ לִכְעוֹס וְשׁוּב יוֹם אֶחָד לִפְנֵי מִיתָתָךְ וֶהֱוֵי
מִתְחַמֵּם כְּנֶגֶד ׳ אוּרָן שֶׁל חֲכָמִים וֶהֱוֵי זָהִיר בְּגַחַלְתָּן שֶׁלֹּא תִכָּוֶה שֶׁנְּשִׁיכָתָן
נְשִׁיכַת שׁוּעָל וַעֲקִיצָתָן עֲקִיצַת עַקְרָב וּלְחִישָׁתָן לְחִישַׁת שָׂרָף וְכָל־דִּבְרֵיהֶם
כְּגַחֲלֵי אֵשׁ:

15. כבוד usual reading. M. ממון, and in v. 17 *vice versa*. M. שֶׁל חכמים. M. שֶׁל
שלא. A.B.C. M.S. שמא ; תלמידים חכ׳.

15. These said three things. R. Eliezer said Let the honour of thine associate be dear to thee as thine own; and be not quick to anger; and repent a day before thy death; and warm thyself at the fire of the Wise, and beware of their glowing coal lest thou be scorched. For their bite is the bite of a fox, and their sting the sting of a scorpion, and their hiss the hiss of a serpent, and all their words like coals of fire.

15—19. Sayings by each of the five disciples already enumerated.

Each is credited with three sayings, but the grouping is not very clearly defined.

15. R. Eliezer's sayings. The first three form the group originally ascribed to him. Those that follow are of a quite different tone, and are not general ethical maxims at all. The first of the group of three is a variant of 'Love thy neighbour as thyself'; the second teachers the lesson of patience and forbearance, and the third the duty of always being ready for the day of death by not deferring repentance. These are simple and obvious and need no comment to explain them.

The succeeding sayings express some very sharp criticism of the Wise, i. e. the Rabbis. The natural clue to the interpretation of them is to be found in the fact that R. Eliezer was in his later years excommunicated by his colleagues, and died while still under the ban. He was not gentle in his disposition, and his bitter words express clearly enough how deeply he felt the severity which had been shown to him, even though he may have acknowledged that the sentence was just. The commentators refer the saying to the words of Torah, on the lines of "The Lord descended upon it (Sinai) in fire" (Exod XIX. 19). But this is a forced explanation, and does not meet the point; for Eliezer spoke of the Wise and of *their* words, *their* sting &c., not of *its* (Torah's) words. If he had meant to teach a lesson of caution in dealing with the words of Torah, he would surely have made that clear, and would scarcely have put so much of suppressed passion into what he said. As a general counsel his words are strained and unnatural; as a piece of self-revelation they are deeply interesting, and awaken sympathy for a great man suffering in lonely bitterness.

R. Eliezer b. Horkenos, often called "the Great", was, until his excommunication, chief among the teachers of his time. His name occurs unnumbered times in the Rabbinical literature. For a full account of him see the article in the Jew. Encyc. The dates of his life are approximately as follows; — he was born in Jerusalem probably about 40 C. E., certainly not later than 50 C. E., for·he must have been at least twenty years of age when he helped R. Johanan b. Zaccai to escape from the city during the siege. His excommunication probably took place in 96 C. E., and he died in or before the סכנה, persecution, under Lusius Quietus in 117 C. E.

The saying "Repent one day &c." is found in b. Shabb. 153ᵃ, and is ascribed to R. Eliezer; his disciples asked him How could a man know when he should die? and he answered 'Let him repent today, for he may die tomorrow'.

For the view that the saying about the Wise is not to be reckoned as one of the three credited to R. Eliezer there is the authority of Maimonides (ad loc.), though he does not suggest their reference to Eliezer's excommunication. Taylor (II. 144) quotes an opinion that these sayings are borrowed from A. R. N. They are found there, (ch. XVI, p. 62), along with the saying 'Repent one day before thy death'. The compiler of A. R. N. may just as well have taken them from Aboth. Until the relation of Aboth to A. R. N. is fully cleared up, a decision on the point is impossible. But it is evident that the commentators felt some difficulty about the words concerning the Wise.

R. Eliezer's excommunication is narrated in b. B. Mez. 59^b and j. M. Kat. 81^d. The immediate point in dispute was a small one, but the real contest was whether the opinion of the majority should prevail. The debate is described in terms of extraordinary boldness; intended no doubt not to be taken literally but to emphasize the importance of the principle at stake. R. Eliezer apparently left the assembly like Jonathan in fierce anger, and R. Akiba offered to go and tell him of the sentence passed upon him. The passage in B. Mez. is one of the most vivid and dramatic in the whole Talmud. R. Eliezer spent the rest of his life, some twenty years, in excommunication; but it does not appear that intercourse between him and his former colleagues entirely ceased.

16. רַבִּי יְהוֹשֻׁעַ אוֹמֵר עַיִן הָרַע וְיֵצֶר הָרַע וְשִׂנְאַת הַבְּרִיּוֹת מוֹצִיאִין אֶת הָאָדָם מִן הָעוֹלָם:

16. R. Jehoshua said: — The evil eye and the evil principle and hatred of mankind drive a man out of the world.

16. R. Jehoshua's three sayings are in reality only one. He mentions three things which drive a man out of the world, the evil eye, the evil inclination and hatred of mankind. These are only three synonyms for selfishness which is by its very nature unsocial. The selfish man cuts himself from human intercourse and the sympathy of his fellows; it is not they but himself to whom is due his exclusion.

R. Jehoshua b. Hananjah, in some respects the foremost man of the time, at all events in his later years. He survived both R. Eliezer and R. Gamliel II, who held the rank of Nasi. He was living in 130 C. E. for he conversed with the Emperor Hadrian in that year. As he helped, along with R. Eliezer, to effect the escape of R. Johanan b. Zaccai from Jerusalem, he must have been born certainly not later than 50 C. E. He had been a singer in the temple. He is not mentioned in connexion with the revolt of Bar Cocheba, 132—135 C. E., so was presumably dead by that time. He took the lead in the controversy with R. Eliezer, but no one could have felt the loss of his former antagonist in debate more than he must have done. It was no unworthy jealousy that parted them. For a full account of him see the article in the Jew. Encyc.

The threefold saying needs little comment. Note that the 'evil eye' is named not by him but by R. Eliezer in answer to R. Johanan's question (above,

v. 14). To drive a man from the world is a phrase which occurs elsewhere, (see below III. 14), and only means exclusion from human fellowship. It does not refer to death, and still less does it imply exclusion from the world to come, as Taylor by his reference (*ad loc.*) to 1 John III. 15 seems to suggest. Some commentators explain the plural '(they) drive him from the world' as referring to the people whom he hates; but the reference to his own selfish nature is simpler and psychologically truer. The selfish man hates, but only the selfish hate him in return. The punishment he receives is what he makes for himself.

17. רַבִּי יוֹסֵי אוֹמֵר יְהִי מָמוֹן חֲבֵרָךְ חָבִיב עָלֶיךָ כְּשֶׁלָּךְ וְהַתְקֵן עַצְמְךָ לִלְמוֹד תּוֹרָה שֶׁאֵינָהּ יְרֻשָּׁה־לָּךְ וְכָל מַעֲשֶׂיךָ יִהְיוּ לְשֵׁם שָׁמָיִם:

17. R. Josē said: — Let the property of thy associate be dear to thee as thine own. And dispose thy self to learn Torah, for it is not an inheritance. And let all thy actions be for the Name of Heaven.

17. R. Josē's three sayings. The first is a variant on that of R. Eliezer but on a lower plane; it is excellent but not inspiring. The second teaches that what knowledge of Torah a man acquires is personal to himself, it cannot be inherited or bequeathed. Torah is in its essence a revelation of divine truth, through the medium of the written or oral word. A man may learn from his teacher how to interpret the word of Torah, may be instructed that such and such truths are contained in it, may be helped in his search for those truths. He in his turn may teach others what has been taught to him. But what he cannot receive from or communicate to another is his own apprehension of the divine truth revealed in the Torah, his own inward vision of "the deep things of God".

The third saying teaches the consecration of one self to the service of God. The principle here implied lies at the heart of Pharisaism, viz that any given act only has worth, moral or religious, when it is done with the purpose of serving God thereby. Merely to do it as an *opus operatum* is nothing; and the only ground on which such action is to be excused or even recommended is that it may lead to action from the higher motive.[1]

---

[1] This is taught in the wellknown sentence b. Pes. 50ᵇ "Ever let a man be occupied with Torah and precepts, even though it be not for its own sake; for while he is doing it not for its own sake, he comes to do it for its own sake." The saying is quoted by R. Jehudah in the name of Rab.

R. Josē the priest is mentioned only very rarely in the Rabbinical literature, and little is known of him. He is called here R. Josē, without his distinguishing epithet; but R. Josē in the Tannaite literature denotes R. Josē b. Halaphta the disciple of R. Akiba (see IV. 8). Nothing is known of the dates of his birth and death; presumably he was much the same in age with R. Eliezer and R. Jehoshua.

18. רַבִּי שִׁמְעוֹן אוֹמֵר הֱוֵי זָהִיר בִּקְרִיאַת שְׁמַע וּבִתְפִלָּה וּכְשֶׁאַתָּה מִתְפַּלֵּל אַל תַּעַשׂ תְּפִלָּתְךָ קֶבַע אֶלָּא רַחֲמִים וְתַחֲנוּנִים לִפְנֵי הַמָּקוֹם שֶׁנֶּאֱמַר כִּי־חַנּוּן וְרַחוּם הוּא אֶרֶךְ אַפַּיִם וְרַב־חֶסֶד וְנִחָם עַל הָרָעָה. וְאַל תְּהִי רָשָׁע בִּפְנֵי עַצְמֶךָ:

18. חסד. M. adds הרע ע יניחם.

18. R. Simeon said: — Be careful in reading the Shema' and in prayer. And when thou prayest, make not thy prayer a fixed form but beseeching and entreaty before God; as it is said (Joel II. 13):— "For he is gracious and merciful, long suffering and plenteous in mercy, and repenteth him of the evil." And be not wicked in thine own sight.

18. R. Simeon's three sayings. The mention of prayer along with the Shema' in the first clause is perhaps due to the second saying which refers to prayer exclusively. Some texts omit "and prayer" in the first saying. But the main point is that to say the Shema' is a solemn duty and ought to be performed with reverence and care, at the right time and in the right way; not because the time or the way are in themselves of any religious importance, but because by observing them the religious act most fully attains its purpose.

Prayer ought to be the free utterance of the heart, see Ber. 28ᵇ; and though prescribed forms and words be used these should be made the means of uttering the inward devotion not of checking it, still less of substituting for it a mere lip-service. This is true whether the reference be to public or to private prayer. The inward spirit must be the master and not the slave of whatever outward form the prayer may assume.

The third saying is obscure in meaning, and is variously interpreted. Rashi explains it "Do not today an act for which tomorrow you will say 'Why did I do this evil'?" Maimonides, and others, explain it "Regard not thyself as (wholly) wicked, since by so doing thou givest up hope of repentance. Regard thyself as partly evil

and partly good; be not either conceited or despairing." Others
explain, "Be not wicked in standing alone, cut not thyself off from
the community, or from common human fellowship." Taylor translates "Be not wicked unto thyself". None of these explanations
seems to be what is required. That of Rashi is not indicated by
R. Simeon's words, but may be founded upon the answer he gave
to the question in v. 14 above. That of Maimonides changes the
force of the saying, from "*Be* not wicked" into "*regard not* thyself
as wicked". The lesson M. deduces is excellent but it does not
naturally follow from the text. The reference to separating from
the community or from human fellowship is far fetched and there
is nothing to suggest it. Taylor's "Be not wicked unto thyself"
might be a good rendering if בפני could mean 'unto'. Keeping
to the grammatical sense of the words,[1] I take the meaning of
the saying to be "Be not wicked in thy own sight" or "Sin not
by thyself". The first rendering would mean "Let not thine own
conscience reproach thee, however much men may condemn thee".
The second would mean "Think not that sin is no sin if there be
none to see it".

R. Simeon b. Nathanel, must not be confused with R. Simeon b. Johai (III. 4)
who is 'R. Simeon' in the Tannaite literature. Of R. Simeon b. Nathanel
little or nothing is known. It is stated in T. A. Zar. III. 10 that he married
the daughter of R. Gamliel I, a statement which Weiss (Dor, dor. II. 80) says
must refer to some other Simeon than the one at present in question. Bacher,
however, (J. Encyc. V. 559) accepts the reference, and this seems warranted.
He is there (A. Zar. *loc. cit.*) said to have been a priest. His marriage must
have taken place before 70 C. E. Beyond this, there is nothing by which
to determine the chronology of his life. Presumably he was much the same
in age as R. Eliezer and R. Jehoshua.

The saying "Make not thy prayer a fixed form &c." has a close parallel
in M. Ber. IV. 4, when R. Eliezer says "If a man makes his prayer a fixed
form, his prayer is not entreaty". As R. Eliezer and R. Simeon were so closely
associated together, one may well have adopted the words of the other. In
the Gemara (Ber. 29[b]) the phrase 'a fixed form' is discussed, and various
meanings attached to it; but there is no reference to the passage in Aboth,
or to R. Simeon b. Nathanel.

---

[1] For the meaning of בפני cp. j. Succ. 53[b] where it is said that in the Synagogue
of Alexandria the various guilds, אומנות, sat each 'by itself', בפני עצמה. In the
passage in Aboth under consideration, the meaning would thus be "by thyself",
separated from others, in solitude.

19. רַבִּי אֶלְעָזָר אוֹמֵר הֱוֵי שָׁקוּד לִלְמוֹד תּוֹרָה וְדַע מַה־שֶּׁתָּשִׁיב לְאֶפִּיקוֹרוֹס
וְדַע לִפְנֵי מִי אַתָּה עָמֵל וּמִי הוּא בַּעַל מְלַאכְתְּךָ שֶׁיְשַׁלֶּם־לְךָ שְׂכַר פְּעֻלָּתֶךָ:

19. שקוד B.C.D.S. שקד A. זהיר M.; ודע B. om. A.C.D.M.; after בלאבתך
B.M.S. add. שישלם לך שכר פעלתך. A. om.

19. R. Eleazar said: — Be alert to learn Torah, and know what
answer to give an 'Epicuros'.[1] And know before whom thou
labourest, and who is the master of thy work to give thee the
wages of thy toil.

19. R. Eleazar's three sayings. The duty of learning Torah needs
no comment, but the context seems to show that in the present
instance the duty has reference to the refutation of opponents. If
the stronghold is to be defended, the defender must be ready for
the assault and have his weapons at hand and be practised in the
use of them. This may be the second of the three sayings, and
indeed must be so regarded if the number three is to be made
up. But unless it be closely connected with the first, that is left
as an almost colourless general maxim, hardly worth the utterance.

The third saying is a reminder to remember that all service is
service of God, who will "render to every man according to his
work" (Ps. LXII. 12).

R. Eleazar b. Arach. He is called here 'R. Eleazar' simply, because he
has already been mentioned as one of the five disciples of R. Johanan
b. Zaccai. In the Tannaite literature 'R. Eleazar' is usually R. Eleazar
b. Shammua (IV. 15). R. Eleazar b. Arach left little mark upon the Tannaite
tradition in spite of the brilliant promise of his youth, (see above, note on
10—12). Yet his companions seem to have retained a deep impression of
his powers. R. Jehoshua met an argument of R. Akiba by saying "Alas [for
thee]! If thou hadst lived in the days of R. Eleazar b. Arach &c." (T. Nedar.
VI. 5). Presumably meaning 'he would have refuted thee'. He went off by
himself after the death of his master, whatever may have been the reason;
and the fruits of his genius were lost to Israel. Nothing can be asserted with
confidence as to his age.

The 'Epikuros' here mentioned is a freethinker, whether of Jewish or
non-Jewish origin, a man who does not accept the Torah as his authority or
his guide. The saying is found in b. Sanh. 38[b], where it is expressly said
that an Epikuros might be either a Jew or a Gentile, and that a Jewish
Epikuros was the more dangerous. The texts in Aboth vary in omitting or

---

[1] 'Epicuros' denotes one who denies God and his commandments. An Epicuros
might be a Gentile, as distinguished from a 'Min', who was usually a Jew. See
my 'Christianity in Talmud and Midrash' p. 120.

retaining the word 'know' before "what thou shalt answer"; but the sense
is clear. This is the first reference in Aboth to controversy in regard to
religion. The maxims hitherto given relate to the duty of the Jew within
the community of Israel. It would be interesting to know what occasion
R. Eleazar had to give this advice to his Jewish brethren. Was his dis-
appearance from the fellowship of Israel perhaps due to the influence of
some Epikuros who weakened his hold on Torah?

20. רַבִּי טַרְפוֹן אוֹמֵר הַיּוֹם קָצָר וְהַמְּלָאכָה מְרֻבָּה וְהַפּוֹעֲלִים עֲצֵלִים
וְהַשָּׂכָר הַרְבֵּה וּבַעַל הַבַּיִת דּוֹחֵק:

20. R. Tarphon said: — The day is short and the work is great,
and the labourers are sluggish, and the wages are high and the
householder is urgent.

21. הוּא הָיָה אוֹמֵר לֹא עָלֶיךָ הַמְּלָאכָה לִגְמוֹר וְלֹא אַתָּה בֶּן־חוֹרִין
לְהִבָּטֵל מִמֶּנָּה אִם לָמַדְתָּ תּוֹרָה הַרְבֵּה נוֹתְנִין לָךְ שָׂכָר הַרְבֵּה וְנֶאֱמָן הוּא
בַּעַל מְלַאכְתְּךָ שֶׁיְּשַׁלֶּם־לָךְ שְׂכַר פְּעֻלָּתֶךָ וְדַע שֶׁמַּתַּן שְׂכָרָן שֶׁל צַדִּיקִים
לֶעָתִיד לָבוֹא:

21. ממנה D.S. הימנה C.M.   A. om.; שכר פעלתך ... הרבה ויאמן.   M. om.

21. He used to say: — The work is not upon thee to finish, nor
art thou free to desist from it. If thou hast learned much Torah
they give thee much wages; and faithful is the master of thy
work who will pay thee the wages of thy toil. And know that the
giving of the reward to the righteous is in the time to come.

20. 21. Two sayings by R. Tarphon. They contain a grave lesson
on the responsibility of life and the duty of earnest faithfulness in
the service of God. The work is great and every one has his part
in it. If many are idle and slothful, yet the faithful servant must
perform his allotted task. It is not for him to survey the whole
field of labour, nor need he be disheartened because he cannot
do all the work. His one thought must be to serve God where
he is placed, for so long as he is bidden to stay there, and in
whatsoever is given him to do. Let him leave the rest in the
hands of God.

R. Tarphon was not one of the group of which R. Johanan b. Zaccai was
the centre, and the reason is not obvious why his sayings were included in
this chapter. Their place may have been suggested by the words of R. Eleazar,
to which they are a fitting supplement. They are reckoned as two sayings;
but the same thought runs through both, and they are practically one.

R. Tarphon did not become prominent until the time after R. Johanan
b. Zaccai had passed from the scene. He once (T. Ḥag. III. 36) said that
he had received a halachah from J. b. Z., but his chief associations were
with younger men, Gamliel II, Eliezer, Jehoshua, and Akiba. He had been
a priest in the Temple (j. Joma 40[b]), an office he could not hold till the age
of twenty years (b. Hull 24[b]). He must therefore have been born not later
than 46 C. E., for he was in the Temple in 66 C. E. (T. Sot. VII. 16), presumably as a priest. He probably met his death in the persecution, סכנה,
of 117 C. E. He is not mentioned in connexion with the war of Bar Cocheba
132—135 C. E. He is sometimes thought to have been the Tryphon of
Justin Martyr; but besides the fact that he was dead some twenty years before the date when the dialogue took place, there is no likeness beyond the
name, and even that is in Jewish tradition always read as Tarphon not
Tryphon. No other instance of the name occurs in the literature of the early
centuries, except as the patronymic of persons who may have been sons of
this Tarphon. It is noteworthy that Tarphon himself has no patronymic;
cp. Hillel, Meir, Nehorai; even Akiba was Akiba b. Joseph.

פרק שליישי CHAP. III.

1. עֲקַבְיָא בֶּן־מַהֲלַלְאֵל אוֹמֵר הִסְתַּבֵּל בִּשְׁלֹשָׁה דְבָרִים וְאֵין אַתָּה בָא לִידֵי
עֲבֵרָה דַּע מֵאַיִן בָּאתָ וּלְאָן אַתָּה הוֹלֵךְ וְלִפְנֵי מִי אַתָּה עָתִיד לִתֵּן דִּין
וְחֶשְׁבּוֹן. מֵאַיִן בָּאתָ מִטִּפָּה סְרוּחָה וּלְאָן אַתָּה הוֹלֵךְ לִמְקוֹם עָפָר רִמָּה
וְתוֹלֵעָה וְלִפְנֵי מִי אַתָּה עָתִיד לִתֵּן דִּין וְחֶשְׁבּוֹן לִפְנֵי מֶלֶךְ מַלְכֵי הַמְּלָכִים
הַקָּדוֹשׁ בָּרוּךְ הוּא:

III 1. המלכים, M. add. הוא before הקדוש.

CHAP. III.

1. Akabja ben Mahalalel said: — Keep in view three things and
thou wilt not come into the power of sin. Know whence thou comest and whither thou goest and before whom thou art to give strict
account. Whence thou comest, — from a fetid drop. Whither thou
goest, — to the place of dust, worms and maggots: and before whom
thou art to give strict account, — Before the king of the kings of
kings, the Holy one blessed be He.

1. This saying is not a mere moralising on the beginning and end
of life, but a counsel how to avoid falling into sin. It is not the beginning and end of life in themselves which are to be remembered,
but the fact that each in its material aspect is loathsome. To bear
in mind his origin is a man's lesson in humility; to remember his

latter end is to keep him unattached to the pleasures of this world; to have in mind the day of reckoning is to make him intent upon that faithful service which is the essence of life according to the Torah. The three virtues to be sought are humility, unworldliness, and the true (not the false) fear of God.

Akabja b. Mahalalel. His date is uncertain, but the fact that he is not called 'Rabbi' shows that he is amongst the earliest Tannaim. Opinions vary as to whether he was contemporary with Hillel or with Gamliel I, or even with Gamliel II. There seems to be no decisive evidence, but what there is seems to me to favour the earlier rather than the later of the dates suggested. The remarkable passage Siphrē, I. Behaaloth. § 105, which is a vindication of Akab. b. M. is based on a phrase of his own, "shall render strict account", which occurs in the saying at present under consideration. The phrase may have been a conventional one, but it is quoted and referred to Ak. b. Mah. in T. Sot. II. 2 by teachers long after his time. His designation of God as "King of the kings of the kings" occurs also in the dying words of R. Johanan b. Zaccai (b. Ber. 28ᵇ). Evidently, Ak. b. M. left a deep impression upon the memory of his countrymen, and was venerated in spite of the sentence of excommunication pronounced against him (M. Edu. V. 6.). If he had been a contemporary, R. Jehudah b. Illai (after 135 C. E.) would have known whether he had been excommunicated or not (M. Edu. *loc. cit.*); and would not have suggested that some other was the real object of the sentence.

2 . רַבִּי חֲנִינָא סְגָן הַכֹּהֲנִים אוֹמֵר הֱוֵי מִתְפַּלֵּל בִּשְׁלוֹמָהּ שֶׁל מַלְכוּת
שֶׁאִלְמָלֵא מוֹרָאָהּ אִישׁ אֶת־רֵעֵהוּ חַיִּים בְּלָעָנוּ׃

2. בלעי D. S. M.   בלענו A. B.

2. R. Hanina the deputy of the priests, said: — Pray for the peace of the government; for, except for the fear of that, we should have swallowed each other alive.

2. A saying quite unlike any that have been recorded in Aboth. It is a reflexion in the Pharisaic mind of the power of the Roman Empire, the power which kept the nations in subjection if not in peace, and according to this teacher prevented the destruction of the Jewish nation. To pray for the peace of the Roman Empire was not a mild platitude from a member of a subject nation, but a deliberate choice in a controversy which ended in war. It is true that the commentators all interpret the saying in reference to kingdoms in general, and draw from it the lesson of sympathy for others; but, for Israel in the first century of the common era, there was only one kingdom or sovereignty which could come under con-

sideration, and that one alone had the power to hold the subject
peoples in control. As a general maxim the saying is flat and commonplace; as a reference to Rome it is extremely interesting and
valuable. Whether it was said before or after the fall of Jerusalem
can hardly be determined, but clearly the author recognised the
overwhelming power of Rome, and by bidding men pray for the peace
of the kingdom he implied that its power was divinely appointed;
Rome was an instrument in the hands of God, as Assyria had been
in former times (Isa. X. 5). The effect of that power was to restrain
the strife of subject peoples, and thereby to preserve Israel from destruction.

R. Ḥanina the deputy of the priests, was another of those who survived
the fall of Jerusalem. In b. Joma 8ᵃ R. Ḥanina סגן הכהנים, the deputy
of the priests, is mentioned along with R. Meir and R. Jose. If this means that
he took part in debate with them, he cannot have held office in the Temple,
yet in T. Zeb. IX. 5 he mentions what his father used to do in the Temple.
The Ḥanina of Joma 8ᵃ was probably a younger descendant inheriting the
title. R. Simeon בן הסגן, (M. Shek. VIII. 5), would seem to show that the
title was inherited, and if so he would be the son of the R. Ḥanina סגן הכ'
who survived the Temple. His office was that of deputy of the High Priest,
to take his place if he were prevented from discharging his functions.
Nothing can be stated with certainty as to the dates of his birth and death.
But he would hardly have held so important an office while still a young
man, and he must have been already holding it while the Temple was yet
standing. It is not unreasonable therefore to conjecture that he must have
been at least fifty years of age when the Temple was destroyed, so that his
birth may be placed at about 20 C.E. The year of his death is not known;
but it is said, in the closing chapter of Meg. Taanith, that he was put to
death on the 25ᵗʰ of Sivan. He is not elsewhere counted amongst the 'political martyrs', הרוגי מלכות, and his death may have been unconnected
with any of the well known persecutions. The reference of his dictum to
Rome is assumed by Grätz, Gsch. IV. 20, Frankel, D. ha-Mish. 60, Bacher
A. T. I. 56, Weiss, Dor dor, I. 191. The last named, (ibid) says that R. Ḥan.
changed his opinion and joined the party of the Zealots. If this be true, (it
is based on A. R. Nᴬ c. XX), it would lend colour to the tradition of his
execution; but the conclusion appears to be without sufficient warrant.

"Should have swallowed ... alive". The MSS vary between בלענו and בלעו.
The former is on the whole more strongly supported (see Taylor II. 146 *ad
loc.*), and is certainly more dramatic. One commentator objects that the
speaker would not have included himself,—"*we* should have swallowed up &c.";
but, in view of the factions and dissensions of his time, this is just what he
would most naturally have said. This saying is quoted, as Mishnah, תנן,
A. Zar. 4ᵃ where the printed text (Wilna ed.) reads בלעו.

3· רַבִּי חֲנַנְיָא בֶּן־תְּרַדְיוֹן אוֹמֵר שְׁנַיִם שֶׁיּוֹשְׁבִין וְאֵין בֵּינֵיהֶם דִּבְרֵי תוֹרָה
הֲרֵי זֶה מוֹשַׁב לֵצִים· שֶׁנֶּאֱמַר וּבְמוֹשַׁב לֵצִים לֹא יָשָׁב· אֲבָל שְׁנַיִם שֶׁיּוֹשְׁבִין
וְיֵשׁ בֵּינֵיהֶם דִּבְרֵי תוֹרָה שְׁכִינָה שְׁרוּיָה בֵּינֵיהֶם· שֶׁנֶּאֱמַר אָז נִדְבְּרוּ יִרְאֵי
יְיָ אִישׁ אֶל־רֵעֵהוּ וַיַּקְשֵׁב יְיָ וַיִּשְׁמָע וַיִּכָּתֵב סֵפֶר זִכָּרוֹן לְפָנָיו לְיִרְאֵי יְיָ
וּלְחֹשְׁבֵי שְׁמוֹ· אֵין לִי אֶלָּא שְׁנַיִם מִנַּיִן אֲפִילוּ אֶחָד שֶׁיּוֹשֵׁב וְעוֹסֵק בַּתּוֹרָה
שֶׁהַקָּדוֹשׁ בָּרוּךְ הוּא קוֹבֵעַ לוֹ שָׂכָר· שֶׁנֶּאֱמַר יֵשֵׁב בָּדָד וְיִדֹּם כִּי נָטַל
עָלָיו:

3. R. Hananjah ben Teradion said:—When two sit and there are
not between them words of Torah, lo, this is 'the seat of the
scornful', as it is said:—'Nor sitteth in the seat of the scornful',
But, when two sit and there are between them words of Torah,
the Shechinah rests between them, as it is said 'Then they that
feared the Lord spake one to another, and the Lord hearkened and
heard; and there was written a book of remembrance before him
for them that feared the Lord and thought upon his name'. I find
here only two. Whence *is it proved* that when even one sits and
occupies himself with Torah the Holy one blessed be He fixes for
him a reward: As it is said 'Let him sit alone and be silent, for
he hath taken upon him'.

3. A variant on the theme of the study of Torah. Expressed in
general terms it teaches that all intercourse between men should
be hallowed in thought and speech by remembrance of the divine
presence. Their conversation should impart, not impair, the influence
which comes through revelation of sacred truth. "The seat of the
scornful" is the company of those who do not "delight in the Torah
of the Lord" (Ps. I. 1). But where two sit together and converse
of Torah, there the divine presence is in their midst. And even if
one sit alone and meditate on holy things, that same divine presence
hallows his solitary musing. Those who think that Pharisaism was
a barren and unspiritual faith would do well to reflect on this deep
and true saying.

R. Hananjah, (or Hanina) b. Teradjon was one of the martyrs in the
terrible slaughter which followed the war of Bar Cocheba, 135 C. E. His
execution is described in ghastly detail b. A. Zar 18[b]; but, as in all great
martyrdoms, the spiritual triumphs over the material, and the nobility of the
man shines out through the horror of his death. The date of his death is
known, but not that of his birth. He left a wife and four children; his
daughter, Beruria, was the wife of R. Meir (see below IV. 12). His home was

in Sichnin. The name Teradjon does not occur elsewhere, except in the case of R. Elazar b. Teradjon (j. Gitt. VII. 4. 48^d) who may have been brother of R. Hananjah. The origin of the name has not been satisfactorily explained.

Three proof-texts are cited to illustrate or establish R. Hananjah's saying. The reference to "the seat of the scornful" Ps. I. 1 is no doubt original, though it only gains its point from the following verse which is not quoted. The quotation from Mal. III. 16 is also probably original, at all events the first clause. There is always, however, room for supposing that the compiler or editor has added the proof-texts by way of giving scripture warrant for the maxims uttered by the several teachers. The passage referring to one who sits alone has all the appearance of an afterthought, intended to carry the argument further than the original teacher had done. For a series of proof-texts cp. nᵒ 7 below, and ch. VI throughout. The phrase אֵין לִי אֶלָּא מִנַּיִן... is the regular academic formula for introducing a proof-text, see Bacher, Terminologie I s. v. מִנַּיִן. Taylor omits the formula, and regards the whole clause as an interpolation. See, for the MS evidence, Taylor II. 147.

4. רַבִּי שִׁמְעוֹן אוֹמֵר שְׁלֹשָׁה שֶׁאָכְלוּ עַל שֻׁלְחָן אֶחָד וְלֹא אָמְרוּ עָלָיו דִּבְרֵי תוֹרָה כְּאִלּוּ אָכְלוּ מִזִּבְחֵי מֵתִים שֶׁנֶּאֱמַר כִּי כָּל־שֻׁלְחָנוֹת מָלְאוּ קִיא צוֹאָה בְּלִי מָקוֹם: אֲבָל שְׁלֹשָׁה שֶׁאָכְלוּ עַל שֻׁלְחָן אֶחָד וְאָמְרוּ עָלָיו דִּבְרֵי תוֹרָה כְּאִלּוּ אָכְלוּ מִשֻּׁלְחָנוֹ שֶׁל־מָקוֹם. שֶׁנֶּאֱמַר וַיְדַבֵּר אֵלַי זֶה הַשֻּׁלְחָן אֲשֶׁר־לִפְנֵי יְיָ:

4. R. Simeon said:—Three who have eaten at one table and have not said over it words of Torah are as if they had eaten of the sacrifices of the dead, as it is said 'For all tables are full of vomit *and* filthiness without God'. But three who have eaten at one table and have said over it words of Torah are as if they had eaten from the table of God, as it is said: 'And he said to me, This is the table which is before the Lord'.

4. A saying on somewhat the same lines as the preceding, and teaching the same duty of "holy conversation", especially in regard to sitting at meals. It may have been suggested by the previous saying.

R. Simeon, here, is R. Simeon b. Johai, one of the most famous teachers of his time. In the Mishnah and the cognate literature, 'R. Simeon' almost always means R. Simeon b. Johai. His history belongs mainly to the period after the war of Bar Cocheba 132—135. He is said to have been one of the seven disciples of R. Akiba who were ordained by R. Jehudah b. Baba, and he certainly helped to carry on the tradition after the older teachers had been swept away. The date of his birth may be put at about 100 C. E., and he died probably about 160 C. E. These dates cannot be far wrong, for Rabbi studied under him in Tekoa, and Rabbi cannot have been born earlier than 135 C. E. For the story of his life, and an account of his work and character see the article in the J. Encycl. XI. 359—362.

The saying about "three who eat &c." is chiefly interesting as an illustration of haggadic exegesis. The moral lesson taught is unexceptionable, but, as the previous saying shows, not original with R. Simeon. No Pharisee would question the truth or importance of it. The point lies in the ingenuity with which the two texts quoted are made to support the lesson taught. The connexion with the first text, Isa. XXVIII. 8 is found in the word מקום 'place', which R. Simeon takes as a designation of God, according to a frequent Rabbinic usage. He was perfectly aware that the prophet had used the word in a quite different sense. For the text Ezek. XLI. 22 the connecting link is the phrase "the table ... before the Lord"; but the argument is really based upon the first clause of the verse, as the commentators point out, where the number three is introduced. No one who contested the lesson which R. Simeon meant to teach would be convinced by his Scripture proof; but those who accepted the lesson might, and no doubt often did, admire the fantastic skill of the demonstration.

5. רַבִּי חֲנִינָא בֶּן־חֲכִינַאי אוֹמֵר הַנֵּעוֹר בַּלַּיְלָה וְהַמְהַלֵּךְ בַּדֶּרֶךְ יְחִידִי
וּמְפַנֶּה לִבּוֹ לְבַטָּלָה הֲרֵי זֶה מִתְחַיֵּב בְּנַפְשׁוֹ:

5. R. Ḥanina ben Ḥachinai said:— He who wakes in the night, and he who walks alone by the way, and he who makes his heart empty for idle thoughts, lo he is guilty against himself.

5. On solitary meditation, and the spiritual danger of an idle and vacant mind. Solitude either by day or night leaves the way open to temptation, and the way to guard against it is to keep the mind closed against idle thoughts. This is an application (whether intended or not) of the injunction in Deut. VI. 7. "Thou shalt talk of them ... when thou walkest by the way, and when thou liest down and when thou risest up". It is one more illustration of that consecration of the whole of a man's waking existence to the service of God which was for the Pharisee the "way of the perfect life". Duty and necessary work demand the application of the mind to many things which are of this world; but what better could there be for the times when there is no work to be done and no social intercourse to engage the attention, than instinctively to turn one's thoughts to God?

R. Ḥanina or Ḥananjah b. Ḥachinai was especially associated with R. Simeon b. Joḥai, and like him a disciple of Akiba. Presumably he was

of much the same age as R. Simeon, possibly somewhat older. There is no
certain evidence that he survived the slaughter after the war of Bar Cocheba,
and one tradition, "some say", includes him amongst the הרוגי מלכות (Midr.
Elleh Ezkerah, in Ozar Midrashim p. 443). This is not in itself unlikely; but
the statement there made, that he lived to the age of 98, makes it quite
impossible that he should have been coeval with R. Simeon, unless he had
long survived the סכנה of 135 C. E.; in which case he would not have been
one of the political martyrs. His birth and death may be dated with fair
probability at 80 C. E. and 135 C. E. respectively.

In suggesting the above interpretation of his saying I have departed widely
from some of the commentators, who seem to have missed the real point,
and given an almost trivial explanation. R. Han. teaches that certain types
of men are "guilty against themselves". These commentators say that there
are three types, (a) the man who wakes in the night, (b) the man who
walks alone, (c) the man who lets his mind lie open to idle thoughts. But
it is absurd to say that one who wakes at night is "guilty against himself".
And it is no less absurd to say that a man who walks alone is guilty against
himself,—even at night; when he may meet the fairies, as the commentator
in the Mahzor Vitry quaintly says. The error (for an error it surely is) arose
from the fact that the MSS vary between (a) מפנה and (b) המפנה. In the
one case, (a), the word refers to and completes both the waking at night and
the walking alone. In the other case (b), it forms a third type along with
the walking in the night and the walking alone, so that all three are pronounced "guilty against themselves". The true interpretation surely is that
a man who wakes in the night and מפנה opens his mind to idle thoughts
is guilty against himself; and equally a man who walks alone and מפנה &c,
is guilty against himself. The reading מפנה is more strongly supported in
the MSS, than המפנה and gives a far better sense. The interpretation quoted
from R. Jonah, in the commentary Magēn Aboth of R. Simeon b. Zemah Duran,
comes nearest to what I believe to be the true sense of the passage. 'To
be guilty against oneself'; literally, 'against one's soul' but theological ideas
should not be imported into the phrase, as if it implied that such a one was
a 'lost soul'.

6. רַבִּי נְחוּנְיָא בֶּן־הַקָּנָה אוֹמֵר כָּל־הַמְקַבֵּל עָלָיו עוֹל תּוֹרָה מַעֲבִירִין
מִמֶּנּוּ עוֹל מַלְכוּת וְעוֹל דֶּרֶךְ אֶרֶץ וְכָל־הַפּוֹרֵק מִמֶּנּוּ עוֹל תּוֹרָה נוֹתְנִין עָלָיו
עוֹל מַלְכוּת וְעוֹל דֶּרֶךְ אֶרֶץ:

6. נותנין :A. גיזרין D.M.

6. R. Nehunjah ben ha-Kanah said: Every one who receives on
himself the yoke of Torah, they remove from him the yoke of the
Kingdom and the yoke of worldly occupation. But every one who

breaks off from him the yoke of Torah, they lay upon him the yoke of the Kingdom and the yoke of worldly occupation.

6. R. Nehunjah's saying. The lesson is that he who devotes himself to the study of Torah is freed from earthly cares, while he who despises Torah goes into bondage to earthly cares with nothing to relieve their sordidness: The yoke is not the symbol of oppression but of obedience. To take the yoke of any person or thing upon one is to devote oneself to the service of that person or thing. No man can serve two masters, it was said. If he takes upon him the yoke of the one, he is freed from the yoke of the other; if he breaks the yoke of the one, the yoke of the other is fastened on him.

R. Nehunjah b. ha-Kanah. A younger contemporary of R. Johanan b. Zaccai, whose disciple he appears to have been. In Pesik. d. R. K. 12^b, and b. B. Bath. 10^b he is named as one of several disciples to whom R. Joh. b. Z. put a question on the interpretation of Prov. XIV. 34. The two versions differ in some details; and it would seem that possibly in both, and certainly in that in B. Bath. 10^b, the accounts of two separate debates have been fused into one. For a discussion of the point see Bacher A. d. T. I. 37—38 n. But in both passages R. Nehunjah b. ha-Kanah appears as the disciple of R. Joh. b. Z., as does also R. Gamliel. He survived the fall of Jerusalem, as R. Ishmael b. Elisha who was then a boy became his disciple; but whether he lived to the great age implied in b. Meg. 28^a is doubted by Bacher who conjectures that the reference in that passage is to Nahum of Gimzo. (See Bacher A. d. T. I. 63 n.) We are thus left without any data for the beginning and end of his life. His patronymic הקנה is always read 'ha-Kanah', and its meaning is uncertain. If it had signified 'the Zealot' we should have expected הקנאי, 'ha-kannai'. This however is Geiger's explanation, on the strength of a variant הקנא. (See Bacher A. d. T. I. 58 n.). R. N. b. h. K.'s saying has a likeness to one by R. Hanina the deputy of the priests, in A. R. N^A. c. XX, where however there is no mention of the 'yoke' either of Torah or of the Kingdom or of worldly occupation. I doubt if there is any political reference in the 'yoke of the Kingdom'. It was one form of non-spiritual care from which a man was released if he gave his mind and the allegiance of his will to Torah. Saint and sinner alike had to endure the burden of civil oppression; but the saint had his way of escape and the sinner had not. If R. Nehun. was a mystic, as tradition says that he was, this interpretation of his saying gains additional point. The phrase *"they remove from him"* is purely general, and does not refer to the angels, the *familia cælestis*.

‏7. רַבִּי חֲלַפְתָּא בֶּן־דּוֹסָא אִישׁ כְּפַר חֲנַנְיָא אוֹמֵר עֲשָׂרָה שֶׁיּוֹשְׁבִין‎
‏וְעוֹסְקִין בַּתּוֹרָה שְׁכִינָה שְׁרוּיָה בֵּינֵיהֶם שֶׁנֶּאֱמַר אֱלֹהִים נִצָּב בַּעֲדַת־אֵל.‎

וּמִנַּיִן אֲפִילּוּ חֲמִשָּׁה שֶׁנֶּאֱמַר וַאֲגֻדָּתוֹ עַל־אֶרֶץ יְסָדָהּ. וּמִנַּיִן אֲפִילּוּ שְׁלֹשָׁה
שֶׁנֶּאֱמַר בְּקֶרֶב אֱלֹהִים יִשְׁפֹּט. וּמִנַּיִן אֲפִילּוּ שְׁנַיִם שֶׁנֶּאֱמַר אָז נִדְבְּרוּ יִרְאֵי
יְיָ אִישׁ אֶל־רֵעֵהוּ וַיַּקְשֵׁב יְיָ וַיִּשְׁמָע ;   וּמִנַּיִן אֲפִילּוּ אֶחָד שֶׁנֶּאֱמַר בְּכָל־הַמָּקוֹם
אֲשֶׁר אַזְכִּיר אֶת־שְׁמִי אָבֹא אֵלֶיךָ וּבֵרַכְתִּיךָ :

7. יקשב יי וישמע.   M. om.

7. R. Halaphta ben Dosa, of Chephar Hananjah, said: when ten
sit together and are occupied with Torah the Shechinah rests
among them, as it is said (Ps. LXXXII. 1):—'God standeth in the
congregation of judges'. And whence *is it proved for* even five?
As it is said (Amos IX. 6):—'He hath founded his troop upon the
earth'. And whence even three? As it is said Ps. LXXXII. 1
'He judgeth among the gods'. And whence even two? As it is
said (Mal. III. 16):—'Then they that feared the Lord spake one to
another and the Lord hearkened and heard'. And whence even one?
As it is said (Exod. XX. 24):—'In every place where I record my
name I will come to thee and bless thee'.

7. Another variation on the theme of the divine presence with
those who are engaged in the study of Torah. See III. 3. 4. above.
The point of the lesson is not in the fact of the divine presence,
for that is assumed, but in the haggadic interpretation which finds
scripture proof for that unquestioned truth. With this saying cp.
n° 3 above, in this chapter.

R. Halaphta [ben Dosa], of Chephar Hananjah. The patronymic 'ben
Dosa' is wanting in several MSS and printed texts. Possibly it is a mistake
for 'Josē', and if so, R. Halaphta would be the son of the wellknown R. Josē
b. Halaphta, who had a son Halaphta (b. Shabb. 118[b]). In b. B. Mez. 94[a] it
is said that "Abba Halaphta of Chephar Hananjah said in the name of
R. Meir" &c. This would be consistent with his being the son of R. Josē
b. Hal., though the epithet 'Abba' is surprising in that case. But there is
evidence that he was considerably older than this would imply. In T. 1
Kelim. IV. 17 we read that "R. Hal. of Ch. Han. said 'I asked Simeon b.
Han. who asked the son of R. Han. b. Teradjon ... and when the answers
were reported to R. Jehudah b. Baba he said &c." The mention of R. Jehudah b. Baba who was killed by the Romans in or about 135 C. E., shows
that this incident took place before that date. If R. Josē b. Hal. was born
100 C. E. or earlier (see on IV. 16) it is possible that he should have had
a son old enough before 135 C. E. to have asked a question of halachah.
All that can be safely said however is that the Halaphta of Ch. Han. was
almost certainly a member of the same family. Rashi, on b. Joma 66[b]; says
that the Halaphta family were of Babylonian extraction. No dates can be

fixed for either the beginning or the end of this Halaphta's life; but he must not be confounded with the Hal. who said that he remembered seeing R. Gamliel I in the Temple. T. Shabb. XIII. 2. The one may have been grandson of the other, or perhaps nephew. That he was living before and after 135 C. E. is all that can be safely stated in regard to his chronology. Cheph. Hananjah is the present Kefr Anan.

The likeness of R. Hal.'s saying to that of R. Han. b. Teradjon (III. 3 above) may be more than accidental. For R. Hal. the elder was associated with R. Han. b. Teradjon, M. Taan. II. 5, and no doubt intimate with him. R. Hal. the younger may well have had opportunities of meeting and hearing R. Han. b. T. His own saying is no more than an expansion of that of the older teacher.

As to the several clauses of his saying, there is considerable variation in the readings of the several MSS and texts. The clause relating to the number ten appears in all. That relating to 'five' is probably a later addition, for it is not contained in the parallel versions Mechilta, Jithro, p. 73[b], b. Ber. 6[a]. The desire for symmetry would easily prompt some later scribe to add it. The proof-text in support of 'two' is used for the same purpose in III. 3, the saying of R. Han. b. Ter.

8. רַבִּי אֶלְעָזָר אִישׁ בַּרְתּוֹתָא אוֹמֵר תֶּן־לוֹ מִשֶּׁלּוֹ שָׁאַתָּה וְשֶׁלְּךָ שֶׁלּוֹ וְכֵן

בְּדָוִד הוּא אוֹמֵר כִּי־מִמְּךָ הַכֹּל וּמִיָּדְךָ נָתַנּוּ לָךְ:

8. איש ברתותא. M. om. and add. בן יהוד'.

8. R. Eleazar of Bartotha said: — Give to Him of what is His, for thou and thine are His; for thus in the case of David *Scripture* says (1. Chron. XXIX. 14): — 'For of Thee cometh all, and of Thine own have we given Thee'.

8. In this saying there is more than merely a lesson in generosity. The author of it was noted indeed for his alms-giving, and knew the secret of true charity. But his thought is that all that a man has, not wealth alone but body and soul and life itself, are what God has entrusted to him. They are a pledge committed to his care, not to be used for any selfish ends, but to be used in the service of God and held at his disposal. The true giving is to devote to his service what he has entrusted to the giver. The thought was perhaps suggested by the words of David, (1. Chron. XXIX. 14), and the quotation of that passage is made not by way of a proof-text but for the sake of the words themselves. The author of the saying gave to the thought contained in them another rendering, which need fear no comparison with the original.

R. Eleazar of Bartotha. Most MSS and texts read R. Eleazar ben Jehudah, of Bartotha. He was a disciple of R. Jehoshua b. Hananjah (see II. 16 above), and a frequent disputant with R. Akiba. These facts afford the only data for the chronology of his life, and merely indicate that he belonged to the period after the fall of Jerusalem. Whether he survived the war of Bar Cocheba is uncertain. For his lavish generosity in almsgiving see b. Taan. 24ᵃ, if the אלעזר איש בירתא there mentioned is the same as R. E. of Bartotha. The identification is accepted by Bacher A. d. T. I. 443. Cod. Monac. reads Bartotha; and in Juhasin (ed. Philipp.) p. 57 the identity is assumed without question; the form of the name is naively illustrated by the author, R. Abraham Zacuto, from his own experience.

In the final clause the implied subject of 'says' in God, speaking through the Scripture.

9. רַבִּי יַעֲקֹב אוֹמֵר הַמְהַלֵּךְ בַּדֶּרֶךְ וְשׁוֹנֶה וּמַפְסִיק מִמִּשְׁנָתוֹ וְאוֹמֵר מַה־נָּאֶה אִילָן זֶה מַה־נָּאֶה נִיר זֶה מַעֲלֶה עָלָיו הַכָּתוּב כְּאִלּוּ מִתְחַיֵּב בְּנַפְשׁוֹ:

9. מה נאה אילן זה. A.M. repeat. and similarly מה נאה נירה זו.

9. R. Jacob said:— He who walks by the way and studies and breaks off his study and says 'How beautiful is this tree, how beautiful is this fallow' Scripture counts it to him as if he were guilty against himself.

9. The lesson of incessant study of Torah is here taught in its extremest form, yet not so much so as it might appear to the Gentile mind. The point is that when the mind is engaged upon the study of Torah its attention ought not to be diverted to common things, or vain talk. Moreover, and this is emphasised by many of the commentators, one who walks alone on a road is exposed to harm from evil spirits; and if he breaks off his Torah, which is his safeguard, he incurs a danger which he might have avoided. If R. Jacob meant really to teach that a man must never utter a word of praise to the creator for the beautiful things he has made in his world, then he spoke for himself alone. The Rabbis themselves provided a benediction expressly for this purpose; and one of them uttered such a benediction on seeing a beautiful Gentile woman. If the strict interpretation of R. Jacob's saying be pressed, it ought not to be made the foundation of a general charge against the Pharisees.

R. Jacob. Some texts have R. Simeon, but R. Jacob is better supported. The argument of one commentator, that R. Jacob must be the right name here because R. Simeon had already been dealt with, III. 4, has little weight since other sayings by R. Jacob occur in IV. 21. 22, and another by R. Simeon in IV. 17.

If R. Jacob be the one usually so called without patronymic, but more fully ben Korshai, then he belonged to the latter half of the second century. He is said (b. Kidd. 39^b) to have been the grandson of Elisha b. Abujah, the famous apostate, a younger contemporary of Akiba. He was certainly one of the teachers of Rabbi. These data may be expressed chronologically, though only by conjecture, if we assume that Elisha b. Abujah was born about 80 C. E. His grandson Jacob would be born about 120 C. E., which would make him about forty when Rabbi was a youth. There is nothing in this to conflict with the statement (b. Hagg. 15^a) that the daughter of El. b. Abujah begged alms of Rabbi. She would be an old woman; and, as the relative of his early teacher, would have a natural claim on him. How long R. Jacob lived is not known, but he is said (b. Hull. 98^a) on somewhat doubtful authority to have been an old man.

The benediction to be said on beholding beautiful things is found in a baraitha, b. Ber. 58^b where it is said that one who beholds beautiful creatures or beautiful trees shall say Blèssed be he who has such things in his world. See also T. Ber. VII. 4, where this is to be said by one who beholds beautiful persons, and not only creatures. According to j. Ber. 13^{b.c} R. Gamliel said it on beholding a beautiful Gentile woman, an act which seemed to some later teachers to call for explanation. The benediction is now found in the Prayerbook.

R. Jacob declared that Scripture condemned the man who said "How beautiful &c.", but no text is alleged, and it is hard to imagine what text would support such a thesis.

10. רַבִּי דוֹסְתַּאי בַּר יַנַּאי מִשּׁוּם רַבִּי מֵאִיר אוֹמֵר כָּל־הַשּׁוֹכֵחַ דָּבָר אֶחָד מִמִּשְׁנָתוֹ מַעֲלֶה עָלָיו הַכָּתוּב כְּאִלּוּ מִתְחַיֵּב בְּנַפְשׁוֹ שֶׁנֶּאֱמַר רַק הִשָּׁמֶר לְךָ וּשְׁמֹר נַפְשְׁךָ מְאֹד פֶּן־תִּשְׁכַּח אֶת־הַדְּבָרִים אֲשֶׁר־רָאוּ עֵינֶיךָ, יָכוֹל אֲפִילוּ תָקְפָה עָלָיו מִשְׁנָתוֹ תַּלְמוּד לוֹמַר וּפֶן־יָסוּרוּ מִלְּבָבְךָ כֹּל יְמֵי חַיֶּיךָ הָא אֵינוֹ מִתְחַיֵּב בְּנַפְשׁוֹ עַד שֶׁיֵּשֵׁב וִיסִירֵם מִלִּבּוֹ:

10. כל ימי חייך. M. om.

10. R. Dosthai bar Jannai, in the name of R. Meir, said: If one forgets a single word of his study, Scripture counts it to him as if he were guilty against himself; as it is said (Deut. IV. 9):— 'Only take heed to thyself and keep thy soul diligently, lest thou forget the things which thine eyes have seen.' One might suppose that this applies even when his study has been too hard for him.

Scripture refutes this when it says: — (*ibid.*) 'And lest they depart from thy heart all the days of the life.' Lo, he is not guilty against himself until of set purpose he turns them away from his heart.

10. Another lesson on close study of Torah, dealing especially with the question of forgetting what has been learned. Here also the censure of Scripture is invoked to declare that one who so forgets is guilty against himself. The recurrence of this phrase may account for the placing of this saying next after that of R. Jacob; and the stringency of both sayings suggests that they were not intended to be applied generally, but were meant for such as for particular reasons engaged in a course of hard and incessant study of Torah. At such a time, and for such special reasons, inattention or forgetfulness would become blameworthy, while under ordinary circumstances they would have no moral importance. Thus, it is right and good to praise the Creator for putting beautiful things in his world; but a man who makes it his duty for the time to concentrate his whole mind on his study of Torah fails in that duty if he looks about him and remarks on what he beholds. So also it is natural and excusable to forget; but the man whose one object for the time is to concentrate his mind on Torah is morally to blame if he forgets, unless his forgetfulness be due to mere weakness of memory and not to his own carelessness. This is the qualification implied in the addition to the saying. Any one may forget, when what he tries to learn is difficult; but only he is to blame who deliberately turns out of his mind what he ought to retain in it. The original saying was felt to be too severe even by such hard students as the Rabbis who created the Mishnah.

R. Dosthai bar Jannai was a disciple of R. Meir, and contemporary with Rabbi, though probably somewhat older. The well known R. Jannai, who belonged to the generation after Rabbi, obviously cannot have been his father, but may well have been a younger relative. The name Dosthai represents the Greek Δοσίθεος, and is one of the many instances of a name of Greek origin borne by a Jew. R. Dos. b. Jannai migrated to Babylon, with R. Jose b. Kipper; but in what year is not known. All that can be said is that he lived in the latter part of the second and the beginning of the third century of the common era.

The clause beginning 'one might suppose' is on the regular lines of discussion in the Rabbinic schools, and is hardly likely to have been part of the original saying. For the technical meaning of יכול ... תלמוד לומר see Bacher, Terminologie I. 199 fol. It should be observed that the saying in the first clause is really from R. Meir, and that R. Dos. b. Jannai repeated it in his name. Possibly R. Dos. b. Jannai's own contribution was the second

clause only, in which he met a difficulty occasioned by the first. "Of set
purpose", literally "sits down" and dismisses them &c. I take the rendering
from Singer's translation in the Daily Prayerbook.

יא. רַבִּי חֲנִינָא בֶּן־דּוֹסָא אוֹמֵר כֹּל שֶׁיִּרְאַת חֶטְאוֹ קוֹדֶמֶת לְחָכְמָתוֹ
חָכְמָתוֹ מִתְקַיֶּמֶת וְכֹל שֶׁחָכְמָתוֹ קוֹדֶמֶת לְיִרְאַת חֶטְאוֹ אֵין חָכְמָתוֹ
מִתְקַיֶּמֶת:

11. R. Hanina ben Dosa said: Everyone whose fear of sin comes
before his wisdom his wisdom endures; and everyone whose wisdom
comes before his fear of sin his wisdom does not endure.

11. The first of a group of three sayings by one and the same
teacher. Each is followed by its negative converse. The first saying
sets up a comparison between 'fear of sin' and 'wisdom', and teaches
that the fear of sin should be primary and wisdom accessory. The
meaning seems to be that fear of sin, if it be present at all, is a
native instinct of the soul, while wisdom is an acquired possession.
Fear of sin is the attitude of the sensitive conscience towards God;
sin is feared, not because of any penalty attaching to it but from
pure love to God. Wisdom is good in so far as it helps a man
to attain this ideal of sinless love to God, by making him better
able to discern what is sinful. But if it is made an end in itself
then it fails, because it lacks its moral foundation, and has no moral
purpose.

R. Hanina (or Hananjah) b. Dosa, famous as a hasid and wonder worker,
belonged to the generation of those who saw the fall of Jerusalem. He
learned Torah from R. Johanan b. Zaccai. He was living at Arab near
Sepphoris in 65 C. E., when he sent a contribution to the Temple, (Koh. R.
I. 2[a], and see Büchler's Die Schauplätze &c., in J. Q. R. 1904, pp. 192, 200).
Joh. b. Zaccai had lived in Arab for eighteen years (j. Shabb XVI. 15[d]) before settling in Jerusalem, and does not appear to have returned to his
former home. R. Hanina presumably learned from him there; for he is never
mentioned in connexion with Jabneh, and only made an occasional visit to
Jerusalem. He is said (j. Ber. 9[d]) to have cured the son of R. Gamliel II,
but not in Jabneh; for it is said that R. Gamliel sent two messengers to him
"in his city", and that the cure was effected at that distance. This incident
must have taken place after Gamliel had become the leader at Jabneh, i. e.
after 80 C. E. or thereabout. Estori Parhi, (in Caph. w. Pherah ch. XLIV.
p. 149[a] ed. Venice), assumes that he was the son of Dosa b. Harchinas; this
is quite possible, but there is no authority for it in the Rabbinical texts.

Taylor conjectures that the negative clause in this and the two following
sayings are later additions. It is true that their absence would be an im-

provement, but there is no MS authority for removing them. The parallel passage A. R. N^A c. XXII contains them, for the first and second sayings. It also adds a proof-text for each, which is some evidence that the proof-texts in Aboth were not original but editorial. The text cited in illustration of the first saying is Ps. CXI. 10, 'The fear of the Lord is the beginning of wisdom'.

12 . הוּא הָיָה אוֹמֵר כֹּל שֶׁמַּעֲשָׂיו מְרֻבִּין מֵחָכְמָתוֹ חָכְמָתוֹ מִתְקַיֶּמֶת וְכֹל שֶׁחָכְמָתוֹ מְרֻבָּה מִמַּעֲשָׂיו אֵין חָכְמָתוֹ מִתְקַיֶּמֶת:

12. He used to say: Everyone whose deeds are more than his wisdom, his wisdom endures. And everyone whose wisdom is more than his deeds his wisdom does not endure.

12. A further saying by the same teacher, and cast in the same form, viz: an opposition between two virtues or excellencies. Here the contrast is between learning and actions, i. e. good works. The lesson is that good deeds, right actions, are essential; without these there can be no true service of God.

Wisdom is not essential. A man who has not much learning can still do good deeds; he may not understand the theory of them, but he can do them with the general intention of serving God. If such learning as he has confirms and helps him in this intention, then it endures, is of permanent worth to him. Moreover, the good deeds are evidence of the 'fear of sin', alluded to in the previous saying; and thus the same position is reached for the positive precepts as was there reached for the negative ones.

If on the other hand, a man have more theoretical knowledge than good deeds to show for it, then his learning does not endure; because his whole life and character are vitiated by his failure to act up to what he knew.

For Han. b. Dosa, see under v. 11. The proof text given in support of this saying in A. R. N. is Exod. XXIV. 7. 'We will do and hear', implying that the doing came first and the hearing or understanding came afterwards. Some texts omit "he used to say" before this and the next verse, thus making the three continuous.

13 . הוּא הָיָה אוֹמֵר כֹּל שֶׁרוּחַ הַבְּרִיּוֹת נוֹחָה הֵימֶנּוּ רוּחַ הַמָּקוֹם נוֹחָה הֵימֶנּוּ וְכֹל שֶׁאֵין רוּחַ הַבְּרִיּוֹת נוֹחָה הֵימֶנּוּ אֵין רוּחַ הַמָּקוֹם נוֹחָה הֵימֶנּוּ:

13. He used to say: Everyone with whom the spirit of mankind is pleased, the spirit of God is pleased with him; and every-

one with whom the spirit of mankind is not pleased the spirit of God is not pleased with him.

13. A further saying by the same teacher, and perhaps of all the three the most difficult to understand. For, on the face of it, the statement is not true that divine favour waits upon and is conditioned by human favour. The commentators have not failed to notice this. The truth of the lesson here taught does not turn upon approval, either human or divine. The phrase "the spirit of ... is pleased with someone" means literally that the spirit is at rest, and its tranquillity proceeds from that person. A human being stands in relations of duty and love towards his fellowmen and also in relations of duty and love towards God. If, in either of those relations, he leaves nothing unfulfilled, than there is no cause of strain or discord between him and the other to whom he is so related. There is peace between them, and that harmony is due to his piety and virtue. Therefore the spirit, either of his fellowmen or of God, is calm and untroubled, neither hurt nor grieved. From this it is clear that if a man in his relation with his fellowmen succeeds in establishing that peace and harmony, so that the spirit of his fellowmen derives rest from him, the spirit of God also will derive rest from him, because there is in him nothing to grieve or displease God. But if in his human relations there is discord due to him, failure on his part to establish the peace and harmony which ought to exist between him and his fellowmen, then the spirit of God is grieved because of him, and finds no rest. The "afflicted saint" may be persecuted and unloved; but God knoweth the heart, and waits for no human approval to give the blessing of his peace to one who "walks before him with a perfect heart, blameless".

R. Han. b. Dosa was a mystic, and in this saying he was perhaps influenced by the thought of a similarity between the heavenly realm and the earthly. But such mystical ideas if present at all are only of secondary importance; and the truth of the lesson here taught needs no extraneous support. It is one of the many instances in which the real meaning of a Rabbinical maxim lies not on the surface where the objector can easily make sport of it, but hidden below where it is discovered only by patient and sympathetic reflexion. I believe I have given the true interpretation of the profound thought contained in this saying; and in doing so I have followed out a hint given in the small but valuable commentary on Aboth called Minhah Hadashah[1], and so far as I am aware not in any other commentary.

---

[1] By Jehiel Michael Moravcyk; first published 1576.

14. רַבִּי דּוֹסָא בֶּן־הָרְכִּינַס אוֹמֵר שֵׁנָה שֶׁל שַׁחֲרִית וְיַיִן שֶׁל צָהֳרַיִם וְשִׂיחַת הַיְלָדִים וִישִׁיבַת בָּתֵּי כְנֵסִיּוֹת שֶׁל עַמֵּי הָאָרֶץ מוֹצִיאִין אֶת־הָאָדָם מִן־הָעוֹלָם:

14. בתי. M. om.

14. R. Dosa ben Harchinas said: Morning sleep and midday wine and children's talk, and sitting in the assemblies of the vulgar drive a man out from the world.

14. A saying of a very different type from the preceding. It warns against various forms of distraction which tend to draw a man away from the strait path of piety. That strait path is the study and practice of Torah, and to this one object a man's whole attention should be devoted. This principle is obviously capable of a very narrow interpretation; and there is nothing to show that the author of the saying intended anything more than a practical warning against hindrances to study. Laziness, unseasonable indulgence in wine, listening to idle talk, and the company of persons who have no care for religion, all tend to turn the mind away from the concerns of the higher life. The lesson is true so far as it goes, but it does not go very far. At least it leaves a good deal unsaid, which a wider and wiser charity would wish to say.

R. Dosa b. Harchinas. Contemporary with R. Johanan b. Zaccai, but perhaps somewhat younger. In a very interesting interview, described in b. Jebam. 16ᵃ, R. Dosa said that he remembered the mother of R. Jehoshua b. Hananjah (see above, II. 16) bringing him in his cradle to the Synagogue. R. Jehoshua was born certainly not later than 50 C. E., so that R. Dosa was born probably not later than 40 C. E., and may very well have been considerably older. For the interview above mentioned took place somewhere about the year 90 C. E., and R. Dosa was then an old man. Moreover, it seems probable that he took part in debates while yet in Jerusalem, along with R. Johanan b. Zaccai. They took opposite sides in regard to a decision by Hanan who was one of the דַּיָּנֵי גְזֵרוֹת in Jerusalem, but their discussion may have taken place at a later date. Yet these two are not mentioned together at Jabneh, after the fall of Jerusalem; and while R. Dosa certainly survived R. Johanan b. Z. (as the passage in Jebam. 16ᵃ indirectly shows) R. Dosa in his old age did not attend the meetings at Jabneh, since it was necessary for the Rabbis who sought his opinion to visit him. On the whole we may with fair probability assign the dates 10 C. E. and 90 C. E. as those of his birth and death, with a margin of a few years later at each end.

The two names, Dosa and Harchinas, are said to be of Greek origin. Krauß (Lehnwörter, pp. 75 and 59) gives as their equivalents Δωσίας and

Ἀρχῖνος. Cp. Dosthai and Δοσίϑεος above, nº 10. The 'vulgar' are the ammē-
ha-aratzoth, those who did not conform to the Pharisaic requirements in their
observance of religious duties. The 'assemblies' are any company where they
might be found. Some texts read בתי כנסירת, which is the technical term for
synagogues; but Cod. M. and other MSS omit בתי, which may well have been
inserted through familiarity with the usual phrase. A. R. N., however, in both
recensions has בתי. The difficulty lies in supposing that persons who were
lax in their religious duties would have been at the trouble of having synagogues
for their own use. Possibly R. Dosa meant to say that a synagogue where the
standard of observance was not as high and strict as he approved was nothing
better than a synagogue of ammē ha-aratzoth, and that to sit there was a
sinful waste of time.

15. רַבִּי אֶלְעָזָר הַמּוֹדָעִי אוֹמֵר הַמְחַלֵּל אֶת־הַקֳּדָשִׁים וְהַמְבַזֶּה אֶת־
הַמּוֹעֲדוֹת וְהַמַּלְבִּין פְּנֵי חֲבֵרוֹ בָרַבִּים וְהַמֵּפֵר בְּרִיתוֹ שֶׁל אַבְרָהָם אָבִינוּ
וְהַמְגַלֶּה פָנִים בַּתּוֹרָה שֶׁלֹּא כַהֲלָכָה אַף עַל פִּי שֶׁיֵּשׁ בְּיָדוֹ תּוֹרָה וּמַעֲשִׂים
טוֹבִים אֵין לוֹ חֵלֶק לָעוֹלָם הַבָּא:

15. שלא כהלכה A.D.M. om.; וחמלבין... M. om.; ברבים.

15. R. Eleazar the Modiite said: He who profanes holy things
and despises the festivals, and shames his associate in public, and
makes void the covenant of Abraham our father, and gives interpretations of Torah which are not according to Halachah, even
though he possess Torah and good deeds he has no portion in the
world to come.

15. A saying which goes near to being a Pharisaic definition of
a heretic. The man being a Jew who did the acts here enumerated
disowned the fellowship of Israel, and by his apostasy forfeited
his part in the world to come. Heresy, in Christian usage, always
refers to doctrinal belief, and doctrinal belief is not here directly
concerned; so that 'heretic' is perhaps not the right word to use.
But the essence of heresy is disregard of the accepted standard
in religious matters and defiance of the authority which sets up
and maintains that standard. This is clearly the nature of the
offence condemned in the present saying; and this is further emphasised by the declaration that much Torah and good works will
not serve to defend a man against such condemnation. For good
or for ill, the Pharisaic system did set up a standard both high
and strict in regard to religious requirements, and is not to be
blamed for defining it precisely. But Pharisaism never persecuted

its heretics, and if it affirmed that they had no part in the life hereafter, at least it did not cut short their life here.

In the present instance the condemnation is after all very reasonable and moderate. It does not deny that the person whose case is dealt with may be learned and good; but it says that by acting as he does he goes contrary to the accepted practice of the community of Israel, disregards what they hold to be essential, undermines the authority which they recognise, and effaces the visible sign of his membership in the community. He may have what seem to him sufficient reason for doing so; but he cannot have it both ways. If he chooses to act as his does, he cannot claim to belong to the community. And if upon the ground of faithful observance of the divine precepts the true member of the community bases his hopes of heaven hereafter, the man who is no longer one of the community cannot upon those grounds share in that hope.

R. Eleazar of Modiim (ha-Modii). He may have been a disciple of R. Johanan b. Zaccai, but the only passage (so far as I know) which mentions them together, b. B. Bath. 10ᵇ, is a combination of two accounts, as Bacher has shown (see above on II. 12. n.). In any case R. Eleazar did not become a conspicuous figure until R. Gamliel II was Nasi at Jabneh. The date of his death is known, for he was killed during the siege of Bethar, 135 C. E., by his nephew the rebel-king Bar Cocheba, upon a groundless suspicion of treason. There is no direct evidence to show how old he was at the time of his death; but as he appeared at Jabneh in the time of R. Gamliel, and was then already an authority whose opinion was much in request, the time during which he was an eminent teacher was not less than forty years. This would suggest that he was not less than seventy at the time of his death.

Modiim, his native place, was the ancient home of the Maccabean family; it lay to the S. E. of Lydda, about seven miles distant.

The distinguishing marks of the 'heretic' call for some explanation. 'Profanes holy things', does not imply sacrilege but merely that he treated holy things as if they were not holy, he did not recognise them as holy. 'Despises the festivals'; another form of the preceding, he would do his ordinary work on a holy day, especially the sabbath as that was of most frequent occurrence. 'Shames his associates in public', is hardly a sign of heresy though it is an offence against the Golden Rule. The clause is found in most of the MSS but cod. Mon. omits it; moreover it is omitted in Siphrë I. § 112 and is only interpolated in b. Sanh. 99ᵃ (see Rabbinowicz ad loc.). It is probably an interpolation in the text of Aboth, due to the fact that the offence was one severely condemned by the Rabbis, so that it might naturally be included in a list of serious offences although of a different nature from the others. 'Makes void the covenant of Abraham', effaces the visible mark of

his circumcision, thereby giving the most decisive proof that he has severed
his connexion with the community of Israel. 'Gives interpretations of Torah
which are not according to halachah'; the words 'which ... halachah' are
omitted in some MSS, but are obviously necessary because there was nothing
heretical in doing what every Rabbi did. The whole point lies in the fact
that the interpretations are unauthorised; they may be good or bad but they
are put forth in disregard of the authority which the community of Israel
accepted as supreme. The phrase מגלה פנים בתורה however occurs without
the addition שלא כהלכה 'which ... halachah', and the example of king
Manasseh is quoted (Siphrē I. § 112) to show the nature of the offence,
viz: — acting insolently against the Torah. Taylor so understands it here,
and omits שלא כהלכה. This may be the original reading, but כהלכה שלא
was evidently added in order to point the definition more precisely against
the heretic. The sin of Manasseh was wholesale apostasy to be held in horror
by all, and not the subtlety of the heretic against whom the faithful Jew
needed to be on his guard.

It is worth remembering in this connexion that the famous ברכת המינים,
the formula for the detection of sectaries and false brethren, especially
Jewish Christians, was added to the Shemoneh Esreh at Jabneh under the
presidency of R. Gamliel[1], and that R. Eleazar was a member of that assembly. He did not himself devise the formula; but his own saying belongs
to the same circle of ideas, and was presumably intended to serve the same
purpose. By the formula, a Min was led to betray himself; in R. Eleazar's
definition, the signs were enumerated by which he might be known. Both
bear witness to the uneasiness which was felt owing to the presence of a rival
to the Jewish religion in the later years of the first century of the common
era.

16. רַבִּי יִשְׁמָעֵאל אוֹמֵר הֱוֵה קַל לְרֹאשׁ וְנוֹחַ לְתִשְׁחוֹרֶת וֶהֱוֵה מְקַבֵּל
אֶת־כָּל־הָאָדָם בְּשִׂמְחָה׃

16. R. Ishmael said: Be submissive to the ruler, patient under
oppression; and receive everyone with cheerfulness.

16. The lesson here taught is that of cheerful acceptance of un-
welcome circumstances. The general meaning is clear, but the
particular application depends upon the interpretation of the several
phrases used, and in regard to this there is considerable difference
of opinion. For the discussion of the point see the paragraph in
smaller type below. Adopting the interpretation there preferred
I take the lesson to be that of ready obedience to the authority

---

[1] For the formula against the Mīnīm, see my Christianity in Talmud and Midrash
pp. 125—136.

of the government in the person of the ruler, willing compliance
with its demands for forced service, and, more generally, a cheerful greeting to everyone. The lesson is thus purely ethical and
quite general, except in so far as it is illustrated by examples
drawn from the social and political conditions of the time. A man
should be in himself such that he shows his best side to whatever
circumstances or persons confront him. If these be favourable and
friendly, he will do so spontaneously; the test of his character
comes when the circumstances are oppressive and the persons un-
congenial or hostile. He is to receive everyone, not his friends
only, with gladness, and to fulfil without grudging or grumbling
the demands of the civil power, although they are imposed on him
by force. He is under outward constraint but is inwardly free;
and, being thus free, he should choose the part of good will and
active beneficence.

R. Ishmael b. Elisha. In the Mishnah and the cognate literature he is always known simply as R. Ishmael. He was the grandson of the Ishmael
b. Elisha the High Priest who was executed at or after the fall of Jerusalem.
He himself was a boy at the time, and according to a story which there
seems no reason to doubt, was taken as a captive and found and released
by R. Jehoshua b. Hananjah. The account in j. Hor. 48[b] und b. Gitt. 58[a]
place the scene of this in Rome, and while it is not improbable that the
young Ishmael should have been taken there, the only occasion on which
R. Jehoshua is known to have been in Rome was in the year 96 C. E., which
is much too late. The account in T. Hor. II. 5 says nothing about Rome, and
if Ishmael was a captive somewhere in the Holy Land immediately after
the fall of Jerusalem, R. Jehoshua might equally well have found him and
released him. In any case, his birth may be placed at about 60 C. E. He
lived certainly till the time of the persecution after the overthrow of Bar
Cocheba, because he himself refers to the "decrees of the wicked kingdom"
b. B. Bath. 60[b]. And there is reason to suppose that he outlived the persecution and died a natural death, (M. Nedar. IX. 10 and see my Christianity
in Talmud and Midrash, p. 131 fol.). His dates may therefore be given as
60—140 C. E. approximately. But see below on IV. 9.

The interpretation of his saying involves several difficulties. The first
phrase, הוי קל לראש, implies doing or being something to 'a head'; the
question is, what head? קל means light, as opposed to heavy; and most of
the commentators take 'head' in the sense of 'superior', 'chief', 'ruler',
although ראש without any qualifying epithet is not a usual term for a dignit-
ary. Still, if קל לראש is the right reading, and it is found in nearly all the
MSS. and the printed texts, there seems no alternative rendering. Taylor,
however, on the strength of his MS 'A' reads קל ראש, and translates "be
pliant of disposition", although there is no reason why קל in this connexion

should mean pliant. קל ראש properly means 'light minded', 'impertinent'; and קלות ראש was a fault of behaviour which the Rabbis were not slow to condemn. It is rebuked even in the very next verse, III. 17. It is not conceivable that R. Ishmael would tell any one to be light minded, in the bad sense; while for the meaning 'light hearted', 'cheerful', which would suit the context very well, there is so far as I know no authority in Rabbinical usage. I follow the general example in reading קל לראש, and taking it to imply deference to a superior.

The word תשחורת presents further difficulties, as it is taken in one of two distinct meanings, either 'youth' or 'forced service'. Probably two words derived from independent roots have acquired the same form. There is I believe no instance in which the meaning 'youth' can be decisively proved for תשחורת, though several in which that rendering is possible, albeit only by figure of speech. On the other hand, one definite meaning of שחר is to exact forced service, ἀγγαρεία; and while this meaning cannot be exclusively established for תשחורת, it goes far to determine the sense of that word. Forced service is a form of compulsion, a pressure of outward circumstance; and I suggest that תשחורת is a general term for the pressure of outward circumstance, not necessarily due to actual demands of the government, but including that as one of its exemplifications. 'Oppression' is the nearest equivalent I can think of; and in most if not in all the instances in which תשחורת is used, 'oppression' suits the context better than any other rendering. Thus j. Taan. 65^b the leader of the prayers on the occasion of a public fast must be שפל ברך ונוח תשחורת, humble and submissive to oppression, where there is no obvious reference to literal forced service. Der. Erez R. c. II העניים הביישנים ושפלי הרוח ונוחין לתשחורת ובעלי הבטחה וגו' i.e. the poor, the shamefaced, the humble in spirit, the submissive to oppression, the trusting &c. Again no literal forced service is implied. In T. d. b. Elijah. R. c. I the literal meaning seems to be required, yet even there no precise forced service is implied. The author says that on one occasion "I walked in the greatest city of the world, והיתה שם תשחורת, and there was oppression, and they seized me and took me into the palace of the king" &c.

Returning now to R. Ishmael's saying, I find there no express reference to forced service but a counsel of submission to oppression in general, the pressure of outward circumstance; the word is a metaphor founded upon actual forced service. (See an article on the Massecheth Derech Eretz, by S. Krauss, R.E.J. XXXVI p. 53. I have found much help from his examples, but I differ from his conclusions.)

For the last clause, see I. 15.

17. רַבִּי עֲקִיבָא אוֹמֵר שְׂחוֹק וְקַלּוּת רֹאשׁ מַרְגִּילִין אֶת־הָאָדָם לְעֶרְוָה: מָסוֹרֶת סְיָג לַתּוֹרָה מַעְשְׂרוֹת סְיָג לָעְשֶׁר נְדָרִים סְיָג לַפְּרִישׁוּת סְיָג לַחָכְמָה שְׁתִיקָה:

17. מסורת סייג לתורה.   M. om.

17. R. Akiba said: Laughter and levity accustom a man to im-
morality. Tradition is a fence for Torah. Tithes are a fence for
riches. Vows are a fence for saintliness. A fence for wisdom is silence.

17. A lesson on temptation and safeguards, which needs but
little exposition. In all the clauses the extreme seriousness of the
higher life is assumed and emphasised. Laughter and levity are
not in themselves sinful, but they open the way for sin by weakening
man's defences against it. They encourage the frame of mind in
which he ceases to be on his guard, and in this way they accustom
him to its hateful presence. The 'fences' against sin are not specified, but they are implied; and therein lies the connexion between
this clause and those which follow. In these are enumerated four
'fences' for four kinds of treasure, tradition for Torah, tithes for
riches, vows for saintliness and silence for wisdom. These do not
all stand on the same plane, and the reason is not apparent why
just these four 'treasures' and their 'fences' were singled out. But
the connecting thought of the whole is the principle that in order
to live the true life of service of God fences are necessary, warnings,
safeguards, to protect the God-fearing man from falling into sin.
This is one of the fundamental principles of Pharisaism, as a system
of practical religion. It is open to abuse and misconstruction, and
has found these in abundance; but in itself it is worthy of the
profoundly earnest men who made it their rule of life. They dreaded
nothing so much as sin, because that was failure in the service of
God; but they did not regard sin as only to be avoided because
there was a fence to warn them back from it. In some cases there
was no fence, and for their own protection they made one. No
one need make a vow; but a vow, if it were made, served to keep
him who made it from doing what he might ignorantly or care-
lessly have done without its help. So there was no natural fence
for the Torah, the treasure of divine revelation; but those to
whom it was committed made a fence for its protection, in the
tradition which ensured that its sacred meaning should be handed
down from age to age unimpaired and unchanged. The maxim that
tithes are a fence to wealth belongs to a different line of thought;
and so, on a higher plane, does the maxim that a fence for wisdom
is silence. These may have been originally said in some other
connexion, and only included here on account of the mention of
a fence.

R. Akiba b. Joseph, the most famous of all teachers of the Tannaite period,
and the one who exerted the most powerful influence upon the life and

thought of the Jewish people in his time. For a full account of him see the article in the J. Encyclop. I pp. 304—310. He was the principal supporter among the Rabbis, of Bar Cocheba, and was put to death by the Romans on that account, during the course of the war, between 132 and 135 C. E. The Roman general by whose order he was executed was Tineius Rufus; and as he was superseded before the end of the war by Julius Severus, it follows that the death of Akiba must be dated earlier than 135 C. E. He was then an old man, although the age of 120 years ascribed to him is only a way of comparing him to Moses and others. The confused stories about him yield no certain conclusion as to the date of his birth; but a careful comparison of the biographical data afforded by the Talmudic literature leads me to the conclusion that he was born in or about the year 50 C. E. He is said to have been of Canaanite ancestry, and he himself probably did not become an adherent of Rabbinical Judaism until he reached the years of manhood. His especial teacher was Nahum of Gimzo, or more probably Nehemjah ha-Emsoni, (N. of Emmaus), with whom he is said to have remained for twenty two years. He was ordained as a Rabbi in oi about 90 C. E., for the interview with R. Dosa b. Harchinas (see on v. 14 above) took place about that time, and Akiba was then famous but not yet a Rabbi. From that time until his death he increased in power and eminence as a teacher and spiritual chief amongst his people; and all that legend has woven round the story of his life tends to show the extraordinary impression made by his personality on the minds of his contemporaries.

In regard to the various clauses in Akiba's saying, that which refers to tithes and riches is omitted by some MSS, and others have the variant "tithes are a fence to Torah". The Midr. Shemuel, unless there is a printer's error in my edition, reads in the text 'tradition is a fence to riches', although in the commentary the reading is the usual 'tithes ... riches'. Evidently the clause about 'tithes ... riches' is not so well attested as the other clauses, and may have been added merely because it contained the same key-word and was in the same form.

‏18. הוּא הָיָה אוֹמֵר חָבִיב אָדָם שֶׁנִּבְרָא בְּצֶלֶם חִבָּה יְתֵרָה נוֹדַעַת לוֹ‎
‏שֶׁנִּבְרָא בְּצֶלֶם אֱלֹהִים שֶׁנֶּאֱמַר כִּי בְּצֶלֶם אֱלֹהִים עָשָׂה אֶת־הָאָדָם: חֲבִיבִין‎
‏יִשְׂרָאֵל שֶׁנִּקְרְאוּ בָנִים לַמָּקוֹם חִבָּה יְתֵרָה נוֹדַעַת לָהֶם שֶׁנִּקְרְאוּ בָנִים‎
‏לַמָּקוֹם שֶׁנֶּאֱמַר בָּנִים אַתֶּם לַיָי אֱלֹהֵיכֶם: חֲבִיבִין יִשְׂרָאֵל שֶׁנִּתַּן לָהֶם כְּלִי‎
‏חֶמְדָּה חִבָּה יְתֵרָה נוֹדַעַת לָהֶם שֶׁנִּתַּן לָהֶם כְּלִי חֶמְדָּה שֶׁבּוֹ נִבְרָא הָעוֹלָם‎
‏שֶׁנֶּאֱמַר כִּי לֶקַח טוֹב נָתַתִּי לָכֶם תּוֹרָתִי אַל־תַּעֲזֹבוּ:‎

18. ‏בצלם‎ (1st). M. add. ‏אלהים; שניתן לחם כלי חמדה‎ (2nd). M. om.

18. He used to say: Beloved is man in that he was created in the image [*of God*]. Greater love was proved to him in that he was created in the image of God, as it is said (Gen. IX. 6):—In the image of God made He man. Beloved are Israel in that they are called sons of God. Greater love was proved to them in that they were called sons of God, as it is said (Deut. XIV. 1):—'Sons are ye to the Lord your God'.

Beloved are Israel in that there was given to them a precious instrument. Greater love was proved to them in that there was given to them the precious instrument whereby the world was created, as it said (Prov. IV. 2):—'For good doctrine I give you, forsake not my Torah'.

18. Another group of sayings by Akiba, dwelling upon the divine love as shown in the creation of man, the calling of Israel, and the giving of Torah. In all three cases there was a general and also a special manifestation of the divine love. It was the act of the divine love that man was created in the image of God; and so it would still have been even if man had never been made aware of the fact. But God added this further mark of his love that he revealed to man the knowledge that he had been created in the image of God. So in the other cases; the calling of Israel to be sons of God was the act of divine love; to make known to Israel this high calling was a further mark of love. It was because of the love of God that the Torah was given to Israel, the Torah being the "precious instrument" where with the world was created. It was the further and special mark of the love of God that Israel was allowed to know that this supreme gift had been committed to him.

There is here no ethical lesson, but the reflexion of a devout mind upon the love of God.

The meaning of the saying of Akiba is, I believe, correctly given above; but, while it is quite clear what is the point of the comparison between the 'love' and the 'greater love', it is by no means easy to extract the meaning from the words of the Hebrew text as they stand. The difficulty is in the clause חבה יתירה נודעת לו שנברא. This means, and can only mean, "Greater love was made known to him that he was created" &c. What the sense requires is חבה יתירה שנודע לו שנברא, "Greater love, in that it was made known to him that he was created" &c. But none of the texts read the clause thus; and it would seem that the interpretation of what Akiba meant is traditional. Apparently some difficulty was felt from the very beginning. A. R. N^A. XXXIX, p. 59^b contains the three clauses giving instances of the divine love, but omits the threefold reference to the greater love. Moreover the saying is there attributed to R. Meir, the disciple of Akiba, A. R. N^B. XLIV, p. 62^b has the sayings in a form which shows acquaintance with the full form in Aboth. They are however ascribed to R. Eliezer b. R. Josē the Galilean, not to Akiba. It combines the first and second clauses by saying that "Beloved are Israel, for they were created in the image" &c; and then adds the remark "If they had not been created and it had not been said to them, they would still have been beloved. Greater love was made known to them in that they were called sons of God". A similar remark follows on the third clause. The variations in the MSS (see Taylor II. 151) are mainly in regard to the word בצלם, and do not touch the main difficulty. All the MSS and texts agree in reading נודעת without the additional שנודע which the sense requires.

The 'greater love' was not merely a further but also a later manifestation of the divine love; for the knowledge was first imparted not to man (or Adam) when he was created, but to Noah (Gen. IX. 6).

19. הַכֹּל צָפוּי וְהָרְשׁוּת נְתוּנָה וּבְטוֹב הָעוֹלָם נָדוֹן וְהַכֹּל לְפִי רוֹב הַמַּעֲשֶׂה:

19. All is foreseen, and free will is given, and the world is judged by goodness; and all is according to the amount of work.

19. Another saying by Akiba, though with nothing except the sequence to show that he was its author. It is a declaration concerning divine foreknowledge and human free will. It attempts no solution of the contradiction between these, but affirms both and rests in the assurance that He who judges is good. Judgment takes account of what man has done. Into these few lines Akiba compressed well nigh the whole Rabbinic philosophy of religion. Perhaps philosophy of religion is hardly the right term, for the Rabbis of the Talmudic period were not exponents of a philosophy. But these words of Akiba give the Rabbinic answer to one of the great problems of the philosophy of religion; and his answer has never been challenged as the expression of the fundamental Jewish conviction, that divine foreknowledge and human freedom were equally real and true, though human wisdom could not intellectually reconcile them. Akiba spoke for the practical needs of the religious and the ethical consciousness of man, not for the theoretical satisfaction of the inquiring mind. In like manner he affirmed, what Judaism has never challenged, that the characteristic of the divine judgment is goodness; whether judgment be, or, according to some, be not, according to the amount of work. Akiba here laid bare

the solid rock on which the whole structure of Rabbinic Judaism
was founded.

For Akiba, see above on v. 17. The texts vary between לפי המעשה and
לא לפי המעשה, with usually the addition of רוב before המעשה in the first.
Apparently the one is the negation of the other; but this is not so in reality.
If the text be read in the affirmative form the meaning is that the judgment
of God takes account of the works of man, judges him according to whether
they are good or bad. This is on the lines of Ps. LXII. 12. The addition of
רוב defines more closely the ground of judgment, as being according to
the preponderance of good or bad deeds respectively. This is judgment of
the individual. The negative form deals with judgment of the world as a
whole, the human race in general; and the meaning is that judgment is not
according to work, because human action is on the whole more bad than
good; and if judgment were according to works the human race would
perish. The sayings included in this verse are found in a somewhat shorter
form in A. R. N^A. § XXXIX and A. R. N^B. § XLIV, and in both places are
ascribed not to Akiba but to R. Eliezer b. R. Josē ha-Galili, in the generation
after Akiba. See on v. 18.

20. הוּא הָיָה אוֹמֵר הַכֹּל נָתוּן בָּעֵרָבוֹן וּמְצוּדָה פְרוּסָה עַל־כָּל־הַחַיִּים
הֶחָנוּת פְּתוּחָה וְהֶחֶנְוָנִי מַקִּיף וְהַפִּנְקָס פָּתוּחַ וְהַיָּד כּוֹתֶבֶת וְכָל הָרוֹצֶה
לִלְוֹת יָבֹא וְיִלְוֶה וְהַגַּבָּאִין מַחֲזִירִין תָּדִיר בְּכָל־יוֹם וְנִפְרָעִין מִן הָאָדָם
מִדַּעְתּוֹ וְשֶׁלֹּא מִדַּעְתּוֹ וְיֵשׁ לָהֶם עַל־מַה־שֶּׁיִּסְמוֹכוּ וְהַדִּין דִּין אֱמֶת וְהַכֹּל
מְתָקָּן לִסְעוּדָה:

20. כל הרוצה ללות יבא וילוה. M.C. om.

20. He used to say: All is given in pledge, and the net is spread
over all the living; the shop is open and the shopman gives credit,
and the account-book is open and the hand writes, and every one
who would borrow let him come and borrow; and the collectors
go round continually every day and exact payment from a man
whether with or without his knowledge. And they have whereon
to rely, and the judgment is a judgment of truth, and all is made
ready for the banquet.

20. A further series of sayings by Akiba, or rather an elaborate
metaphor worked out in detail. The theme is the divine justice
and the retribution with which it visits good deeds and bad ones.
The solemn force of the thought is not helped by the terms of the
comparison with a tradesman or moneylender keeping his books
and collecting his debts. It would be quite untrue and unjust to

charge the Rabbis on the strength of this passage with teaching that the relation of man to God is merely that of debtor and creditor. Akiba used a metaphor which no doubt would go home to some of his hearers; but what he was illustrating was the justness of God in dealing with men. And the point of the lesson is not that God is severe but that he can be trusted. "They have whereon to rely, and the judgment is a judgment of truth". This affirmation of the absolute justice of God is one of the unshakeable foundations of the Jewish religion through all its history. The last clause means that all have their part in the future life, and enter upon it after they have, in terms of the metaphor, paid their debts. The sinner after he has suffered the retribution imposed upon him by the divine justice, is thence forward no longer a sinner, and may enter the "banquet".

This saying is also ascribed in A. R. N^A. XXXIX to R. Eliezer b. R. Josē ha-Galili, but without the conclusion "they have on whom to rely, &c." It would be interesting to know why the shorter version of all these sayings of Akiba was ascribed, with no mention of him, to a less eminent teacher as early as the next generation. Many references to Akiba, and sayings ascribed to him, are to be found in A. R. N.; but of those in Aboth only a part of v. 17 above, which occurs in A. R. N^B. XXXIII. This is one of the many points which make it difficult to understand the relation of A. R. N. to Aboth. Schechter in his preface makes an attempt to solve the problem, but does not get very far.

21. רַבִּי אֶלְעָזָר בֶּן עֲזַרְיָה אוֹמֵר אִם אֵין תּוֹרה אֵין דֶּרֶךְ אֶרֶץ אִם אֵין דֶּרֶךְ אֶרֶץ אֵין תּוֹרָה. אִם אֵין חָכְמָה אֵין יִרְאָה אִם אֵין יִרְאָה אֵין חָכְמָה. אִם אֵין דַּעַת אֵין בִּינָה אִם אֵין בִּינָה אֵין דַּעַת. אִם אֵין קֶמַח אֵין תּוֹרָה אִם אֵין תּוֹרָה אֵין קֶמַח:

21. R. Eleazar ben Azariah said:— If there is no Torah there is no worldly occupation, and if there be no worldly occupation there is no Torah. If there is no wisdom there is no fear, and if there is no fear there is no wisdom. If there is no knowledge there is no understanding, and if there is no understanding there is no knowledge. If there is no meal there is no Torah, if there is no Torah there is no meal.

21. A saying by R. Eleazar b. Azariah, expressed in a series of pairs denoting things which cannot exist without the other member of the pair. The form is such as to arrest attention, which was no

doubt the author's purpose; and like so many Jewish maxims, its meaning does not lie on the surface. Taken literally, it is a series of contradictions, and implies that none of the things enumerated can be acquired at all, since each depends on the previous existence and presence of the other. But in all the pairs of contrasted things there is one unifying thought; that which has its source within the mind needs for its complement that which has its origin without. The inner and the outer realm form a harmony, and neither is complete without the other. Torah is the divine revelation, given indeed from without but apprehended in the mind; "derech eretz" is life in the world, practical life, the acting out of what is discerned within. Without Torah, such "life in the world" becomes the existence of a heathen or an animal, degraded from its true meaning and dignity. Without life in the world, Torah becomes a wasted treasure, and occupation with it the self-indulgence of a futile piety. In like manner, wisdom belongs to the inner realm, and fear has regard to the outer; not indeed to the material realm, for the object of the fear is God, but to the objective as opposed to the subjective sphere of consciousness. Wisdom that knows no fear of God is self-centred and worthless. Fear that is without wisdom is the feeling of a mere animal towards its master, not that of an intelligent and moral being towards God his maker, judge and father. Knowledge and understanding are similarly linked together, knowledge being that which is acquired from without, while understanding is that which is contributed from within. Without understanding, the acquisition of facts and truths from without is useless 'cramming'; without knowledge, the faculty of understanding is left with nothing on which to work. Lastly, the lesson is taught, with that excellent good sense and practical wisdom which characterise Jewish ethics, that bodily food and mental food are both necessary, for man to live as he was intended to live. If the meaning of this saying has been correctly given, then it is independent of the particular definition to be given to the various terms enumerated and contrasted. The commentators spend much time upon the various possible interpretations suggested by the different shades of meaning, but without as it seems to me getting to the underlying thought of the whole.

R. Eleazar b. Azariah was a prominent member of the assembly at Jabneh after R. Gamliel II had succeeded R. Johanan b. Zaccai as the president. When R. Gamliel was deposed, R. Eleazar b. Azariah was chosen to fill his place. For a general account of him, see the article in the Jew. Encyclopedia. His dates may be given with some probability as follows:—He was born somewhere about 70 C. E., and was dead before 135 C. E. When he was chosen to succeed R. Gamliel, which must have been at some date between 90 and 95 C. E., he is said to have been eighteen years old (b. Ber. 28ᵃ) and that this is meant literally and not figuratively is shown by the fact that at the interview with R. Dosa b. Harchinas (see above on v. 14) described in b. Jeb. 16ᵃ, he was a very young man, so young that R. Dosa did not know of his existence, and exclaimed "Has then our associate Azariah a son"?. This interview took place somewhere about 90 C. E. Eleazar, accordingly, must have been born not earlier than 70 C. E. The date of his death cannot be determined with certainty. He outlived R. Eliezer, for he was one of four Rabbis who met after R. Eliezer was dead to consider halachic decisions given by him. (T. Gitt. IX. 1—5 and elsewhere.) Now R. Eliezer died probably in or about the time of the persecution of 117 C. E., so that Eleazar must have survived that event. But he is nowhere mentioned in connexion with the war of Bar Cocheba, as he could hardly have failed to have been if he were then still living. The leadership which he held along with R. Gamliel passed to R. Tarphon and especially to R. Akiba. He had property in Sepphoris and may have retired there and ended his days in obscurity.

The saying contained in the present passage is found in A. R. Nᴬ XXXVIII, but without the last clause. In A. R. Nᴮ XXXIV the series is complete but divided into two groups, the second being introduced by "He used to say". The order of the several pairs varies in the three versions.

22. הוּא הָיָה אוֹמֵר כָּל־שֶׁחָכְמָתוֹ מְרֻבָּה מִמַּעֲשָׂיו לְמָה הוּא דוֹמֶה לְאִילָן שֶׁעֲנָפָיו מְרֻבִּין וְשָׁרָשָׁיו מוּעָטִין וְהָרוּחַ בָּאָה וְעוֹקַרְתּוֹ וְהוֹפַכְתּוֹ עַל פָּנָיו שֶׁנֶּאֱמַר וְהָיָה כְּעַרְעָר בָּעֲרָבָה וְלֹא יִרְאֶה כִּי־יָבֹא טוֹב וְשָׁכֵן חֲרֵרִים בַּמִּדְבָּר אֶרֶץ מְלֵחָה וְלֹא תֵשֵׁב. אֲבָל כָּל־שֶׁמַּעֲשָׂיו מְרֻבִּין מֵחָכְמָתוֹ לְמָה הוּא דוֹמֶה לְאִילָן שֶׁעֲנָפָיו מוּעָטִין וְשָׁרָשָׁיו מְרֻבִּין שֶׁאֲפִילוּ כָּל־הָרוּחוֹת שֶׁבָּעוֹלָם בָּאוֹת וְנוֹשְׁבֹת בּוֹ אֵין מְזִיזִין אוֹתוֹ מִמְּקוֹמוֹ שֶׁנֶּאֱמַר וְהָיָה כְּעֵץ שָׁתוּל עַל מַיִם וְעַל יוּבַל יְשַׁלַּח שָׁרָשָׁיו וְלֹא יִרְאֶה כִּי יָבֹא חֹם וְהָיָה עָלֵהוּ רַעֲנָן וּבִשְׁנַת בַּצֹּרֶת לֹא יִדְאָג וְלֹא יָמִישׁ מֵעֲשׂוֹת פֶּרִי:

22. כל שמעשיו. M. שמ׳ מי כל. מי כל.

22. He used to say: One whose wisdom is greater than his deeds what is he like? A tree whose branches are many and its roots few. And the wind comes and roots it up and overturns it on its face, as it is said (Jer. XVII. 6):— 'And he shall be like a tamarisk in the desert, and he shall not see when good cometh, and shall

inhabit the parched places in the wilderness, a land that is salt
and undwelt in'. But one whose deeds exceed his wisdom what is
he like? A tree whose branches are few and its roots many; so
that even if all the winds that are in the world come and blow
upon it they stir it not from its place, as it is said (*ib.* 8): — 'He
shall be like a tree planted by the water, and that sendeth forth
its roots by the river; and it shall not see when heat cometh, and
its leaf shall be green, and in the year of drought it shall not be
troubled nor cease from yielding fruit'.

22. A further saying by R. Eleazar b. Azariah, in which the thought
expressed by R. Hanina b. Dosa (see above, v. 12) is expanded and
illustrated. The lesson is that good deeds are the practical proof
of true service of God as well as the enduring fruits of it, while
wisdom is vain unless there is something to show for it. The two
types of character are illustrated by picturesque figures of the tree
with feeble roots which cannot withstand drought and storms, and
the tree with strong roots which stands firm though all the winds
of heaven blow upon it.

For R. Eleazar b. Azariah see on the preceding verse. The illustration of
the two trees is picturesque and forcible, and no doubt is due to R. Eleazar
himself. Two proof-texts are added, the first from Jer. XVII. 6 verbatim, the
other apparently meant for Ps. I. 3, but with hardly more than a suggestion
of the words referred to. Possibly the point of the allusion is to be found
in the concluding words "all that he doeth shall prosper". But it is not unlikely that the proof-texts here and elsewhere are an editorial addition.

A. R. N^A XXXVIII contains this saying with the two proof-texts. A. R. N^B
XXXIV contains it, but without the proof-texts; and it adds another illustration of the same thought by R. Simeon b. Eleazar, who must not be taken
to be a son of R. Eleazar b. Azariah. He was the son of R. Eleazar b. Shammua
(see below IV. 15). The only known son of R. Eleazar b. Azariah was called
Ishmael.

‏23. רַבִּי אֶלְעָזָר חִסְמָא אוֹמֵר קִנִּין וּפִתְחֵי נִדָּה הֵן הֵן גּוּפֵי הֲלָכוֹת‎
‏תְּקוּפוֹת וְגֵמַטְרִיָאוֹת פְּרַפְרָיוֹת לַחָכְמָה:‎

23. ‏הלכות‎. S.B.C.D. ‏תורה‎ A.M.

23. R. Eleazar Hisma said: Offerings of birds and purifications
of women, these, yea these, are the essential precepts. Astronomy
and geometry are but fringes to wisdom.

23. A saying by R. Eleazar Hisma. If it was intended to teach
a general lesson, then the meaning would seem to be that those

parts of Torah which might seem to be of least importance, and with which a man in virtue of his sex has no direct concern, are of more worth than secular sciences which are highly thought of. But it is not unlikely that R. Eleazar, who was famous for his attainments as a student of astronomy and physics, meant to disarm opposition on the part of those who disapproved of his favourite studies. He therefore declared that the least item in the Torah (or what seemed to be the least) shared in the divine character of the whole, while secular knowledge however great was only an external embellishment.

R. Eleazar Hisma (not ben Hisma) was a disciple of R. Jehoshua b. Hananjah and of R. Akiba. There are no sufficient data to determine the years of his birth and death; but he was brought by R. Jehoshua to the notice of R. Gamliel during the voyage to Rome, 96 C.E., and was by the latter given an appointment to provide him with a living, as he was in extreme poverty (see b. Hor. 10ᵃ and Siphre on Deut. § 16). But how long he lived and what became of him there is nothing to show. His name 'Hisma', which may be rendered 'tongue-tied' is explained in Vajik. R. § 23, where it is told how he was scoffed at for being ignorant of his duties as a Rabbi, and how he prevailed on R. Akiba to teach him what to do and say; after which he returned to those who had scoffed at him and delighted them by his readiness, so that they said "this is R. Eleazar the tongue-tied"! What are here translated "offerings of birds" and "purifications of women", קינין and פתחי נדה refer to the offerings brought by women after childbirth and for reasons arising out of the monthly periods. To explain them fully would need a minute knowledge of halachah and is not necessary for the present purpose. The point is that they are declared to be of the very essence of Torah. The commentators lay stress on the fact that they contain very profound meaning. The word translated "fringes" is פרפרות, and "fringes" is not a literal rendering. It is only used in order to bring out what is evidently the point of R. Eleazar's saying. The origin of the word is uncertain, but it has been taken to represent either περιφορά or περιφέρεια. The former word means 'dainties' served either before or after a meal, slight additions to the main courses, what Taylor calls 'after-courses'. The latter word means 'circumference'. The word in its former meaning occurs elsewhere in the Rabbinical literature, and most of the commentators upon the present passage adopt this meaning. Krauß, Lehnwörter I, p. 280, holds that neither of these meanings can be applied to the present passage in Aboth, and himself suggests that the word represents πληροφορία in the sense of "that which gives support or confirmation". He translates "astronomical and geometrical studies give full support to wisdom". The suggested derivation seems to be rather hazardous, for it involves what he calls a "leicht erklärliche Contraction" of the first two syllables; but more than that, it misses the point of R. Eleazar's saying. He was urging not the importance but the unimportance of astronomy and geometry in comparison with halachah. It would have spoiled his case to have shown how astronomy &c. were a valuable support to wisdom. On the contrary he wished to teach that astronomy &c. was all very well in its way, but lay quite far from the real centre the real truth that mattered. This point is brought out whether 'פר represent περιφορά or περιφέρεια, and the commentators have mostly assumed the former. They have also demurred to the disparagement of sciences in which many Jews have become famous. It is allowable to render 'גמ by 'geometry', although it usually denotes a form of deduction based upon the numerical value of the letters of the alphabet. The latter rendering would not bear out R. Eleazar's point, and the rendering 'geometry' is suggested by the word itself, which is only a Hebrew form of γεωμετρία.

CHAP. IV. פרק רביעי

א. בֶּן זוֹמָא אוֹמֵר אֵיזֶהוּ חָכָם הַלּוֹמֵד מִכָּל־אָדָם שֶׁנֶּאֱמַר מִכָּל־מְלַמְּדַי הִשְׂכַּלְתִּי כִּי עֵדְוֹתֶיךָ שִׂיחָה לִי: אֵיזֶהוּ גִּבּוֹר הַכּוֹבֵשׁ אֶת־יִצְרוֹ שֶׁנֶּאֱמַר טוֹב אֶרֶךְ אַפַּיִם מִגִּבּוֹר וּמוֹשֵׁל בְּרוּחוֹ מִלּ֫כֵד עִיר: אֵיזֶהוּ עָשִׁיר הַשָּׂמֵחַ בְּחֶלְקוֹ שֶׁנֶּאֱמַר יְגִיעַ כַּפֶּיךָ כִּי תֹאכֵל אַשְׁרֶיךָ וְטוֹב לָךְ. אַשְׁרֶיךָ בָּעוֹלָם הַזֶּה וְטוֹב לָךְ לָעוֹלָם הַבָּא. אֵיזֶהוּ מְכֻבָּד הַמְכַבֵּד אֶת הַבְּרִיּוֹת שֶׁנֶּאֱמַר כִּי מְכַבְּדַי אֲכַבֵּד וּבֹזַי יֵקַלּוּ:

1. Ben Zoma said: Who is wise? He who learns from every man. As it is said Ps. CXIX. 99:—"From all my teachers I get understanding, for thy testimonies are my meditation." Who is strong? He who controls his passions, as it is said Prov. XVI. 32:— 'Better is the long suffering than the mighty, and one that ruleth his spirit than one who taketh a city.' Who is rich? He who rejoiceth in his portion, as it is said Ps. CXXVIII. 2:—'When thou eatest of the labour of thy hands happy art thou and and *it shall be* well with thee'. Happy art thou in this world, and *it shall be* well with thee in the world to come.

Who is honoured? He who honours mankind, as it is said 1. Sam. II. 30 'For them that honour me will I honour, and they that despise me shall be lightly esteemed'.

1. A group of definitions of certain types of character, the wise, the strong, the rich and the honourable. By means of these definitions their author, Ben Zoma, teaches the virtues of true wisdom, self control, contentment and courtesy; but the teaching is raised

above mere commonplace by the force and aptness of the definitions. He who learns from every man is wise because he has an open mind, ready to acquire knowledge, and has also the sympathy and humility which are not restrained by pride from seeking knowledge wherever it is to be found. He is truly strong who is master of himself; he is rich who finds enough in what he has and is not craving for more. He is deserving of honour who himself honours his fellows.

The lessons are so plain that they hardly need any explanation. They deserve to be remembered as amongst the best epigrams which Jewish moralists have produced.

Ben Zoma, more fully Simeon b. Zoma, was a disciple of R. Jehoshua b. Hananjah, but it is not possible to fix the dates of his birth and death. All that can be said is that he lived in the later years of the first century C. E., and that he died young. The proof-texts are again probably editorial; they are not always very appropriate and add nothing to the force of the original saying. The text Ps. CXIX. 99 does not prove Ben Zoma's point, neither does the text 1. Sam. II. 30, as will be seen on referring to the several passages. Ben Zoma's sayings are given in A. R. N^A XXIII, and A. R. N^B XXXIII. In the latter passage is an addition not found in Aboth. Ben Zoma is another instance of a Jewish teacher with a Greek name. Zoma represents ζωμός, which means broth or soup. It has no connexion with זורהמא, filth.

2. בֶּן עַזַּי אוֹמֵר הֱוֵי רָץ לְמִצְוָה קַלָּה וּבֹרֵחַ מִן הָעֲבֵרָה שֶׁמִּצְוָה גּוֹרֶרֶת מִצְוָה וַעֲבֵרָה גּוֹרֶרֶת עֲבֵרָה שֶׁשְּׂכַר מִצְוָה מִצְוָה וּשְׂכַר עֲבֵרָה עֲבֵרָה:

2. Ben Azai said: Be swift towards a light precept, and flee from transgression; for precept leads to precept and transgression to transgression. For the reward of a precept is a precept and the reward of a transgression is a transgression.

2. A saying by Ben Azai, the last clause of which is widely known outside the circle of the Rabbinical literature. The lesson that a light precept should count as much as a weighty one is taught in the saying of Rabbi already considered, (above, II. 1); but Ben Azai teaches it from a different point of view and raises it to a higher plane. A precept, 'mitzvah' is to be welcomed and sought for, because it will lead to another, and every precept is an opportunity offered for serving God. It is a privilege not a burden, a gain not a loss; therefore there can be no truer reward for a mitzvah than another mitzvah; as a poet has said,

"And we will ask for no reward
"Except to serve Thee still".

The other half of the lesson is the stern but necessary converse of the first. A transgression is a spurning of the service of God, it is a loss and a burden, an injury inflicted upon oneself, and it brings others after it. The retribution for such transgression is further transgression; the loss becomes greater, the burden heavier, the injury more deadly, and thus the sinner is, by the solemn justice of God, requited for his sin. The gate of repentance is doubtless ever open to him; but the teacher leaves the lesson in its grim simplicity. This is one of the great words of Jewish ethical teaching.

Ben Azai, more fully Simeon b. Azai [1] is frequently mentioned along with Ben Zoma his contemporary. He was closely associated with R. Akiba as disciple and, though probably much younger, as companion, חבר. Both owned R. Jehoshua b. Ḥananjah as their teacher. Ben Azai, like Ben Zoma, was for some reason never ordained, and is never called Rabbi. As a rare exception to Jewish practice he was never married, though there was a report (b. Kethub. 63ᵃ) that the daughter of Akiba was secretly married to him, doing what her mother had done for Akiba himself. It is possible to imagine, perhaps dimly to discern, the traces of a romance and a tragedy in the hint of a secret marriage, a parting from the woman he loved, thenceforth his passionate devotion to the study of Torah, and his answer to those who wondered at his remaining solitary, "my soul has drunk of the Torah; others can maintain the human race".

As for the chronology of his life, all that can be said in addition to the relations with R. Jehoshua and R. Akiba above mentioned, is that he was present at Jabneh when R. Gamliel was deposed (M. Zebaḥ. I. 3), and that his name occurs in one list (Ech. R. II. 2) of the הרוגי מלכות, those killed in the persecution after the war of Bar Cocheba. He does not appear amongst those at Usha and Jabneh after the persecution. He is mentioned (b. Ber. 62ᵃ, Jeb. 4ᵃ) along with R. Jehudah who did not become eminent till after the war, but such intercourse may have taken place at Jabneh before that date, as R. Jehudah is known to have been a disciple of R. Akiba, and would therefore have many opportunities of meeting Ben Azai.

The saying under consideration is found in A. R. N.ᴬ XXV, and A. R. N.ᴮ XXXIII, in both cases in an expanded form, but in both the final clause in its severe simplicity is left untouched. See also Debar R. VI. 4 where part of the saying is rather feebly illustrated, and in Tanḥuma, Ki Tētzē I, where Ben Azai is not even mentioned, and only the illustrations of Debar. R. repeated.

---

[1] The name Azai is a contracted form of Azariah; cp. Zaccai for Zechariah, Johai for Johanan, Illai perhaps for Eleazar, Nittai for Nathanjah, Shammai perhaps for Shemariah, more probably for Shemajah.

‎3. הוּא הָיָה אוֹמֵר אַל תְּהִי בָז לְכָל־אָדָם וְאַל תְּהִי מַפְלִיג לְכָל־דָּבָר‎
‎שֶׁאֵין לְךָ אָדָם שֶׁאֵין לוֹ שָׁעָה וְאֵין לְךָ דָּבָר שֶׁאֵין לוֹ מָקוֹם:‎

3. He used to say: Despise not any man and regard nothing as
impossible; for you find no man who has not his hour, and no thing
which has not its place.

3. Another saying by Ben Azai, simple in expression but wide
in range. Some take it as a mere counsel of prudence, Beware of
consequences, since a seemingly trivial thing may lead to great
results, for evil no less than for good. One commentator even draws
the lesson Despise no man, for the time may come when he will
be able to do thee a mischief. This is surely to place a harsh and
cynical interpretation upon Ben Azai's words, which is in no way
called for. The real lesson seems to be this: — Call no man and
no thing contemptible; for in God's world there is not a man or
a thing unneeded or useless. Great and small alike they have their
part to play, and their set time in which to fulfil their Maker's
purpose. The lesson is thus that of a living sympathy with all
created beings, and even with their Creator, and an insight born
of that sympathy into the deep-lying unity beneath the infinite
variety of the world.

For Ben Azai see on the preceding v. This saying does not appear to
be included in A. R. N., though other sayings of Ben Azai are found there
A. R. N^A XXV and A. R. N^B XXXIII besides those mentioned above which
are not in Aboth.

‎4. רַבִּי לְוִיטַס אִישׁ יַבְנֶה אוֹמֵר מְאֹד מְאֹד הֱוֵה שְׁפַל רוּחַ שֶׁתִּקְוַת אֱנוֹשׁ‎
‎רִמָּה:‎

4. ‎מאד מאד‎. M. once only.

4. R. Levitas of Jabneh said: Be exceeding humble, for the hope
of mortal man is the worm.

4. A maxim of humility which needs no expansion to explain its
meaning.

R. Levitas is mentioned only here and in Pirkē de R. Eliezer. The present
maxim is repeated in A. R. N^B XXXIV. There are no data by which to fix
his chronology. This is an instance which shows that the compiler of Aboth
was not concerned to choose sayings only by eminent teachers; also that the
teachers whose sayings he did choose cannot all have been regarded as the
'Fathers' named in the title of the book. The compiler seems to have made
his selection according to the importance of the maxim not according to the

eminence of the teacher who gave it; the importance, that is, for his own
purpose whatever it may have been. In the present instance the lesson on
humility is taught with a certain extravagance of expression, מְאֹד מְאֹד הֱוֵי שְׁפַל,
which may have struck the compiler as worth preserving, and he found a
suitable place for it after Ben Azai's fine saying.[1]

Te name Levitas represents Λευίτης, so that we have here an instance of
a Jew bearing a Greek name which was formed from a Hebrew original.

5. רַבִּי יוֹחָנָן בֶּן־בְּרוֹקָה אוֹמֵר כָּל־הַמְחַלֵּל שֵׁם שָׁמַיִם בַּסֵּתֶר נִפְרָעִין
מִמֶּנּוּ בַּגָּלוּי אֶחָד [בְּ]שׁוֹגֵג וְאֶחָד [בְּ]מֵזִיד בְּחִלּוּל הַשֵּׁם:

5. בשוגג ... במזיד. M. om. ב.

5. R. Johanan ben Barokah said: He who profanes the Name of
Heaven in secret they exact the penalty from him openly. Ignorant
and wilful are all one in regard to profaning the Name.

5. A lesson on profanity, a sin which includes not merely im-
pious speech but any act or word which offends against the majesty
of God. Retribution follows upon every such offence whether it
were done wilfully or in ignorance; and though the offence were
in secret the retribution is inflicted openly. According to the commentators the sin aimed at is the hypocrisy of the man who is
outwardly pious and holy while inwardly he is corrupt and un-
clean. Retribution falls upon him openly when his hypocrisy is
exposed. This is true, but it hardly covers the whole case; for
hypocrisy is a sin of wilfulness not of ignorance. But a man might
ignorantly or inadvertently do something which when brought
to light is seen to be a profanation of the Name; and in that ex-
posure, which shows him the real nature of his offence, consists
the retribution which is inflicted openly. In this way retribution
awaits alike the wilful and the ignorant offender; but Maimonides
well observes that they are alike in the fact of their punishment
not in the greatness of it. The hypocrite whose false piety is ex-

---

[1] R. Levitas' saying, however, is not his own. It is a quotation from Ecclus.
VII. 17, where the Hebrew text of the recovered fragments gives the exact words.
It is well known that Ben Sira is several times quoted in the Talmud; but the
book was not included in the Canon, and it is certainly remarkable that Rabbi
should have included in his list a teacher, whose one maxim was a quotation from
Ben Sira. In R. E. J. XXXV, p. 53, thus before the discovery and publication of
the Hebrew fragments, F. Perles showed by comparison of the Syriac text that the
passage in Aboth gave the Hebrew original. He suggested a Christian interpolation
in the Greek text.

posed feels a deeper shame than the man who knew not that he
did wrong and is filled with remorse when he realises it.

R. Johanan b. Baroka was a disciple of R. Jehoshua b. Hananjah, and is
mentioned (b. Hag. 3ᵃ) as visiting his teacher along with R. Eleazar Hisma
(see above III. 23) in Pekiin, at some date after the deposition and restoration
of R. Gamliel at Jabneh. He must have survived the war of Bar Cocheba
and the persecution which followed it, for he is mentioned in connexion with
R. Meir and R. Jehudah. In b. R. h. Sh. 32ᵃ it is said that he was present
and active at Usha; but j. R. h. Sh. 50ᵇ has R. Ishmael b. R. Joh. b. Baroka,
Siphra p. 101ᵇ has R. Hanina b. Joh. b. Baroka. The probability is in favour
of R. Ishmael.

6. רַבִּי יִשְׁמָעֵאל בְּנוֹ אוֹמֵר הַלּוֹמֵד עַל מְנָת לְלַמֵּד מַסְפִּיקִין בְּיָדוֹ לִלְמוֹד
וּלְלַמֵּד וְהַלּוֹמֵד עַל מְנָת לַעֲשׂוֹת מַסְפִּיקִין בְּיָדוֹ לִלְמוֹד וּלְלַמֵּד לִשְׁמוֹר
וְלַעֲשׂוֹת:

6. בנו. So A.B.M.   C.S. om. some texts have בר רבי יוסי.

6. R. Ishmael his son said: He who learns with a view to teaching they give him the opportunity to learn and to teach. And he
who learns with a view to doing they give him the opportunity to
learn and to teach, to observe and to do.

6. A saying by R. Ishmael, son of the preceding. The meaning
is not quite clear, and some of the commentators felt a difficulty.
On the face of it the meaning is merely that whether a man studies
Torah for a lower or for a higher purpose the opportunity is given
him to do so, a lesson of no particular value. A contrast is evidently
intended between mere *learning* of Torah, for self improvement,
and the *doing* of it whereby also others are benefitted. And this
contrast would be clear if it were not that the (mere) teaching and
not mere learning is set in contrast to the doing of Torah. If a
man studies Torah in order to teach it he is surely unselfish; for
he benefits others, and it is a needless assumption that he only aims
at winning renown and honour as a teacher. The passage would
be much more intelligible if it were read "He that studies Torah
in order to *learn*". In that case there would be point in saying
that such as one is given the opportunity to learn *and to teach*. If
his purpose were merely selfish he is given the chance of acting
unselfishly. The rest of the saying then follows naturally; if his
purpose be the higher one of *doing* the Torah, then he is given
the opportunity of *doing* and *keeping* and also of *learning* and
teaching it, he finds the full blessing which can come from occupation with Torah.

R. Ishmael b. R. Johanan b. Baroka, son of the preceding. He was one of the assembly which met at Usha after the persecution, and later. But there are no data by which to fix the termini of his life. In general he was contemporary with R. Simeon b. Gamliel from 140 C.E. onwards. The saying under consideration is found in A.R. N^A XXXII with a notable difference; it reads in the first clause אין מספיקין "they do not give him the opportunity", a reading which is contradicted by experience. Also, the author of the saying is called R. Ishmael without anything to show which R. Ishmael is intended. A few lines further down a saying is given by R. Ishmael b. R. *Hanina* b. Baroka, which shows that the compiler attributed the previous saying to some other R. Ishmael.

Duran, in his commentary Magen Aboth, says that the man who teaches in order that they may call him Rabbi is allowed the opportunity to carry out his purpose; but he is not found worthy to "keep and to do", and this is his sufficient penalty. "And" (Duran adds) "we have seen many 'hachamim' such as he, who do nothing, and they are a burden to the world".

7. רַבִּי צָדוֹק אוֹמֵר אַל תִּפְרוֹשׁ מִן הַצִּבּוּר וְאַל תַּעַשׂ עַצְמְךָ כְּעוֹרְכֵי
הַדַּיָּנִין וְאַל תַּעֲשֶׂה עֲטָרָה לְהִתְגַּדֶּל־בָּה וְלֹא קַרְדּוֹם לֶאֱכוֹל מֵהֶן וְכַךְ הָיָה
הִלֵּל אוֹמֵר וּדְאִשְׁתַּמַּשׁ בְּתָגָא חֲלָף הָא לָמֵדְתָּ כָּל־הַמְּהֶנֶה (נ"א הַנֶּאֱוֹת)
מִדִּבְרֵי תוֹרָה נוֹטֵל חַיָּיו מִן הָעוֹלָם:

7. תפרוש מן הצבור...הדריינין ואל. M. om.
לֶאֱכוֹל מֵהֶן. A.C.D.M. B.S. לחתוך בהם. Some texts have לחפור בה.
לָמֵדְתָּ. A.C.D.M. om. and read הא כל הנאות.
S. הא למדת שכל האוכל ה'.

7. R. Zadok said: Separate not thyself from the congregation and make not thyself as they who prepare the judges; and make not—(*it* or *them*)—a crown wherewith to magnify thyself nor a 'dish' wherewith to eat. And thus Hillel used to say 'and he who serves himself with the crown passes away'. Here thou hast learned that everyone who makes profit from the words of Torah removes his life from the world.

7. A saying which if the text is correct is mainly made up of quotations from earlier teachers. The maxim of Jehudah b. Tabbai (I. 8 first clause) is combined with a saying of Hillel (II. 5 first clause), and another saying by him (I. 13). The two former may be interpolations, but the third can hardly be so, for it is brought in to prove the assertion in the last clause, which alone is R. Zadok's own contribution. The lesson is that Torah must not be made a means of gain, no teacher of Torah must earn his living by teaching.

The practice of the Tannaim was in accordance with this precept; in later times religious teachers, both Jewish and Christian, have looked at the question from a different standpoint, and arrived at a different conclusion. The commentators serve to illustrate the change both of theory and of practice.

R. Zadok was one of a family in which the names Zadok and Eliezer (or Eleazar) were repeated for several generations in succession, so that it is not easy to decide which Zadok or which Eliezer b. Zadok is meant in a given case. Hyman in his very useful and valuable "Toldoth Tannaim ve-Amoraim" I. pp. 201—5 has disentangled the family history with considerable success, and I refer the reader to his analysis. The Zadok with whom we are at present concerned is most probably the one who is said to have been spared after the fall of Jerusalem in 70 C. E. at the intercession of R. Johanan b. Zaccai. He lived several years afterwards as an honoured member of the assembly at Jabneh; and if it be true that he fasted for forty years before the siege he must have been an old man at his death. On these lines his life would cover the greater part of the first century C. E. Hillel died only a few years before he was born, and his great reputation would make one of the earliest and strongest impressions on the mind of the young Zadok. This would supply a reason for the reference to Hillel's words in his own saying; and, for what it is worth, it gives some slight colour to the suggestion (see Introduction § C) that R. Zadok may have been the author of ch. I of Aboth. R. Gamliel of Jabneh held him in exceptional honour; and if he left in R. Gamliel's possession at his death the list of the older teachers ending with the fall of Jerusalem, that list would naturally pass in time to R. Gamliel's grandson, Rabbi, the editor of the Mishnah. The possession of that list, coming from a man so distinguished as R. Zadok, might naturally induce Rabbi to enlarge the collection by including in it sayings by other teachers which seemed to him worthy of remembrance, and such a historical note as is found in II. 10—12. This is pure conjecture, but at least it serves to make more intelligible the gradual formation of Aboth.

The two clauses in this v., beginning "Separate thyself . . ." and "make not thyself . . ." are not found in the older texts and commentaries (see Taylor II. 156). The author of the "Midrash Shemuel" knew of their being found in some texts but only by hearsay. They are probably interpolated, but for what reason is not apparent, since they have already been given in connexion with their original authors in Aboth.

. R. Zadok's own saying begins with "Make not . . . a crown wherewith to magnify thyself". The implied object of 'make' is not 'a crown' but either 'Torah' or 'words of Torah'; and the latter is probably intended, as the better reading is "make not them", אל תעשם. This would seem to show that the first clause, now lost, made some reference to "words of Torah"; and in that case the two really irrelevant maxims were put in to fill the gap left by the omission of the original clause. There is considerable variation in the clause "Make not ... a crown &c.". The word קרדום, axe or spade, is found in all the texts, but the verb which defines its use varies being either 'to eat with', 'to dig with', 'to cut with'. The first variant shows that there must have been an alternative to קרדום, but what it was is not known. Hillel's maxim, quoted by R. Zadok in support of his own, is in Aramaic, and forms the last clause of I. 13.

8. רַבִּי יוֹסֵי אוֹמֵר כָּל־הַמְכַבֵּד אֶת־הַתּוֹרָה גּוּפוֹ מְכֻבָּד עַל הַבְּרִיּוֹת
וְכָל־הַמְחַלֵּל אֶת־הַתּוֹרָה גּוּפוֹ מְחֻלָּל עַל הַבְּרִיּוֹת:

8. R. Josē said: Every one who honours Torah is himself honoured of men, and every one who dishonours the Torah is himself dishonoured of men.

8. A lesson on reverence for the Torah; but whether for the Torah as divine revelation or the written Torah contained in a scroll is not defined. The commentators, by the illustrations which they give, mostly adopt the latter interpretation. This is certainly one of the ways in which reverence for Torah would naturally show itself; but the lesson loses its impressiveness if its scope is thus restricted, and its accordance with experience is open to question. To be scrupulous in respect for a Sepher Torah is not always a sure way to win popular esteem. The truth of the saying becomes most apparent and its ethical value greatest if the term Torah be understood in its highest and most inclusive sense of the divine revelation. Reverence for Torah is then reverence for the revelation and for the Revealer; and where such reverence fills a man's mind and inspires his character, his fellowmen instinctively respect him and respond to his unconscious influence.

R. Josē, without patronymic, is in the Tannaite literature R. Josē b. Halaphta, one of the disciples of Akiba who became eminent after the Hadrianic persecution. For the dates of his life a *terminus a quo* is given by the fact (which he mentions himself, T. Shebi. IV. 4) that he, along with R. Jehudah, had been in the company of R. Tarphon. Now R. Tarphon died in or about 117 C.E., and R. Josē cannot have been less than twenty years of age at the time, so that he must have been born not later than 97 C.E. possibly earlier. On the other hand he lived to be one of the chief supporters of Rabbi, of course after the death of Rabbi's father, R. Simeon b. Gamliel. This event took place at some time between 160 and 170 C.E. Grätz places it in 165 C.E. (G. d. J. IV. 471). R. Josē must therefore have been still living some years after this. He survived R. Meir (b. Kidd. 52[b]); and after his death, Rabbi relied on his authority against that of R. Meir (b. Gitt. 67[a]). If he lived

to an advanced age, his death cannot be placed much later than 180 C. E.
For a general account of his life see the article in J. E. R. Josē's saying is
found in A. R. N.^A c. XXVII with the addition of a proof-text (1. Sam. II. 30),
which does not indeed establish the truth of the saying though it tends to
confirm the interpretation given above. A. R. N.^B c. XXXII gives the saying
without the proof-text.

9. רַבִּי יִשְׁמָעֵאל אוֹמֵר הַחשֵׂךְ עַצְמוֹ מִן הַדִּין פּוֹרֵק מִמֶּנּוּ אֵיבָה וְגָזֵל
וּשְׁבוּעַת שָׁוְא, וְהַגַּס לִבּוֹ בְּהוֹרָאָה שׁוֹטֶה רָשָׁע וְגַס רוּחַ:

.בו. 9.   M.S. ברבי יוסי.

9. R. Ishmael ben R. Josē said: He who shuns the office of judge
escapes enmity theft and perjury; but he who is haughty in his
teaching is foolish wicked and arrogant.

9. A lesson rather of practical experience than of ethical precept. To perform the duty of a judge is to run the risk of moral
danger; for, by the decision which he gives, he lays himself open
to the ill will of the loser in the suit, he may become unwittingly
a party to a wrongful disposition of property, and he may be the
means of leading some witness to swear falsely. It is prudent
therefore for a man to excuse himself from acting as judge. But
the teacher does not say that a man ought to, or even that he
may, so excuse himself. If his duty consists in his filling that office then he must do his duty. The teacher is pointing out what
makes the duty especially hard and morally dangerous, and his
intention may be to warn any who are inclined to magnify their
office as judge. The second part of the saying continues the warning, at least if it refers to a man who acts as judge. One who
is haughty on the judgment-seat takes away all moral worth from
his decisions, by showing himself foolish wicked and arrogant. The
clause, however, may refer to teachers in general and not to judges,
since it is not the function of a judge to teach at all, but to administer justice. Yet the remark is none the less true when applied
to a judge.

R. Ishmael. This is R. Ishmael b. Josē b. Halaphta. The texts vary between
'Ishmael his son' and 'Ismael b. R. Josē'. A variant is 'Simeon his son'.
In any case he was the son of R. Josē, the author of v. 8. From this fact
some indication may be obtained as to his chronology. There is no evidence
that he remembered or had any part in the Hadrianic persecution, but he
says himself that he saw R. Ishmael b. Elisha (b. Jeb. 104^a). This goes to
confirm what is said above (see on III. 16) that R. Ish. b. Elisha survived the

persecution; and if so, then the date of his death must be late enough to allow of the younger R. Ishmael having seen him while not remembering the persecution. The year 145 C. E. would meet the case, if the younger Ishmael were born not later than 135 C. E. On the other hand he lived to old age, and was closely associated with Rabbi, presumably in Sepphoris where R. Ishmael had spent most of his life and whither Rabbi removed seventeen years before his death. This would bring the death of R. Ishmael into the third century C. E. Rabbi died in 219 C. E. R. Ishmael probably but a few years earlier, say 210 C. E.

For a general account of R. Ishmael b. J. see the article in the J. E. His saying about the office of a judge gains force from the fact that he was him-self a judge and noted for his integrity (b. Macc. 24ª). He drew enmity upon himself by aiding the Roman government to arrest robbers, the criminals being of his own people (b. B. M. 84ª).

10. הוּא הָיָה אוֹמֵר אַל תְּהִי דָן יְחִידִי שֶׁאֵין דָּן יְחִידִי אֶלָּא אֶחָד וְאַל
תֹּאמַר קַבְּלוּ דַעְתִּי שֶׁהֵן רַשָּׁאִין וְלֹא אָתָּה:

10. He used to say: Judge not alone, for there is none save one who judgeth alone. And say not Receive my opinion, for they are entitled and thou not.

10. Another saying by the same teacher, and, like the preceding, concerned with the function of a judge. It is also a counsel founded on experience. In a matter so important as judging between a man and his neighbour it is not safe for the judge to rely on himself alone; he should share his responsibility and be supported by the wisdom and authority of others. God alone can judge alone. More-over, the judge must not force his opinion upon those whom he judges (or perhaps upon his colleagues), for they are as competent to judge as he is.

For R. Ishmael b. J. see the preceding note. His saying is quoted as Mishnah, j. Sanh. 18ª, *a propos* of an opinion by R. Abahu a century later upon the subject. If the practice of judging alone had not been known there would have been no need of a warning against it nor of an explanation of what it implied. Duran in his commentary, *ad loc.*, is at pains to justify the practice.

This saying and the preceding are found in A. R. N.ᴮ XXXIV, but are there attributed to R. Eliezer son of R. Eleazar ha-Kappar, better known as Bar Kappara. The two were contemporary.

יא. רַבִּי אוֹמֵר כָּל־הַמְקַיֵּם אֶת־הַתּוֹרָה מֵעֹנִי סוֹפוֹ לְקַיְמָהּ מֵעֹשֶׁר וְכָל־
הַמְבַטֵּל אֶת־הַתּוֹרָה מֵעֹשֶׁר סוֹפוֹ לְבַטְּלָהּ מֵעֹנִי:

11. יונתן. So B.D.S.   A.M. יוחנן.

11. R. Jonathan said:—He who fulfils Torah when he is poor
will fulfil it in the end when he is rich. And he who makes void
the Torah when he is rich will in the end make it void when he
is poor.

11. Self denial for the sake of Torah demands an effort of will;
and one who has so devoted himself is less likely to forsake the
Torah when the need for effort becomes less. Wealth has its
temptations no less than poverty; but, while wealth tempts to the
neglect of Torah, through pressure of worldly interests and claims,
poverty presents difficulties indeed and hardship but spurs a man
on to the goal of his aspiration. In either case, what is begun in
youth is not likely to be altered in age.

R. Jonathan, in the Mishnah and cognate literature, is Jonathan b. Josē or
Joseph; but his father was not the well known Josē b. Halaphta. Josē was
a very common name. R. Jonathan is sometimes called R. Nathan, and must
be distinguished from R. Nathan the colleague of R. Simeon b. Gamliel and
later of Rabbi. R. Jonathan was older, having been a disciple possibly of
R. Akiba and certainly of R. Ishmael b. Elisha. He says (b. Hull. 70ᵇ) that
he once spoke to Ben Azai, who asked him what was the opinion of R. Ishmael
upon the point in question, and lamented that he himself had never studied
under R. Ishmael. This must have been previous to 138 C. E. if Ben Azai
was killed in the persecution (see above on IV. 2). R. Jonathan is usually
mentioned along with R. Joshiah, another disciple of R. Ishmael. There is
no evidence to show when he died. A R. Jonathan is mentioned (b. B.
Mez. 90ᵇ) as asking a question of R. Simai, a younger contemporary of
Rabbi; but as the questioner would seem to have been younger than
R. Simai, he can hardly have been the R. Jonathan who was the disciple of
R. Ishmael.

The reading R. Johanan, adopted by Taylor on the strength of his MS. A,
also in Cod. Mon., is, as Bacher says, (A. T. II. 354, n. 2), manifestly a
corruption. It is impossible that the name of the great Amora should
have been inserted in the Mishnah, and no other can be meant when
R. Johanan is mentioned without patronymic. Taylor does not notice
the difficulty. The saying is given in A. R. Nᴬ XXX, and A. R. Nᴮ XXXV,
with some additions. In the former passage the teacher is called R. Nathan
b. Joseph.

‫12. רַבִּי מֵאִיר אוֹמֵר הֱוֵי מְמַעֵט בְּעֵסֶק וַעֲסוֹק בַּתּוֹרָה וֶהֱוֵה שְׁפַל רוּחַ‬
‫בִּפְנֵי כָל־אָדָם וְאִם בָּטַלְתָּ מִן הַתּוֹרָה יֶשׁ־לְךָ בְּטֵלִים הַרְבֵּה כְּנֶגְדָּךְ וְאִם‬
‫עָמַלְתָּ בַּתּוֹרָה יֶשׁ־לוֹ שָׂכָר הַרְבֵּה לִתֶּן־לָךְ׃‬

12. R. Meir said: Do little in business and be busy with Torah,
and be humble of spirit before all men. And if thou hast been
idle in respect of Torah there will be many idle things in thy
way, and if thou hast laboured at Torah there will be for him
much reward to give thee.

12. The first and second clauses of this verse are hardly more
than a repetition of lessons already taught in Aboth. The duty of
studying Torah is enjoined over and over again; and the virtue
of humility is one of the chief features in the Pharisaic conception
of the perfect type of character. The third clause however teaches
a lesson which is not a mere echo of former words. Neglect of
Torah brings its punishment through the things for which Torah
has been neglected. The opportunity lost, the duty left undone,
have consequences that are not merely negative; they set up other
occasions for action which make it the harder to recover the lost
ground of service to God through devotion to Torah. And, by re-
sisting the temptation to neglect Torah, there will be so much the
more of reward, in the true sense of reward, the approval of God
to the faithful servant of his will.

R. Meir was, next after his teacher R. Akiba, the most eminent and the
most original of all the Tannaim. The fact that he should be represented
in Aboth, (not including ch. VI), by only the one saying here given would
seem to show that the compiler, whatever his purpose may have been, was
not concerned to choose especially characteristic sayings of each teacher.
It bears out what is suggested in the Introduction, (§ B. p. 7) that the compiler merely gathered together sayings by various teachers which he thought
worth noting, and added them as a kind of appendix to his work.
R. Meir is one of the best known, and also one of the least known, of the
Tannaim. His words are to be found on well-nigh every page of the Mishnah; and, although Rabbi gave to the Mishnah its final form, it is known
that his work owed much to the previous labours of R. Meir, as R. Meir himself had built upon the foundation laid by R. Akiba. Yet of his birth and
parentage and place of origin nothing is known; even his name is in doubt
(b. Erub. 13[b] and Dik. Soph. *ad loc.*) and the name of his father is never mentioned, nor his family except in the extraordinary legend that he was a descendant of the Emperor Nero, (b. Gitt. 56[a]).
R. Meir was one of the seven mentioned as having been ordained by

R. Jehudah b. Baba during the Hadrianic persecution b. Sanh. 14ᵃ;[1] it is said, indeed (*ibid.*) that he was ordained by R. Akiba, but that his ordination was not recognised. Rashi (ib.) says that this was owing to Meir's youth. But a probable explanation is suggested on the same page of Sanh., viz that an ordination performed "outside the Land" was not valid, and that R. Akiba had ordained him while on one of his journeys. It is stated (b. Jebam. 121ᵃ) that Meir accompanied R. Akiba, though in another ship, to Kapōtkia.[2] This took place before the outbreak of the Bar Cocheba War, therefore previous to 135 C.E. Meir could hardly have been much less than twenty five years of age, so that the year of his birth cannot be placed later than 110 C.E. He died at some time after Rabbi had already succeeded his father, R. Simeon b. Gamliel, as Patriarch, but before the death of R. Jose (b. Kidd. 52ᵇ). This gives the years 165 C.E. and 180 C.E., as approximate limits of the period within which his death took place.

R. Meir's saying is referred to in A. R. Nᴬ XXIX, and more nearly reproduced in A. R. Nᴮ XXXIII (see Bacher, A. T. II. 11, n. 6).

13. רַבִּי אֶלִיעֶזֶר בֶּן־יַעֲקֹב אוֹמֵר הָעוֹשֶׂה מִצְוָה אֶחָת קוֹנֶה לוֹ פְּרַקְלִיט אֶחָד וְהָעוֹבֵר עֲבֵרָה אֶחָת קוֹנֶה לוֹ קַטֵּגוֹר אֶחָד תְּשׁוּבָה וּמַעֲשִׂים טוֹבִים כִּתְרִיס בִּפְנֵי הַפּוּרְעָנוּת:

13. R. Eliezer ben Jacob said: He who does one precept gains for himself one advocate, and he who commits one transgression gains for himself one accuser. Repentance and good works are as a shield in face of punishment.

13. A lesson on the retributive effect of both obedience and sin. A man's actions in respect of Torah will witness for or against him in the judgment. The best defence against punishment is to be found in repentance and good works.

R. Eliezer b. Jacob is the name of two Tannaim, one a contemporary of R. Johanan b. Zaccai who reported various things about the Temple and who is said to have been the chief authority for the treatise of the Mishnah entitled Middoth, and the other a disciple of R. Akiba, one of those who assembled at Usha after the Hadrianic persecution. There is no evidence to determine which of the two was the author of the saying under consideration. Neither are there any data by which to fix more precisely the chronology of either. It is worth noting however that the teachers named in vv. 12—17, are amongst the seven disciples of Akiba or who are mentioned as having

---

[1] But see on R. Jehudah, v. 16 below.

[2] If Kapotkia is Cappadocia, it has no seacoast, and could not be reached by a ship. Presumably the travellers landed at Tarsus, and made their way up country.

been ordained by R. Jeh. b. Baba b. Sanh. 14[a1] and who met in Usha, to re-organise the religious life of the community after the persecution. The list is given j. Hag. 78[d], Ber. R. LXI, and Koh. R. XI. 6. This would seem to show that the R. Eliezer b. Jacob whose saying is quoted was the later not the earlier of that name. His saying is found in A. R. N.[B] XXXV.

14. רַבִּי יוֹחָנָן הַסַּנְדְּלָר אוֹמֵר כָּל־כְּנֵסִיָּה שֶׁהִיא לְשֵׁם שָׁמַיִם סוֹפָהּ
לְהִתְקַיֵּם וְשֶׁאֵינָהּ לְשֵׁם שָׁמַיִם אֵין סוֹפָהּ לְהִתְקַיֵּם:

14. R. Johanan the sandalmaker said: Every assembly which is for the sake of Heaven will in the end be established, and *every assembly* which is not for the sake of Heaven will in the end not be established.

14. A saying about assemblies, with however no indication to show what assemblies are meant. If it be taken as a general maxim it is a variant of the saying of R. Hananjah b. Teradjon, III. 3, and the meaning is that if men assemble for a purpose such as God can approve, for some service of him, then that purpose will be fulfilled. If for some other purpose such as God cannot approve, then it will fail. Common experience would seem to con-tradict this maxim; but it is a deeper truth that God does not allow wholly to fail what is done for his sake; and the whole history of the Jewish people in their dispersion confirms that truth.

R. Johanan ha-Sandelar, the sandalmaker, a native of Alexandria, (j. Hag 78[d]), and in an especial degree a disciple of R. Akiba, as he said to R. Meir "I have served Akiba standing, longer then thou hast served him sitting", i. e. as a student before him. After the death of Akiba, whom he managed to consult while a prisoner, (j. Jeb. 12[d]) he planned to escape to Nisibis along with R. Eleazar b. Shammua, (Siphrē D. § 80), but both turned back on the frontier of the Land, unable to forsake it even in their peril. After the persecution was over he was one of the Rabbis who met at Usha. How long he lived there is no evidence to show; but he is seldom mentioned ex-cept in connexion with the men of his own standing, such as R. Meir. Bacher (A. T. II. 365) suggests that his saying in Aboth may have been intended as an encouragement and a warning to those who after the persecution were trying to re-organize the life of the community, by collective efforts of some kind.

The saying is found, anonymously, in A. R. N.[A] XL, and A. R. N.[B] XLVI. In each case examples are given of the two kinds of assembly, the one being Israel at Sinai, the other the builders of the Tower of Babel. Taylor, *ad loc.*

---

[1] But see on R. Jehudah, v. 16 below.

gives as the first example in A. R. N. the Great Synagogue, but this is not
mentioned in either of the two versions nor in Schechter's note on the
passage.

15. רַבִּי אֶלְעָזָר בֶּן־שַׁמּוּעַ אוֹמֵר יְהִי כְבוֹד תַּלְמִידְךָ חָבִיב עָלֶיךָ כִּכְבוֹד
חֲבֵרְךָ וּכְבוֹד חֲבֵרְךָ כְּמוֹרָא רַבָּךְ וּמוֹרָא רַבָּךְ כְּמוֹרָא שָׁמָיִם:

בֶּן שמוע. So M.S.; ‏כשלך‎ ;M.S. So A.B.C.D. ‏ככבוד הברך‎ .15. So M.S.; A.C.D. om.

15. R. Eleazar ben Shammua said: Let the honour of thy disciple be dear to thee as the honour of thy associate; and the
honour of thy associate as the fear of thy teacher, and the fear
of the teacher as the fear of Heaven.

15. On the duty of paying honour and reverence to both learners
and teachers of Torah. That study is the bond which links together
disciple, associate, teacher and God who gave the Torah. There
is subordination of rank amongst these, and the honour shown to
one is not the same in amount or expression as that due to another. But it is as much a duty to show to the disciple the honour
due to the disciple as it is to show to an associate, or to a teacher,
or to God himself, the honour that is respectively due to them.
And this removes the difficulty that the teacher appears to be
made equal to God, since the reverence due to the one is said to
be equal to that due to the other; a point which Gentile critics
have not failed to make. But the Rabbis never taught such an
equality. They taught that there was a reverence due to the
teacher of Torah (by reason of the sacredness of Torah) and a reverence due to God the giver of Torah; and that to pay that reverence was an equal obligation in each case.

R. Eleazar b. Shammua is R. Eleazar of the Mishnah. He was another of
the seven who were said to have been ordained by R. Jehudah b. Baba during
the persecution[1] (b. Sanh. 14[a]), a fact which gives some indication of his
age. He cannot have been born later than 115 C. E., and he may have been
somewhat older than this would indicate. He was near enough in age to
R. Meir to call him "Meir", as he says himself, (M. Naz. VII. 4). He was not
amongst the Rabbis who met at Usha, and does not seem to have held any
intercourse with those who gathered round R. Simeon b. Gamliel and Rabbi.
Yet the latter was placed by his father under the care of R. Eleazar to learn
Torah, so that there could have been no animus against him. He is said to
have lived to be old, (b. Meg. 27[b]) and a late tradition says that he died at

_____
[1] But see on R. Jehudah, v. 16 below.

the age of 105 years (Midr. Elleh Ezkerah); but as it includes him among
the ten Martyrs, which is manifestly impossible, its evidence is unreliable.
The date of his death is quite unknown; but if his old age is admitted, his
life covered the greater part of the second century C. E.

In form this saying is like that of R. Eliezer, (II. 15), and this likeness may
have produced the uncertainty of the text which varies between כבוד חברך
and כשלך for both these terms occur in R. Eliezer's saying. The reading
חברך 'כ is however amply supported in the present passage, and makes a
better sequence in the thought.

The saying is found in A. R. N.^A XXVII, and A. R. N.^B XXXIV. In the
latter passage it is ascribed to R. Nathan, and is accompanied by proof-texts
(Exod. XVII. 8, and VII. 2); and in both the text reads כשלך instead of
כ' חברך.

16. רַבִּי יְהוּדָה אוֹמֵר הֱוֵה זָהִיר בְּתַלְמוּד שֶׁשִּׁגְגַת תַּלְמוּד עֹלָה זָדוֹן:

16. R. Jehudah said: Be cautious in teaching; for error in teaching
may amount to intentional sin.

16. On the consequences of careless teaching. Where the whole
body of religious teaching rested on tradition it was clearly of
vital importance that no error should be made in what was trans-
mitted. There might be differences of interpretation; but that which
was to be interpreted must not be varied in the slightest degree.
If a teacher, through carelessness, did so vary what he was bound
to teach exactly, that would be at the moment a שגגה, a sin committed unwittingly; but, in its consequences, by perpetuating error
and leading to false deductions on the part of those who in all
good faith accepted the erroneous teaching as being true, it amounts
to זדון, intentional sin on the part of the original teacher.

R. Jehudah is R. Jehudah b. Illai one of the most eminent of the Tannaim.
He is said to have been another of the disciples of R. Akiba who were ordained by R. Jehudah b. Baba during the persecution. The difficulty of understanding why these men were not ordained by R. Akiba himself is greatest
in the case of R. Jehudah, for he was apparently the oldest among them,
and he had learned from all the chief teachers of the time before the war,
R. Jehoshua, R. Tarphon, R. Eleazar b. Azariah, R. Akiba and R. Ishmael. He
could not have been still a young man at the time of the persecution; and
the fact that he learned from R. Tarphon as he says himself, (b. Meg. 2^a)
shows that he must have been born near the beginning of the century, since
R. Tarphon died in 117 C. E. Schlatter (Der Trajanstag 21. n.) makes the
bold suggestion that the names of the men ordained by R. Jehudah b. Baba
were lost and their place supplied in Talm. Babli by those of the men who
did in fact revive the tradition after the persecution. It is certainly remarkable

that the brave deed of R. Jeh. b. B. is not mentioned in the Palestinian tradition, and is first reported by Rab. No doubt he learned the fact of the
ordination from his Palestinian teachers; but he may well have drawn his
own conclusion as to the names of the men ordained, from his knowledge
that R. Meir and the others were the men who first came forward after the
persecution was ended. Hard as it is to dissociate their names from the
splendid memory of R. Jeh. b. Baba and his ordination, and no less hard to
be deprived of the names of the brave men who received ordination in the
face of death, I am bound to admit that I believe Schlatter's suggestion to
be well founded. If this be accepted, then there is no difficulty in allowing
that R. Jehudah b. Illai and his companions were no longer young at the
time of the persecution; and this also makes it easier to understand how
they could at once take the lead after the persecution was over.

As to the length of his life, he outlived R. Meir (b. Kidd. 52ᵇ), and R. Josē
(b. Succ. 18ᵃ), so that his death may be dated at about 180 C. E.

For the severe judgment upon error in teaching, cp. III. 10, above. As
for the character of the act, a שגגה could not *become* a זדון; but in view of
its serious consequences it could be accounted a זדון, Taylor cp. b. Ḥag. 5ᵃ.

17. רַבִּי שִׁמְעוֹן אוֹמֵר שְׁלֹשָׁה כְתָרִים הֵן כֶּתֶר תּוֹרָה וְכֶתֶר כְּהוּנָה
וְכֶתֶר מַלְכוּת וְכֶתֶר שֵׁם טוֹב [עוֹלֶה] עַל גַּבֵּיהֶן:

17. צוּלה. So A.B.C.S. D.M. om.

17. R. Simeon said: There are three crowns, the crown of Torah
the crown of the priesthood and the crown of kingship but the
crown of a good name excels them.

17. A lesson on the excellence of personal character as compared with acquired dignity. The crown is the symbol of pre-
eminence, and the metaphor can readily be applied to any gradation
of rank or character. Priesthood and kingship are dignities conferred upon a man, without any necessary reference to his character.
Even the crown of Torah, the fame of a great teacher, might con-
ceivably be acquired by one who was personally unworthy. But
the crown of a good name is the tribute paid to personal worth
and upright character, and is better than all the others because it
alone is indispensable.

For R. Simeon, who is R. Simeon b. Johai, see above III. 4. The commentators have found some difficulty in this verse. Duran objects that a good
name cannot be called a crown; and Bartenora cannot find support in scripture for more than the three crowns. The phrase "Excels them all" is taken
by one to mean that a good name can only be obtained by 'kingship', 'priesthood' or 'Torah', while another takes the opposite view that none of these

are of any worth without a good name. R. Simeon's saying seems to me to carry its own meaning without the need of explanation, as a fine ethical epigram which is only spoiled by laboured interpretation.

The saying is found in A. R. N.^A XLI, and A. R. N.^B XLVIII.

18. רַבִּי נְהוֹרַאי אוֹמֵר הֱוֵה גוֹלֶה לִמְקוֹם תּוֹרָה וְאַל תּאֹמַר שֶׁהִיא
תָּבוֹא אַחֲרֶיךָ שֶׁחֲבֵרֶיךָ יְקַיְּמוּהָ בְּיָדֶךָ וְאֶל־בִּינָתְךָ אַל תִּשָּׁעֵן:

18. ר' נחוראי וגי'. M. omits, and substitutes ר' או עשה רצונו וגי' as in II. 4.

18. R. Nehorai said: Betake thyself to a place of Torah, and say not that it shall come after thee, for thine associates will fulfil it through thee. And rely not on thine own understanding.

18. Knowledge of Torah, as the highest of all, is to be sought and striven for, and not expected to come of itself. For its sake, a man should go like an exile away from his home if he cannot learn Torah where he is, and seek it where it is to be found. There he will not only learn it but help to fulfil it, by aiding the associates whom he will meet there. If he stayed at home he would learn nothing, and have only his own untaught understanding to rely upon.

R. Nehorai is a shadowy figure in the Mishnah. Even in the Talmud there is uncertainty as to his real name. He is there variously identified with R. Meir, R. Nehemjah and the earlier R. Eleazar b. Arak. None of these identifications is possible, because R. Nehorai is found in debate with R. Meir, (b. Sanh. 99^a); and in A. R. N.^B XL R. Nehemjah speaks in the name of R. Nehorai. R. Eleazar b. Arak never could have come into contact with R. Meir. The little that is known about R. Nehorai shows that he took part in the assembly at Usha, after the persecution; and the passage just quoted from A. R. N.^B XL speaks of him as a disciple of R. Tarphon.

Nothing more is known of him. There was another R. Nehorai in the period of the Amoraim.

His saying is understood by some of the commentators to be a reflexion by R. Eleazar b. Arak on the lesson of his own wasted life and opportunity thrown away. This cannot be accepted; but on the other hand it is possible that the interpretation of the saying on these lines suggested the identification of the teacher with R. Eleazar b. Arak. The saying is found in A. R. N.^A XXIII, and A. R. N.^B XXXIII.

The Munich MS omits the saying and gives in place of it the saying of R. Gamliel already recorded, II. 4, but ascribes it to Rabbi.

19. רַבִּי יַנַּאי אוֹמֵר אֵין בְּיָדֵינוּ לֹא מִשַּׁלְוַת הָרְשָׁעִים וְאַף לֹא מִיִּסּוֹרֵי
הַצַּדִּיקִים:

19. R. Jannai said: There is not in our hands either the security of the wicked or the chastisements of the righteous.

19. A saying of which the lesson is by no means certain. Some interpret it to mean that it is not in human power to *explain* either the security of the wicked or the afflictions of the righteous. Others take it to mean that it is not in human power to *allot* the portion either of the wicked or the righteous; if it were, they would not have allotted security to the wicked nor afflictions to the righteous. Their lot is in the hands of God alone. Others interpret the saying to mean we do not enjoy the security of the wicked nor suffer the afflictions of the righteous. We are not hopelessly bad, nor perfectly good; our hope is not destroyed, but we are not to think that we need make no further effort in the service of God. Of these interpretations the last keeps nearest to the grammatical construction, and on that account seems preferable. Moreover, it is not a truism as the others are, but a comment on life of salutary application. If Israel does not enjoy security, at least in that respect he does not share the lot of the wicked. If he suffers, he suffers for his sins and is not to think that he is an afflicted saint.

The name R. Jannai denotes in almost every case the Amora of the third century, of the generation after Rabbi. But either there was a Tanna of that name, or the present saying is an interpolation made after the close of the Mishnah. The latter is not impossible; and the fact that the Munich MS omits the saying may be taken as pointing in that direction. But, if there was a Tanna by name R. Jannai, then it is hardly warrantable to have recourse to an interpolation. Moreover, if the saying of one Amora was to be interpolated into the Mishnah why not the sayings of others also? The father of R. Dosthai b. Jannai (III. 11 above) was R. Jannai, as is shown in A. R. N.ᴬ III, and R. Dosthai b. J. was a disciple of R. Meir. Also, in j. Taan. IV. 2, R. Levi says that a book of 'Juhasin', pedigrees, was found in Jerusalem which gave the ancestry of several persons, amongst them R. Josē b. Halaphta, (R ...) ben Jehudah, R. Jannai, R. Nehemjah. Apart from those who are unknown, R. Hija is the only one who was later than the Mishnah, and he was only just later. Presumably all were of the Mishnah period; for it is quite incongruous with the context to assume with Geiger (Urschr. p. 111) that Jannai denotes king Jannai the Hasmonean. The incongruity would be just as great if the reading דבית ינאי (Ber. r. 98) were preferred to the reading ר' ינאי of the Jerushalmi. Geiger does prefer it, but it does not help his assumption. There seems no reason to doubt that R. Jannai, in the Mishnah, denotes the father of R. Dosthai in which case he would be contemporary with R. Meir. His comparative obscurity is no argument against the choice of a saying by him to be included in Aboth, as it has already appeared that the teachers therein named were by no means always the most famous in their time. The saying is found in A. R. N.^B XXXIII, with an addition which bears out the interpretation preferred above.

20. רַבִּי מַתִּתְיָא בֶּן־חָרָשׁ אוֹמֵר הֱוֵה מַקְדִּים בִּשְׁלוֹם כָּל־אָדָם וֶהֱוֵה
זָנָב לָאֲרָיוֹת וְאַל תְּהִי רֹאשׁ לַשּׁוּעָלִים:

20. See this quoted as מ״ת in opposition to the מתלא j. Sanh. 22^b IV. 10.

20. R. Mattithiah ben Ḥarash said: Be first in greeting every man; and be a tail to lions and not a head to foxes.

20. There does not appear to be any connexion between the two clauses of this saying. The first is a counsel of courtesy, perhaps also of prudence in a state of society where good-will to the Jew could not be counted on. The second is an epigram of which the contrary would be equally plausible. It may have been a popular proverb applied by the teacher who quotes it here to his own case.

R. Mattithiah (or Matthia) b. Ḥarash, a disciple of R. Eliezer as he said himself (b. Joma 53^b). If the name 'Eliezer' can be relied on, and is not a mistake for some later Eleazar, R. Matthia must have been very young at the time. He escaped from Palestine before the Bar Cocheba War (or possibly in the early stages of it) as did also R. Jehudah b. Bethira and R. Ḥananjah the nephew of R. Jehoshua b. Ḥananjah. He made his way to Rome, where he appears to have spent the rest of his life. He was there when R. Simeon b. Joḥai came thither on his mission to obtain a relaxation of the penal laws against the Jews, and no more is heard of him. From the nature of the case he came but seldom in contact with the Palestinian Rabbis; and his isolation in this respect may have prompted him to make, or adopt, the remark about being the tail of lions rather than the head of foxes.

The saying is found in A. R. N.^B XXXIV in the name of R. Matt. b. H.; but in A. R. N.^A it is included (הוא היה אומר) among the sayings of R. Isaac b. Pinhas. In j. Sanh. IV. 10 it is quoted as Mishnah in opposition to the proverb "Be a head to foxes rather than a tail to lions".

21. רַבִּי יַעֲקֹב אוֹמֵר הָעוֹלָם הַזֶּה דּוֹמֶה לִפְרוֹזְדּוֹר בִּפְנֵי הָעוֹלָם הַבָּא
הַתְקֵן עַצְמְךָ בִּפְרוֹזְדּוֹר כְּדֵי שֶׁתִּכָּנֵס לַטְרַקְלִין:

21. R. Jacob used to say: This world is like a vestibule before the world to come; prepare thyself in the vestibule that thou mayest enter into the banquet hall.

21. One of the best known and most often quoted sayings in Aboth. It speaks for itself, and teaches its lesson without the need of any explanation.

R. Jacob is the same who is quoted above, III. 9. At least that is to be
presumed in the absence of any evidence to the contrary. The present
R. Jacob is certainly R. J. b. Kurshai, for the saying in this v. is found in
Koh. R. IV. 6 with the full name of the teacher.

פרוזדור is usually taken to represent προθύρα, vestibule. Taylor contends
that the reading פרוזדוד is to be preferred, and remarks truly enough that
the likeness between פרוזדור and προθύρα is not as close as might be expected. But פרוזדוד occurs hardly anywhere else; and if it be meant for
πρόσοδος, the two ד are unexplained. There is ample authority for the
reading פרוזדור, and it is assumed by Rashi and most of the commentators:[1]
טקרלין is triclinium.

The saying is found in A. R. N.B XXXIII, and in T. Ber. VII. 21 where it
is anonymous and is introduced in opposition to the Mīnīm, (heretics), who
maintained that this world was the only one.

22. הוּא הָיָה אוֹמֵר יָפָה שָׁעָה אַחַת בִּתְשׁוּבָה וּמַעֲשִׂים טוֹבִים בָּעוֹלָם
הַזֶּה מִכֹּל חַיֵּי הָעוֹלָם הַבָּא וְיָפָה שָׁעָה אַחַת שֶׁל קוֹרַת רוּחַ בָּעוֹלָם הַבָּא
מִכֹּל חַיֵּי הָעוֹלָם הַזֶּה:

22. He used to say: Better is one hour of repentance and good
works in this world than all the life of the world to come; and
better is one hour of calmness of spirit in the world to come than
all the life of this world.

22. A further lesson on the contrast between the present world
and the world to come, expressed in two vivid paradoxes. The
passage has given much trouble to the commentators, since the
one clause appears directly to contradict the other. I believe that
the teacher intended to show what was the real difference between
this world and the world to come. The former is a state of existence in which change, (especially change of mental and spiritual
condition), can take place; the latter is a state of existence in
which such change cannot take place. In a world of change, the
highest and best form of change is that which is expressed in repentance and good works, because these are the acts of the soul
consciously turning to God and serving him. One hour of such

---

[1] The difficulty of taking פרוזדור as representing προθύρα is that פרו would be
expected to represent προς rather than προ. Krauß in the first vol. of his Lehnwörter, p. 101, accepts פרוזדור = προθύρα. But in vol. II, p. 484, the suggestion
of I. Löw is accepted, according to which the right reading is פרוזדיר = προστάς
or in the gen. case προστάδος. I give this on the authority of F. Perles, as I have
not been able to refer to Krauß' second vol.

consciously active seeking of God is better than an eternity of static bliss, the conditions of this world being what they are. On the other hand, in a world where there is no change, the highest and best form of existence is that of perfect peace in the beholding of God, as it is said (Ps. XVI. 11):—"In thy presence is fulness of joy". One hour of such bliss is better, under the conditions of such a world, than all "the changes and chances of this mortal life". The difficulty of the passage is due (if this explanation be correct) to the fact that the teacher does not explicitly state the real difference between the two worlds, viz:— change and changelessness, but only shows the consequences which follow from that difference. Both his statements are seen to be true when their hidden basis is supplied; without it, they remain paradoxes, but only the more striking on that account.

The above explanation is given after a study of many commentators, but is not taken from any of them. The author of Midrash Shemuel, perhaps the most ingenious amongst them, rejects all their explanations on the ground that they depend on a comparison of things which cannot be compared, — this world and the world to come. There is no question, he says, of a comparison in this saying. The מ in the phrase מכל חיי העולם הזה is not the מ of comparison but the מ of causation. The meaning accordingly is that in this world repentance and good works which are caused by, or due to, or prompted by the thought of, the world to come are יפה fair, excellent, or whatever be the right equivalent of that word. In the world to come, the quietness of spirit which is caused by, or is due to, or has been attained through, all the life of this world, is also יפה. The lesson is finely worked out by this commentator, and in itself is undeniably good; but, though not grammatically impossible, it seems very forced. יפה ... מ' almost irresistibly compels the reader to assume that a comparison of some kind is intended; and all the other commentators have so understood it.

The saying is found in A. R. N.ᴮ XXXIII.

23. רַבִּי שִׁמְעוֹן בֶּן־אֶלְעָזָר אוֹמֵר אַל תְּרַצֶּה אֶת חֲבֵרְךָ בִּשְׁעַת כַּעְסוֹ וְאַל תְּנַחֲמֵהוּ בְּשָׁעָה שֶׁמֵּתוֹ מֻטָּל לְפָנָיו וְאַל תִּשְׁאַל לוֹ בִּשְׁעַת נִדְרוֹ וְאַל תִּשְׁתַּדֵּל לִרְאוֹתוֹ בִּשְׁעַת קַלְקָלָתוֹ:

23. R. Simeon ben Eleazar said: Soothe not thy associate in the hour of his anger, and console him not in the hour when his dead lies before him; and question him not in the hour of his vow, and seek not to see him in the hour of his disgrace.

23. A lesson against unintended provocation, the wellmeant word which only hurts instead of healing. When a man is under the

sway of strong emotion it is well to refrain from speaking to him, until he is in a condition to receive calmly what is said. Job's three friends were more truly comforters while they sat silent on the ground before him, "for they saw that his grief was very great". It was when they began to talk to him that they did the harm and gave the pain. True, the world would have lost much if that silence had not been so splendidly broken; but Job felt the pain none the less.

R. Simeon b. Eleazar. It is often assumed that he was the son of R. Eleazar b. Shammua, but in fact it is quite uncertain who was his father. Eleazar was a very common name, and his father is nowhere called Rabbi. R. Simeon b. E. was intimate with R. Meir, as his young attendant and disciple; and in his later years was the companion and opponent in debate of Rabbi.

A curious chance has preserved the record that two famous teachers of a later generation, R. Johanan and R. Samuel b. Naḥmani, both heard R. Simeon b. Eleazar when they were little boys, young enough to ride on the shoulder of their grandfathers. Each mentions this himself, R. Johanan in j. Maas. 48^b, and R. Samuel b. N. in Ber. R. IX. 5.

Now R. Johanan was born in 200 C, E., and R. Samuel b. N. died in extreme old age in 299 C. E. If the incident took place in or about 215 C. E. (or somewhat earlier in the case of R. Johanan) that would allow of R. Simeon b. Eleazar having been born about 140 C. E., which would suit well his relation to R. Meir. These dates may be taken as fairly reliable.

His saying is found in A. R. N.^A XXIX but spoken by him in the name of R. Meir. Bacher, A. T. II. 9, n.^3, holds this to be the original reading. It is found in A. R. N.^B XXXIII in R. Simeon b. E.'s own name. It is not obvious why the authority of A. R. N., and that only in one version, should prevail over the reading of the Mishnah. No doubt R. Simeon b. E. often spoke in the name of R. Meir; but surely he said some things that were not mere quotations.

24. שְׁמוּאֵל הַקָּטָן אוֹמֵר בִּנְפֹל אוֹיִבְךָ אַל תִּשְׂמָח וּבִכָּשְׁלוֹ אַל יָגֵל לִבֶּךָ׃
פֶּן יִרְאֶה יְיָ וְרַע בְּעֵינָיו וְהֵשִׁיב מֵעָלָיו אַפּוֹ׃

24. Samuel the small said (Prov. XXIV. 17):—'Rejoice not when thine enemy fall and when he stumbleth let not thine heart be glad'. (ib. 18):—'Lest the Lord see it and it be evil in his sight, and he turn away his anger from him'.

24. The words ascribed to the teacher in this verse are not his own but are a quotation from Scripture, Prov. XXIV. 17. 18. There are many quotations from Scripture in Aboth but only in this one instance is a Scripture text adopted by a teacher as his own. Pre-

sumably, he was in the habit of quoting it frequently. Cp. for a somewhat similar case, IV. 4 above.

Samuel ha-Katan, the small. In my "Christianity in Talmud and Midrash" pp. 132—134, I have dealt with the chronology of Samuel the small (ha-Katan), and have brought evidence to show that he died not earlier than about 80 C. E. and was then a very old man. This is contrary to the usual view, that he died young; but I have seen no reason to alter the opinion formerly expressed. The fact that he was called upon by R. Gamliel at Jabneh to draw up the formula against the Minim, (b. Ber. 28ᵇ) is in favour of his being no longer young but a man of recognised age and position. The fact that only a year afterwards he himself forgot, in reciting the prayers, the very words he had composed is much more in keeping with old age than with youth, as is also the great forbearance that was shown to him on that occasion. Even R. Gamliel, who publicly disgraced R. Jehoshua b. Ḥananjah and was party to the excommunication of R. Eliezer, did not rebuke Samuel when he had disobeyed the orders of the Nasi, (j. Sanh. 8ᶜ) but addressed him in words of reverent praise, as one whose character was known to all Israel. This is far more intelligible in the case of a very old man than in that of a young one. There is indeed nothing in what is recorded about him to support the tradition that he died young, for his name does not imply youth and is not so interpreted by any of the commentators. The fact that he is not called Rabbi is no proof of his youth, for it fits equally well the view that he was older than the time when that title came into use. Duran, in his commentary on Aboth, *ad loc.* quotes a passage from a Midrash to the effect that "four men died at the age of fifty two years, Samuel the Ramathite, Solomon the king, Samuel the small and Samuel b. Abba". Duran does not give the reference to this Midrash, and I have not been able to verify the quotation; but it shows that the common opinion as to the early death of Samuel was not universally held. That he was young when he died is nowhere stated, so far as I know, in the Talmudic literature, and I believe it to rest on nothing more than a conjecture from his name. For chronological purposes, I should regard him as contemporary with R. Joḥanan b. Zaccai; and should place his birth in the very early years of the common era, and his death about 80 C. E.[1]

The saying does not appear to be included in A. R. N. In some texts it is repeated in v. 24, and in others found only there.

---

[1] My conjecture as to the old age of Samuel is independently confirmed by Hyman, in his Toldoth Tannaim ve-Amoraim p. 1148. He says there, "without any doubt Samuel the small was amongst the disciples of Hillel, and it is known that Hillel died about sixty years before the חורבן, so that Samuel would be about twenty at the time." This would make Samuel about ninety when he died, which is not impossible. In any case, Hyman recognises that Samuel was an old man and not a youth when he died. I would here express my indebtedness to Hyman's valuable work, from which I have derived much help.

25. אֱלִישָׁע בֶּן־אֲבוּיָה אוֹמֵר הַלּוֹמֵד יֶלֶד לְמָה הוּא דוֹמֶה לִדְיוֹ כְּתוּבָה
עַל נְיָר חָדָשׁ וְהַלּוֹמֵד זָקֵן לְמָה הוּא דוֹמֶה לִדְיוֹ כְּתוּבָה עַל נְיָר מָחוּק:

25. Elisha ben Abujah said: He who learns when a youth, to
what is he like? To ink written on new paper. And he who learns
when old to what is he like? To ink written on erased paper.

25. A lesson on the duty of learning Torah while one is young,
on the ground that what is learned then will remain longest, and
that what is learned in old age is retained only with difficulty.

Elisha b. Abujah. He is not called Rabbi, and perhaps was never ordained;
but the omission of the title may be due to the fact that he fell away and
became an apostate from the religion of his people. He was born probably
about 80 C. E., although, if the story in j. Hag. 77[b] could be relied on in
all its details, he was born in Jerusalem before the siege. But the point of
that story is not his age but his apostasy. If he had been born when the
story says he was, R. Eliezer and R. Joshua would not have been the two
principal guests at his מילה banquet. They would only in the view of a
later age appear to be such; and, whatever elements of historical truth the
passage contains, it is much more like a finished haggadah than a personal
recollection. See above, on R. Jacob, III. 9 for reasons which point to a date
not later than about 80 C. E. for Elisha's birth. How long he lived is not
known; but he witnessed the persecution under Hadrian, and R. Meir his
faithful friend and former disciple was already established as a teacher. His
death may be dated at somewhere near the middle of the second century C.E.

Some of the commentators explain that Elisha b. Abujah probably uttered
this maxim before he became an apostate, since the words of such a one
would never be given a place in the Mishnah. This is by no means certain.
The fact that a teacher of such high authority as R. Meir never wavered in
his devotion to Elisha shows that there was something to be felt if not much
to be said for him. Moreover, if no halachic decision of his is to be found
in the Mishnah, there is mention of one (b. M. Kat. 20[a]) which is quoted as
authoritative without reservation. See, on this passage an excellent remark
by Weiß, Dor, II. 140, n. 1. A whole series of sayings by Elisha b. A. is
found in A. R. N.[A] XXIV. They express rather the experience of an old
man than the opinions of a young one. The compiler of Aboth may well
have thought that the saying he has recorded was worth preserving for its
own sake, knowing also that its author, in spite of his defection, had been
a notable man in his time.

26. רַבִּי יוֹסֵי בַּר יְהוּדָה אִישׁ כְּפַר הַבַּבְלִי אוֹמֵר הַלּוֹמֵד מִן הַקְּטַנִּים
לְמָה הוּא דוֹמֶה לְאוֹכֵל עֲנָבִים קֵהוֹת וְשׁוֹתֶה יַיִן מִגִּתּוֹ וְהַלּוֹמֵד מִן הַזְּקֵנִים
לְמָה הוּא דוֹמֶה לְאוֹכֵל עֲנָבִים בְּשׁוּלוֹת וְשׁוֹתֶה יַיִן יָשָׁן:

26. R. Josē bar Jehudah of Chephar ha-Babli said: He who learns from the young to what is he like? To one who eats unripe grapes and drinks wine from his wine-press. And he who learns from the old to what is he like? To one who eats ripe grapes and drinks old wine.

26. Another comparison, or rather contrast, between the young and the old, in regard not to learning but to teaching. It puts the case from the point of view of the old, as the following saying (v. 27) is a rejoinder from the point of view of the young. On the one side is ripe experience, on the other the fresh mind and new ideas. Youth and age will always differ on the point. The terms of the comparison need no elucidation.

R. Josē b. Judah, of Chephar ha-Babli is, on account of his epithet, to be distinguished from the far better known R. Jose b. R. Jehudah (b. Illai). It is probable, though not certain, that he is the man to whom an extraordinary series of names is ascribed (b. Pes. 113^b. Joma 52^b), amongst them Joseph ha-Babli and Isi b. Jehudah. A man bearing the latter name is mentioned by Rabbi as a disciple of R. Eleazar b. Shammua (b. Men. 18^a cp. T. Zeb. II. 17). Rabbi said (*ibid.*) that when he went to study under R. Eleazar b. Shammua he found Joseph ha-Babli there. This would be somewhere about 160 C. E. This is the only clue to his chronology. As he was already the chief disciple of R. Eleazar b. S., he was presumably somewhat older than Rabbi. There is nothing to show how long he lived. The saying of Rabbi immediately following his in this chapter, may be a playful retort, and in any case would only have any point if Rabbi though young was already recognised as a teacher, after the death of his father, in or about 165 C. E. Moreover, this interpretation implies that Josē b. Jehudah's own saying was aimed at Rabbi, the young teacher as compared with (presumably) R. Eleazar b. Shammua, Jose's own venerated teacher. There is no need to assume any ill-feeling in this interchange of pleasantries. Rabbi would hardly have included his fellow-student's maxim in Aboth if he had been unfriendly towards him; and no harm was done if he thereby was able to get in his own rejoinder.

The saying of Jose b. J. is found in A. R. N.^{B} XXXIV, and is there attributed to R. Dosa ha-Babli, whose name does not occur elsewhere.

27. רַבִּי אוֹמֵר אַל תִּסְתַּכֵּל בְּקַנְקָן אֶלָּא בְּמָה שֶׁיֶּשׁ בּוֹ יֵשׁ קַנְקָן חָדָשׁ מָלֵא יָשָׁן וְיָשָׁן שֶׁאֲפִילוּ חָדָשׁ אֵין בּוֹ:

27. Rabbi said: Look not at the pitcher but at that which is in it. There is a new pitcher which is full of old *wine* and an old pitcher which has not even new *wine* in it.

27. The reply of youth to age. See on the preceding v. and for
Rabbi, above, II. 1. If the interpretation given in the preceding
v. be correct, then the "old pitcher which does not contain even
new wine" is doubtless meant for R. Josē b. Jehudah. This and the
preceding saying are found together in A. R. N.ᴮ XXXIV.

28. רַבִּי אֶלְעָזָר הַקַּפָּר אוֹמֵר הַקִּנְאָה וְהַתַּאֲוָה וְהַכָּבוֹד מוֹצִיאִין אֶת־
הָאָדָם מִן הָעוֹלָם:

28. R. Eleazar ha-Kappar said: Envy and desire and ambition
drive a man out of the world.

28. A lesson against selfishness, in three of its most fatal forms.
In what sense these "drive a man out of the world" is open to
question, but not the fact that selfishness in any form is unsocial.
It breaks the ties which should unite a man to his fellowmen, and
whether or not it leads to physical death, it destroys his higher
life as a moral being, made in the likeness of God.

R. Eleazar ha-Kappar was a close companion of Rabbi; but beyond that
fact there are no data by which to determine his chronology. He was, in
all probability (see Bacher, A. T. II. 500—502), the father of the better
known Eliezer bar Kappara, who outlived Rabbi. The meaning of the name
ha-Kappar is uncertain. It may denote some trade, like sandelar, lablar.
This saying and the following are found in A. R. N.ᴮ XXXIV, but are there
ascribed to R. Eliezer the son of R. Eleazar ha-Kappar.

29. הוּא הָיָה אוֹמֵר הַיִּלּוֹדִים לָמוּת וְהַמֵּתִים לִחְיוֹת וְהַחַיִּים לִדּוֹן לֵידַע
וּלְהוֹדִיעַ וּלְהִוָּדַע שֶׁהוּא [אֵל הוּא] הַיּוֹצֵר הוּא הַבּוֹרֵא הוּא הַמֵּבִין הוּא
הַדַּיָּן הוּא הָעֵד [הוּא] בַּעַל דִּין הוּא עָתִיד לָדוּן בָּרוּךְ הוּא שֶׁאֵין לְפָנָיו
לֹא עַוְלָה וְלֹא שִׁכְחָה וְלֹא מַשּׂוֹא פָנִים וְלֹא מְקַח שֹׁחַד וְדַע שֶׁהַכֹּל לְפִי
הַחֶשְׁבּוֹן וְאַל יַבְטִיחֲךָ יִצְרְךָ שֶׁשְּׁאוֹל בֵּית מָנוֹס לָךְ שֶׁעַל כָּרְחָךְ אַתָּה נוֹצָר
וְעַל כָּרְחָךְ אַתָּה נוֹלָד וְעַל כָּרְחָךְ אַתָּה חַי וְעַל כָּרְחָךְ אַתָּה מֵת וְעַל
כָּרְחָךְ אַתָּה עָתִיד לִתֵּן דִּין וְחֶשְׁבּוֹן לִפְנֵי מֶלֶךְ מַלְכֵי הַמְּלָכִים הַקָּדוֹשׁ
בָּרוּךְ הוּא:

29. שבשאול ;A.C.D.M. om. לָךְ. M. שחשאיל ;ובעל. M. הוא בעל. A.C.M. om. אל הוא.

29. He used to say: Those that are born are for death, and the
dead are for life, and they that live (again) are to be judged; to

know, to make known and to be made aware that He is God, He is the Maker, He the Creator, He the Discerner, He the Judge, He the witness, He the adversary and He will judge; blessed be He in whose presence there is neither obliquity nor forgetfulness, nor respect of persons nor taking of bribes. And know that all is according to reckoning. Let not thy nature persuade thee that the underworld will be a refuge for thee. For not of thy will wast thou formed and not of thy will dost thou die, and not of thy will art thou to give just account and reckoning before the King of the kings of the kings, the Holy One, Blessed be He.

29. This group of sayings is a kind of meditation on human destiny and judgment, divine justice and retribution. Apparently it is placed here as a suitable close to the chapter. Possibly it was originally the end of the collection which now forms the third and fourth chapters. The thoughts expressed in it find their echo in the teaching of well-nigh every Jewish moralist. There is a certain solemnity of language as well as of thought in the passage, which marks it off from the immediately preceding sayings. One might almost conjecture that it was taken from some sermon or religious address.

For R. Eleazar ha-Kappar and his son see on the preceding verse.

The construction of the first half of the passage is unusually elaborate. The triple arrangement in the first clause is carried through the other clauses as well, and this explains the three verbal forms, לְהוֹדִיעַ, לֵידַע, and לְהִוָּדַע. The first corresponds to הֵיל' לָמוּת; the second to הֵמֵת' לַחֲיוֹת, and the third to הֶחָיֵ' לִידוֹן. In like manner the knowledge implied in these three forms of יֵדַע is three-fold, though the division is not clearly marked. To לֵידַע corresponds שֶׁהוּא הָאֵל; to לְהוֹדִיעַ corresponds הוּא הַבּוֹרֵא הוּא הַיּוֹצֵר הוּא (שׁ); and to לְהוֹדַע corresponds הוּא הַמֵּבִין הוּא הַדַּיָּין הַדִּין וְגו' (שׁ). The general sense of the passage is thus: — The living are destined to die, that they may know that God is. Death is the final proof that God is supreme; none can escape or defy his decree. The dead are destined to live again, and thereby to make known the creative power of God. The living, that is those who have been made alive after death, are to be judged, so that they may be made aware that God is the supremely just, the witness the discerner the judge in whose sight there is no respect of persons.

The remainder of the saying develops the thought that there is no escape from the justice of God, and that human will counts for nothing against the will of the King of Kings.

פרק חמישי CHAP. V.

‫א. בַּעֲשָׂרָה מַאֲמָרוֹת נִבְרָא הָעוֹלָם וּמַה תַּלְמוּד לוֹמַר וַהֲלֹא בְּמַאֲמָר‬
‫אֶחָד יָכוֹל לְהִבָּרְאוֹת אֶלָּא לְהִפָּרַע מִן הָרְשָׁעִים שֶׁמְּאַבְּדִין אֶת־הָעוֹלָם‬
‫שֶׁנִּבְרָא בַּעֲשָׂרָה מַאֲמָרוֹת וְלִתֵּן שָׂכָר טוֹב לַצַּדִּיקִים שֶׁמְּקַיְּמִין אֶת־הָעוֹלָם‬
‫שֶׁנִּבְרָא בַּעֲשָׂרָה מַאֲמָרוֹת:‬

V. 1. ‫ומה תלמוד לומר‬. M. om.; ‫אלא‬ M. add. ‫כדי‬.

1. By ten sayings the world was created. And why does *Scripture* teach this? Could it not have been made with *only* one saying? But *it was in order* to exact penalty from the wicked who destroy the world which was created by ten sayings, and to give good reward to the righteous who establish the world which was created by ten sayings.

The contents of this chapter differ for the most part from those of the preceding chapters in the form in which they are cast. N[os] 1—18 are arranged in groups, based upon the numbers ten, seven, four;[1] and are not ascribed to any teacher by name. N[os] 19—22 are not numerical, (n° 22 is partially so), and are also anonymous. Only n[os] 23—26 are ascribed to some teacher by name. It will be shown that there is considerable divergence amongst the several authorities for the text in regard to the concluding verses, which form the end not merely of this chapter but of the original Aboth, as it was incorporated in the Mishnah. The non-personal character of this chapter goes to show that the compiler of 'Aboth', if he gave that title to his collection, did not mean to give a series of 'Fathers' illustrated by their sayings. Chapter V has hardly any 'Fathers'; and of those in the earlier chapters several, as has been shown, are so obscure that they can only be called 'Fathers' if every teacher in the Tannaite period is entitled to that name.

1. By ten sayings the world was created. These are the divine utterances in Gen. I, "and God said". There are however only nine such utterances in the series, and the tenth is supplied variously by different teachers, either from Gen I. 1 or II. 18 or from Ps. XXXIII. 16. Ten is evidently a round number. The point of

---

[1] Another numerical series is found in b. B. Bathra 17ᵃ. A collection of the chief instances of numerical grouping in the Talmud is given by Rosenthal, "Zusammenhang der Mischnah" I § 86, pp. 138—140.

the passage is not in the number ten but in the idea of many
divine utterances as compared with one. This is shown by the
question why could not the world have been created by one divine
utterance only? The reason given is to show the greater guilt
of those who would destroy, and the greater virtue of those who
would maintain, a work upon which so much divine care was
bestowed.

The purpose of the author of this haggadah was not, as in some other
passages, to collect ten examples of some object or event, but to draw a
lesson from the fact that the words "and God said" were repeated so many
times in the account of the creation; nine times explicitly and one im-
plicitly. Jom-tob well says (*ad loc.*) Creation was not so ordered as to lead
to the punishment of the wicked &c., but Scripture in narrating the creation
teaches this lesson. This is shown by מה תלמוד לומר.

This saying is found in A. R. N.^B XXXVI, and the beginning of it (^A) XXXI.

---

2. עֲשָׂרָה דוֹרוֹת מֵאָדָם וְעַד נֹחַ לְהוֹדִיעַ כַּמָּה אֶרֶךְ אַפַּיִם לְפָנָיו שֶׁכָּל־
הַדּוֹרוֹת הָיוּ מַכְעִיסִין וּבָאִין עַד שֶׁהֵבִיא עֲלֵיהֶם אֶת־מֵי הַמַּבּוּל:

2. Ten generations from Adam to Noah, to show how much long-
suffering is before Him, for all the generations went on provoking
Him until He brought upon them the waters of the Flood.

---

3. עֲשָׂרָה דוֹרוֹת מִנֹּחַ וְעַד אַבְרָהָם לְהוֹדִיעַ כַּמָּה אֶרֶךְ אַפַּיִם לְפָנָיו שֶׁכָּל־
הַדּוֹרוֹת הָיוּ מַכְעִיסִין וּבָאִין עַד שֶׁבָּא אַבְרָהָם אָבִינוּ וְקִבֵּל שָׂכַר כֻּלָּם:

3. נח ... אברהם. M. אדם ... נח, as in v. 2.

3. Ten generations from Noah to Abraham, to make known how
much long-suffering is before Him; for all the generation went
on provoking him until Abraham our father came and received
the reward of them all.

2. 3. Another lesson from a Scripture record, that of the ten
generations from Abraham to Noah, and another ten from Noah
to Abraham. These show the long-suffering of God, since the men
of those generations continued to provoke him, and only in the
tenth did He bring the Flood upon the earth to destroy the sinners.
There were righteous men in those generations, as Enoch and Noah
himself, and no clear distinction could be drawn between this series
and the next to show why their terminations were so different, —

in the one case destruction by the Flood, in the other case pardon'
through the merits of Abraham. The haggadist took the two
statements of Scripture, first that there were ten generations beginning with Adam and ending with the Flood, and second that
there were ten generations beginning with (the sons of) Noah and
ending with Abraham, and from both these statements he drew
a religious lesson, viz: — that God is longsuffering.

By an error of the scribe the Munich MS repeats the first series as the
second.

A. R. N.[B] XXXVI repeats Aboth V. 1—6 with little variation, and in
ch. XXXVII, after an interruption, it adds several more groups of ten.
A. R. N.[A] XXXII follows the line of Aboth but with much expansion.

4. עֲשָׂרָה נִסְיוֹנוֹת נִתְנַסָּה אַבְרָהָם אָבִינוּ וְעָמַד בְּכֻלָּם לְהוֹדִיעַ כַּמָּה
חִבָּתוֹ שֶׁל אַבְרָהָם אָבִינוּ:

4. With ten trials Abraham our father was tried, and he bore
them all, to make known how great was the love of Abraham
our father.

4. The ten trials of Abraham. The Scripture does not say that
there were ten trials, and the commentators differ in the way in
which they make up the number. But from the point of view of
the haggadist there is no importance in the number; it is merely
a convenient aid to memory, the fact to be remembered being that
Abraham endured many trials and bore them all. The real subject
offered for meditation is the endurance of Abraham, and the love
which enabled him to endure. The commentators do not add to
the force of the lesson by enumerating the several trials, since
these only draw away the attention from the main thought of the
passage.

The number ten is not suggested in Scripture, as in the preceding passages. It may have been chosen as in some sense a sacred number, and to
that extent as having an importance of its own; but the fact remains that
the real lesson taught in this haggadah turns not on the number ten but on
the love of Abraham.

5. עֲשָׂרָה נִסִּים נַעֲשׂוּ לַאֲבוֹתֵינוּ בְּמִצְרַיִם וַעֲשָׂרָה עַל הַיָּם:

5. M. om. במצרים ועשרה, but gives it in margin; after ים M. adds סוף.

5. Ten wonders were done for our fathers in Egypt and ten by
the Sea.

5. A pair of Scripture series merely stated and calling for no comment. The compiler, having started on a series of groups of ten, includes in it an observed fact of Scripture. No lesson is drawn from the fact.

6. עֶשֶׂר מַכּוֹת הֵבִיא הַקָּדוֹשׁ בָּרוּךְ הוּא עַל הַמִּצְרִיִּים בְּמִצְרַיִם וְעֶשֶׂר עַל הַיָּם:

6. M. omits the whole verse.

6. [Ten plagues did the Holy One, blessed be He, bring upon the Egyptians in Egypt, and ten by the Sea.]

6. A double series of ten plagues; mentioned with the like brevity.

There seems no reason why this series should not have been included with as much fitness as that in v. 5. But it is doubtful whether it was so included in the original Aboth. The clause is marked as doubtful in some printed texts.[1] A. R. N.[A] XXXIII refers to the series but does not give it in the form in which it would have been given if the author had found it in Aboth. It is as if the omission in Aboth were noted in A. R. N., and the omission supplied in the prayer-books which now contain the clause. The Munich MS omits it altogether.

7. עֲשָׂרָה נִסְיוֹנוֹת נִסּוּ אֲבוֹתֵינוּ אֶת־הַקָּדוֹשׁ בָּרוּךְ הוּא בַּמִּדְבָּר שֶׁנֶּאֱמַר וַיְנַסּוּ אוֹתִי זֶה עֶשֶׂר פְּעָמִים וְלֹא שָׁמְעוּ בְּקוֹלִי:

7. With ten trials did our fathers try the Holy One, blessed be He, in the wilderness, as it is said (Num. XIV. 22): — And they tempted me these ten times, and hearkened not to my voice.

7. Ten occasions when Israel tried God, the same word being used as in the preceding series. The meaning in each case is the same, — put to the test; but whereas it is part of the divine discipline that man is put to the test by what is laid upon him to endure, it is human insolence which tries the patience of God, and dares to put even him to the test. There is a certain daring simplicity, which perhaps only a Jew can fully appreciate, in thus linking together the trials which God and Israel brought on each other. This daring simplicity of thought is one of the characteristic features of the Haggadah in general, and one which is seldom understood or rightly judged by the Christian reader.

---

[1] Jomtob in his commentary *ad loc.*, mentions how he delivered a *derashah* in Cracow, on Hoshana Rabbah, in which he proved that this clause was not part of the Mishnah, and that there was no obligation to read it as such.

After all, this passage is only a statement of what is recorded in Scripture, in the text (Num. XIV. 22) expressly quoted. In this instance the text may be accepted as original, and not as an editorial addition. The number ten is explicitly given. The commentators are at pains to make out the list, but they do not agree amongst themselves.

‫8. עֲשָׂרָה נִסִּים נַעֲשׂוּ לַאֲבוֹתֵינוּ בְּבֵית הַמִּקְדָּשׁ. לֹא הִפִּילָה אִשָּׁה‬
‫מֵרֵיחַ בְּשַׂר הַקֹּדֶשׁ, וְלֹא הִסְרִיחַ בְּשַׂר הַקֹּדֶשׁ מֵעוֹלָם, וְלֹא נִרְאָה זְבוּב‬
‫בְּבֵית הַמִּטְבָּחַיִם וְלֹא אֵרַע קֶרִי לְכֹהֵן גָּדוֹל בְּיוֹם הַכִּפֻּרִים, וְלֹא כִבּוּ‬
‫הַגְּשָׁמִים אֵשׁ שֶׁל עֲצֵי הַמַּעֲרָכָה, וְלֹא נִצְּחָה הָרוּחַ אֶת־עַמּוּד הֶעָשָׁן,‬
‫וְלֹא נִמְצָא פְסוּל בָּעֹמֶר וּבִשְׁתֵּי הַלֶּחֶם וּבְלֶחֶם הַפָּנִים, עֹמְדִים צְפוּפִים‬
‫וּמִשְׁתַּחֲוִים רְוָחִים, וְלֹא הִזִּיק נָחָשׁ וְעַקְרָב בִּירוּשָׁלַיִם מֵעוֹלָם, וְלֹא אָמַר‬
‫אָדָם לַחֲבֵירוֹ צַר לִי הַמָּקוֹם שֶׁאָלִין בִּירוּשָׁלָיִם:‬

8. ‫לַאֲבוֹתֵינוּ‬ M. om. In M. the order of the ‫נִסִּים‬ is as in the text, except that (5) and (6) are transposed. ‫מֵעוֹלָם‬ M. om. twice.

8. Ten wonders were done for our fathers in the Sanctuary. (1) No women miscarried through the smell of the sacred flesh. (2) The sacred flesh never stank. (3) No fly was seen in the slaughter house; (4) and no uncleanness befell the High Priest on the Day of Atonement; and (5) no rain quenched the fire of the wood-pile, and (6) no wind overcame the column of smoke and (7) no defect was found in the sheaf and the two loaves and the shew bread; (8) *the people* stood close together but had room to bow themselves. (9) No serpent or scorpion did harm in Jerusalem. (10) And no one said to his associate The place is too narrow for me that I should lodge in Jerusalem.

8. A list of ten wonders associated with the Temple. It amounts merely to a quantitative expression of the holiness of the Temple in terms of miracle. That such terms are entirely inadequate for the expression of holiness or any other divine quality may be freely admitted, without denying that the Temple was holy.

There are discrepancies in the commentaries as to the contents of the list of wonders, and how they are to be reckoned. For details see Taylor, notes on the text *ad loc.* The number ten in this connexion is not suggested by anything in Scripture, and one can only suppose that the author of the list assumed the number ten as a sacred number and set himself to compile a list of wonders to the required amount. Note that some of the wonders

were done in Jerusalem and not in the Temple. This is remarked in the
Talmud, (b. Joma. 21ᵃ).

The passage is found in A. R. N.ᴬ XXXV, and (ᴮ) XXXIX.

9. עֲשָׂרָה דְבָרִים נִבְרְאוּ בְּעֶרֶב שַׁבָּת בֵּין הַשְּׁמָשׁוֹת וְאֵלּוּ הֵן. פִּי הָאָרֶץ
פִּי הַבְּאֵר פִּי הָאָתוֹן הַקֶּשֶׁת וְהַמָּן וְהַמַּטֶּה וְהַשָּׁמִיר הַכְּתָב וְהַמִּכְתָּב
וְהַלֻּחוֹת. וְיֵשׁ אוֹמְרִים אַף הַמַּזִּיקִין וּקְבוּרָתוֹ שֶׁל מֹשֶׁה וְאֵילוֹ שֶׁל אַבְרָהָם
אָבִינוּ וְיֵשׁ אוֹמְרִים אַף צְבָת בִּצְבַת עֲשׂוּיָה:

9. קבורתו M. קברו.

9. Ten things were created on the eve of Sabbath, between the
suns. And these are they: The mouth of the earth, the mouth of
the well, the mouth of the ass, the bow, the manna, the rod, the
shamir, the writing and the pen and the Tables; some say also the
evil spirits, and the grave of Moses and the ram of Abraham our
father, and some say also the tongs made with the tongs.

9. Ten things formed "between the suns", i. e. between the sixth
day of creation and the seventh on which the Creator rested. They
are all associated with some special divine activity different from
that manifested in the ordinary objects and works of nature. Therefore they were not regarded as being included in the classes of
things created in the six days as recorded in Scripture. On the
other hand they could not have been created after the sixth day,
when the work of creation was finished. Therefore they must have
been created last of all, before the seventh day. The ten objects
specified with the exception of the tenth, which is admitted to be
open to question, — "some say", — are all mentioned in Scripture.
It is not impossible that beneath this series of unique creations,
especially the last, there is concealed some attempt at the solution
of a philosophical problem; but I am unable to define what it was.

There is an extended reference to this passage in b. Pes. 54ᵃ where it is
given as a baraitha. The list of ten things is substantially the same though
the order is different, and two or three additions are suggested. These are
put forward not as being new, but as tradition of what was originally in the
list. The teachers who thus criticise the form of the tradition were R. Joshiah,
R. Nehemiah, who spoke "in the name of his father", and R. Judah. The
mention of these men, all Tannaim, shows that the list was already traditional in their time; and the fact that R. Nehemiah quoted the opinion of
his father carries it a stage earlier. It is clear therefore that the passage is
not due to the compiler of Aboth, and that he found it already in existence.

On the same page, (b. Pes. 54ᵃ), are other lists on somewhat similar lines. The compiler of Aboth either found and incorporated in his work a collection of numerical groups already made, or else he made his own selection from existing material. Why he chose some and omitted others there is nothing to indicate, as there is no apparent reason why he included the sayings of some teachers and omitted those of others equally or often more distinguished. I am confirmed in the opinion expressed in the Introduction, that Aboth contains just what happened from time to time to impress the compiler as worth recording, and discloses as a whole no logical plan or continuous purpose.

In regard to the several objects mentioned, the "mouth of the earth" means the fact that on occasion the earth "opened her mouth" and swallowed up evil doers, as in the case of Korah, (Num. XVI. 32). The "mouth of the well" refers to the well in Num. XXI. 16—18. Every well has a mouth; but this well produced water where till then there had been none. (Duran.) The "mouth of the ass" denotes the power of speech given to Balaam's ass. The bow is the rainbow which was given as a sign, (Gen. IX. 13). The manna dropped miraculously from heaven, (Exod. XVI. 15 fol.). The rod of Aaron became a serpent, and then a rod once more, (Exod. VII. 10). The shamir, in Scripture, is merely the diamond (Jer. XVII. 1, Ezek. III. 9, Zech. VII. 12); but in the Rabbinical literature it appears as a minute worm, having an irresistible power to penetrate the hardest rock. (See the art. Shamir in J. E. XI. 229 fol.) Its mention here is due to the belief that Solomon used it in the building of the temple. Writing, כתב, is by some commentators explained as the art of making the forms of the characters used to denote sounds; writing, מכתב, is the art of combining the characters so as to form words and thus to express ideas. Duran remarks that he does not know why these should be distinguished. He gives a more plausible explanation by connecting כתב and מכתב with the לוחות, as the writing on the tables, the instrument with which it was written, and the tables themselves. In this way, all three objects are associated with special divine action, and are suited to be included in the list. The evil spirits are not mentioned in the creation story; they must have been created at some time because they exist (according to the general belief of the period), and since the creator "saw all that he had made and behold it was very good", the evil spirits must have been created after that declaration had been made. The grave of Moses is included (by some) because its locality was known only to God (Deut. XXXIV. 6). The ram of Abraham is the one which was provided as a substitute for Isaac (Gen. XXII. 13.) The "tongs made with tongs" are not Scriptural at all. They are a symbol of unexplained beginnings. If tongs are needed wherewith to make other tongs, how were the first tongs made? By including them in the list, as some teachers wished, the lesson would be taught that all such unexplained beginnings were brought about by divine action.

The parallel passages A. R. N.ᴮ XXXVII, Mechilta, Beshall. IV. 5, Siphre, Deut. § 355, b. Pes. 54ᵃ, show that more than ten objects were thought of

as having been created in the last hours of the Creator's work. The list of
ten was variously computed; but the fact of that variation shows that the
subject was not new when the compiler of Aboth included one such list in
his collection. If he were looking for groups of ten things he would naturally
find a place for so striking an example.

10. שִׁבְעָה דְבָרִים בְּגֹלֶם וְשִׁבְעָה בְּחָכָם, חָכָם אֵינוֹ מְדַבֵּר לִפְנֵי מִי שֶׁגָּדוֹל
מִמֶּנּוּ בְּחָכְמָה וּבְמִנְיָן, וְאֵינוֹ נִכְנָס לְתוֹךְ דִּבְרֵי חֲבֵרוֹ, וְאֵינוֹ נִבְהָל לְהָשִׁיב,
שׁוֹאֵל כָּעִנְיָן וּמֵשִׁיב כַּהֲלָכָה, וְאוֹמֵר עַל רִאשׁוֹן רִאשׁוֹן וְעַל אַחֲרוֹן אַחֲרוֹן,
וְעַל מַה־שֶּׁלֹּא שָׁמַע אוֹמֵר לֹא שָׁמָעְתִּי, וּמוֹדֶה עַל הָאֱמֶת, וְחִלּוּפֵיהֶן
בְּגֹלֶם:

10. לפני. M. בפ׳. After נבהל להשיב the order of the clauses in M. is ועל מה
שלא וג׳ ואומר על ראשן וג׳ ומודה על האמת וחלופין וג׳.

10. Seven things are in an uneducated man and seven concerning a wise man. A wise man does not speak in the presence
of one who is greater than he in wisdom, and does not interrupt
the words of his associate, and does not hasten to reply. He
questions according to the subject and answers according to rule.
He speaks of the first thing first, and of the last thing last, and
concerning what he has not heard he says I have not heard. He
acknowledges the truth. The opposites of these are *found* in the
uneducated man.

10. A series of seven, summing up the characteristics of a wise
man and by contract those of a rude, undisciplined man. The wise
man, here, is not the philosopher but the Rabbi or the disciple
of the Rabbi. "The Wise" is the standing term in the Mishnah to
denote the Rabbis, as authoritative exponents of Torah. The lesson
is not so much ethical as academical.

This group is found A. R. N.^A XXXVII, and (^B) XL, where it is expanded
to ten characteristics. גולם is literally the *foetus* the unborn human being,
unformed and unfinished. By metaphor it denotes the man who is mentally
unformed and unfinished as contrasted with the Wise.

11. שִׁבְעָה מִינֵי פֻּרְעָנוּיוֹת בָּאִין לָעוֹלָם עַל שִׁבְעָה גּוּפֵי עֲבֵרָה: מִקְצָתָן
מְעַשְּׂרִין וּמִקְצָתָן אֵינָן מְעַשְּׂרִין רָעָב שֶׁל בַּצֹּרֶת בָּא מִקְצָתָן רְעֵבִים
וּמִקְצָתָן שְׂבֵעִים: גָּמְרוּ שֶׁלֹּא לְעַשֵּׂר רָעָב שֶׁל מְהוּמָה וְשֶׁל בַּצֹּרֶת בָּא:
וְשֶׁלֹּא לִטּוֹל אֶת הַחַלָּה רָעָב שֶׁל כְּלָיָה בָּא: דֶּבֶר בָּא לָעוֹלָם עַל מִיתוֹת

הָאֲמוּרוֹת בַּתּוֹרָה שֶׁלֹּא נִמְסְרוּ לְבֵית דִּין וְעַל פֵּירוֹת שְׁבִיעִית: חֶרֶב בָּאָה
לָעוֹלָם עַל עִנּוּי הַדִּין וְעַל עִוּוּת הַדִּין וְעַל הַמּוֹרִים בַּתּוֹרָה שֶׁלֹּא כַהֲלָכָה:
חַיָּה רָעָה בָּאָה לָעוֹלָם עַל שְׁבוּעַת שָׁוְא וְעַל חִלּוּל הַשֵּׁם: גָּלוּת בָּאָה
לָעוֹלָם עַל עוֹבְדֵי אֱלִילִים וְעַל גִּלּוּי עֲרָיוֹת וְעַל שְׁפִיכוּת דָּמִים וְעַל שְׁמִטַּת
הָאָרֶץ:

11. שביעית A.M. שביעיות; עובדי אלילים, M. ז״ט.

11. Seven kinds of penalties come to the world for seven chief transgressions. When some give tithes and some do not, famine through drought comes, some go hungry and some are full. If they have decided not to give tithes *at all* famine through tumult and drought comes. And *if they have decided not to give* the cake of dough a famine of extermination comes. Pestilence comes to the world on account of the sins for which the penalty of death is appointed in the Torah, and which have not been brought before a court of justice; also for fruits of the seventh year. The sword comes to the world on account of the delay of justice and the perversion of justice, and on account of those who interpret the Torah not according to the halachah. The wild beast comes to the world on account of false swearing and profaning the Name. Exile comes to the world on account of idolatry and incest and bloodshed and *neglect of* the release of the earth.

11. A series of seven forms of retribution for so many kinds of transgression. The acts upon which retribution follows are many more than seven, and can only be made to correspond with that number by arbitrary grouping. The seven forms of retribution are a deduction from Lev. XXVI. 14 fol., where indeed the number seven is not strictly adhered to but where the refrain is repeated "I will chastise you seven times more for your sins". The passage is practically a commentary on this portion of Scripture; and its validity as a statement depends upon the view which is taken of the teaching of the chapter in Leviticus. The logic of the passage is this, that since the offences were transgressions against the divine commands, expressly denounced in the Torah, the displeasure of God would be shown by such signal punishments as those mentioned. Judged by the standard of Torah all the offences were alike deserving of punishment as being all alike in their quality of disregard of the divine command. And so long as they are judged by that standard the objection is irrelevant that the with-

holding of tithes is not morally in the same class with extortion
false swearing or bloodshed. The 'release of the earth' means the
letting it lie fallow.

The passage is found in A. R. N.^{A} XXXVIII and (^{B}) XLI with considerable
expansion in both.

12. בְּאַרְבָּעָה פְּרָקִים הַדֶּבֶר מִתְרַבֶּה בָּרְבִיעִית וּבַשְּׁבִיעִית וּבְמוֹצָאֵי
שְׁבִיעִית וּבְמוֹצָאֵי הֶחָג שֶׁבְּכָל שָׁנָה וְשָׁנָה: בָּרְבִיעִית מִפְּנֵי מַעְשַׂר עָנִי
שֶׁבַּשְּׁלִישִׁית בַּשְּׁבִיעִית מִפְּנֵי מַעְשַׂר עָנִי שֶׁבַּשִּׁשִּׁית, בְּמוֹצָאֵי שְׁבִיעִית
מִפְּנֵי פֵּירוֹת שְׁבִיעִית, בְּמוֹצָאֵי הֶחָג שֶׁבְּכָל שָׁנָה וְשָׁנָה מִפְּנֵי גֶּזֶל מַתְּנוֹת
עֲנִיִּים:

12. שבכל שנה M. שלכל.

12. At four seasons pestilence increases, in the fourth *year*, in
the seventh, in the year after the seventh and the time after the
Feast in each year. In the fourth because of the tithe for the
poor in the third; in the seventh because of the tithe for the poor
in the sixth. In the year after the seventh because of the fruits
of the seventh; and in the time after the Feast because of the
robbery of the gifts assigned to the poor.

12. This passage takes up one of the themes of the preceding,
the sending of pestilence upon the earth. The group number is
four instead of seven. The sins punished are in form ritual transgressions, punishable as being acts of disobedience to the divine
commands given in the Torah. But they are also acts of de-
frauding the poor, breaches of the command "Thou shalt love thy
neighbour as thyself". The connexion between transgression and
such scourges as famine and pestilence is one which the Talmudic
teachers never questioned; and though the connexion would be
interpreted now in a manner widely different from theirs, their
ethical insight was not at fault in discerning that retribution must
follow in some form upon all transgression.

The four seasons mentioned are not the four divisions of the year but
four periods in the cycle of seven years, very unequally placed with regard
to each other. The passage teaches that there are four periods at which
certain precepts ought to be observed, and that if they are not observed
pestilence will increase. It does not teach that there is at each of these
periods an increase of pestilence, so that an outbreak could be confidently
expected.

13. אַרְבַּע מִדּוֹת בְּאָדָם הָאוֹמֵר שֶׁלִּי שֶׁלִּי וְשֶׁלְּךָ שֶׁלָּךְ זוֹ מִדָּה בֵּינוֹנִית
וְיֵשׁ אוֹמְרִים זוֹ מִדַּת סְדוֹם, שֶׁלִּי שֶׁלְּךָ וְשֶׁלְּךָ שֶׁלִּי עַם הָאָרֶץ, שֶׁלִּי שֶׁלְּךָ
וְשֶׁלְּךָ שֶׁלָּךְ חָסִיד, שֶׁלְּךָ שֶׁלִּי וְשֶׁלִּי שֶׁלִּי רָשָׁע:

13. Four characters of men: He who says, what is mine is mine
and what is thine is thine.[1] This is the average type: some say
it is the character of Sodom. *He who says* What is mine is thine
and what is thine is mine, is undisciplined. *He who says* What is
mine is thine and what is thine is thine is a saint. *He who says*
What is thine is mine and what is mine is mine is wicked.

13. In this and the following passages 14—17, the same method
is used to distinguish the four types severally enumerated. First
some quality or feature is specified (*A*) along with its opposite (*B*).
Each of these may be modified in opposite ways, (+ or —). Thus
four results follow, expressed in the form (+ *A* — *B*), (— *A* + *B*),
(+ *A* + *B*), (— *A* — *B*).[2]

The group number four is probably suggested by the fact that
four is the number of possible combinations of ideas so treated.

The first 'four' group classifies men according as they are selfish
or unselfish in regard to their possessions. The ordinary average
man goes by the rule of "each for himself". The undisciplined
man disregards all rules, makes no distinction. The saint is wholly
unselfish; the wicked is wholly selfish.

The type described as that of the ordinary man is said to be termed by
some 'the type of Sodom'. It is remarkable that the name of that exception-
ally wicked city should be applied to a type of conduct which is defined
as that of the average man. There is of course no implication that ordinary
men are as wicked as those of Sodom. The author of the remark, ('some
say'), probably meant to express his strong dissent from the view that the
rule of 'each for himself' was the one followed by the average man. That
rule was the most intensely selfish of the four mentioned, because it denied
all relation whatever between a man and his fellowmen, and left each shut
up in himself. The reference to Sodom is probably based on Ezek. XVI. 49,
which describes her indolent and heartless pride. "She strengthened not
the hand of the poor and needy".

The undisciplined man is the *am haaretz*, who disregarded the Torah and
the instruction of those who expounded it. See above on III. 14.

The passage is found in A. R. N.[B] XLV.

---

[1] Unfortunately no translation can reproduce the effect of the original מה שׁל־
שׁלי ומה שׁלד שׁלד.

[2] The signs + and — are not to be taken arithmetically, but merely indicate
that a person has (+) or has not (—) the quality in question.

14. אַרְבַּע מִדּוֹת בְּדֵעוֹת, נוֹחַ לִכְעוֹס וְנוֹחַ לִרְצוֹת יָצָא הֶפְסֵדוֹ בִּשְׂכָרוֹ, קָשֶׁה לִכְעוֹס וְקָשֶׁה לִרְצוֹת יָצָא שְׂכָרוֹ בְּהֶפְסֵדוֹ, קָשֶׁה לִכְעוֹס וְנוֹחַ לִרְצוֹת חָסִיד, נוֹחַ לִכְעוֹס וְקָשֶׁה לִרְצוֹת רָשָׁע:

14. חפסדו . . . שכרו. M. transposes, and similarly in the second clause.

14. Four types of dispositions: Easy to provoke and easy to pacify, his gain is cancelled by his loss. Hard to provoke and hard to pacify, his loss is cancelled by his gain. Hard to provoke and easy to pacify, he is pious. Easy to provoke and hard to pacify, he is wicked.

14. The basis of the ethical distinction here drawn is gentleness, good nature, good will; its opposite is harshness, ill nature, ill will. These are arranged according to the formula given above, the qualifying term being readiness to show the one or the other of the two opposite qualities. The third and fourth combination are said to characterise respectively the saint and the wicked. To the first and second no such definition is attached; in place of it another pair of opposites is introduced. In the case of the first man it is said that his gain is cancelled by his loss; in the case of the second, his loss is cancelled by his gain. In each case, therefore, the net result is the same, and there is no preponderance to which an ethical term could be applied. The only difference between them is that the first is a weaker and the second a firmer character.

Note that it is not required of the saint in this classification that he should never be angry. "That," says Duran, "is only possible to angels. Who could "be more perfect than Moses? And yet Moses on occasion was angry." (Comment. *ad loc.*)

15. אַרְבַּע מִדּוֹת בְּתַלְמִידִים מָהִיר לִשְׁמוֹעַ וּמָהִיר לְאַבֵּד יָצָא שְׂכָרוֹ בְּהֶפְסֵדוֹ קָשֶׁה לִשְׁמוֹעַ וְקָשֶׁה לְאַבֵּד יָצָא הֶפְסֵדוֹ בִּשְׂכָרוֹ מָהִיר לִשְׁמוֹעַ וְקָשֶׁה לְאַבֵּד [זֶה חֵלֶק טוֹב] קָשֶׁה לִשְׁמוֹעַ וּמָהִיר לְאַבֵּד זֶה חֵלֶק רָע:

15. בתלמידים, M. has הכם A.M. ,זֶה חלק טוב בלמדים לפני חכמים ;

15. Four characters of disciples. Quick to learn and quick to lose his gain is cancelled by his loss. Slow to learn and slow to lose, his loss is cancelled by his gain. Quick to learn and slow to lose, this is a good portion. Slow to learn and quick to lose, this is an evil portion.

15. Four types of disciples. The structure of the classification is the same as in the preceding verse, and there is the same balancing of gain and loss in regard to the first two types. The distinction of the several types is clear without need of explanation.

16. אַרְבַּע מִדּוֹת בְּנוֹתְנֵי צְדָקָה הָרוֹצֶה שֶׁיִּתֵּן וְלֹא יִתְּנוּ אֲחֵרִים עֵינוֹ
רָעָה בְּשֶׁל אֲחֵרִים יִתְּנוּ אֲחֵרִים וְהוּא לֹא יִתֵּן עֵינוֹ רָעָה בְּשֶׁלּוֹ, יִתֵּן וְיִתְּנוּ
אֲחֵרִים חָסִיד לֹא יִתֵּן וְלֹא יִתְּנוּ אֲחֵרִים רָשָׁע:

16. Four characters of almsgivers. He who wishes that he should give and that others should not give, his eye is evil towards what belongs to others. *He who wishes* that others should give and that he should not give his eye is evil towards what is his own. *He who wishes* that he should give and that others should give is a saint; that he should not give and that others should not give, is wicked.

16. Four types of almsgivers. The same structure of classification as before, with a variation "the evil eye" in regard to the first and second. One is inclined at first to think that the man who wishes others to give while not giving himself is a meaner character than the man who wishes that neither should give. But the author of the passage is right. For where there are two sources of alms it is open to a man to wish that both shall be used, or one, or the other, or neither; and clearly the last is the most selfish. The evil eye denotes the grudging temper. If almsgiving is a pious duty whose reward is the divine approval, then the man whose eye is "evil towards the alms of others" begrudges to them the reward given to them; and, if he wish that others should give while he himself does not give, then he prevents a blessing from coming to himself which otherwise would have come.

17. אַרְבַּע מִדּוֹת בְּהוֹלְכֵי בֵית הַמִּדְרָשׁ הוֹלֵךְ וְאֵינוֹ עֹשֶׂה שְׂכַר הֲלִיכָה
בְּיָדוֹ, עֹשֶׂה וְאֵינוֹ הוֹלֵךְ שְׂכַר מַעֲשֶׂה בְּיָדוֹ, הוֹלֵךְ וְעֹשֶׂה חָסִיד, לֹא הוֹלֵךְ
וְלֹא עֹשֶׂה רָשָׁע:

17. Four characters of them that go to the house of learning. He who goes and does not perform, has the reward of going. He who goes not but performs, has the reward of doing. He who goes and performs is a saint. He who neither goes nor performs is wicked.

17. Four types of men classified according to their attendance at the house of learning and their performance of the duty they are taught there. The persons here in question are not in any technical sense disciples, as they have been dealt with already, v. 15. Here the reference is to ordinary people who are concerned to be taught their duty, mitzvoth, and for whom the 'house of learning' is the place where they would be taught. There is the same structural basis of classification as before, with again a variation in regard to the first and second terms. Both types of men are imperfect, in opposite ways, but each is given credit for so much as is good in his action.

18. אַרְבַּע מִדּוֹת בְּיוֹשְׁבִים לִפְנֵי חֲכָמִים סְפוֹג וּמַשְׁפֵּךְ מְשַׁמֶּרֶת וְנָפָה:

סְפוֹג שֶׁהוּא סוֹפֵג אֶת־הַכֹּל וּמַשְׁפֵּךְ שֶׁמַּכְנִיס בְּזוֹ וּמוֹצִיא בְזוֹ מְשַׁמֶּרֶת

שֶׁמּוֹצִיאָה אֶת־הַיַּיִן וְקוֹלֶטֶת אֶת־הַשְּׁמָרִים וְנָפָה שֶׁמּוֹצִיאָה אֶת־הַקֶּמַח

וְקוֹלֶטֶת אֶת־הַסֹּלֶת:

18. After this v. M. has vv. 20—21.

18. Four characters of those who sit before the Wise. A sponge, a funnel, a strainer and a sieve. A sponge because it sucks up everything; a funnel, because it receives at one end and lets out at the other; a strainer because it lets out the wine and keeps back the dregs, a sieve[1] because it lets out the coarse meal and keeps the fine flour.

18. Four types of those who sit before the Wise. The author of this verse evidently arranged his four types on a structural basis similar to that used in the preceding verses, according as the disciple (a) takes everything and keeps it, (b) take everything and lets it all go, (c) keeps the worthless and lets go the good, or (d) lets go the worthless and keeps the good. But the classification is diversified by a comparison between each of the types and, some familiar utensil. The author's intention is successfully carried out in regard to the first three; but in regard to the fourth his ingenuity breaks down, for no sieve was ever devised which would let the coarse meal pass through and keep only the fine flour.

19. כָּל־אַהֲבָה שֶׁהִיא תְלוּיָה בְדָבָר בָּטֵל דָּבָר בְּטֵלָה אַהֲבָה, וְשֶׁאֵינָה

תְלוּיָה בְדָבָר אֵינָהּ בְּטֵלָה לְעוֹלָם, אֵיזוֹ הִיא אַהֲבָה שֶׁהִיא תְלוּיָה בְדָבָר

זוֹ אַהֲבַת אַמְנוֹן וְתָמָר, וְשֶׁאֵינָהּ תְּלוּיָה בְדָבָר זוֹ אַהֲבַת דָּוִד וִיהוֹנָתָן:

---

[1] A correspondent informs me that in Arabic the words equivalent to קמח and סולת mean, or can mean, 'fine flour' and comparatively 'coarse flour,' respectively. This would justify the 'sieve' but in that case there would be no distinction between the 'strainer' and the 'sieve'; (c) and (d) would be the same.

19. All love which depends on some thing, if the thing ceases the love ceases. Love which does not depend one some thing never fails for ever. What love is that which depends on some thing? This is the love of Amnon and Tamar. And *that* which does not depend on some thing? This is the love of David and Jonathan.

19. The numerical basis for distinction of types is now abandoned, and a series of general propositions is given relating to virtues or types of character.

The first proposition distinguishes between two kinds of love, and is illustrated by the two examples (a) of Amnon and Tamar, and (b) David and Jonathan. The first case is that of love which seeks some gratification of self, not necessarily of so gross a kind as that which Amnon pursued; the other is the case where love is purely unselfish, where it seeks only the good of the one who is loved, and enters with that one into a union of mutual affection. The latter is the only love that endures, that takes no heed of the changes of outward appearance or outward fortune, but lives in timeless joy and peace.

20. כָּל־מַחֲלֹקֶת שֶׁהִיא לְשֵׁם שָׁמַיִם סוֹפָהּ לְהִתְקַיֵּם וְשֶׁאֵינָהּ לְשֵׁם שָׁמַיִם אֵין סוֹפָהּ לְהִתְקַיֵּם, אֵיזוֹ הִיא מַחֲלֹקֶת שֶׁהִיא לְשֵׁם שָׁמַיִם זוֹ מַחֲלֹקֶת הִלֵּל וְשַׁמַּי, וְשֶׁאֵינָהּ לְשֵׁם שָׁמַיִם זוֹ מַחֲלֹקֶת קֹרַח וְכָל־עֲדָתוֹ:

20. Every controversy which is for the Name of Heaven will in the end be established. And *every one* which is not for the Name of Heaven will not in the end be established. What controversy is that which is for the Name of Heaven? This is the controversy of Hillel and Shammai. And that is not for the Name of Heaven? This is the controversy of Korah and all his company.

20. A general axiom in regard to contention, especially controversy in regard to religion. If the object of the controversy be to establish truth and not to flout authority, then the truth will in the end be established and the authority will be vindicated. The service of truth is an action done for the name of heaven, or in other words for the sake of God. Both the contending parties may be equally sincere in their desire to serve the truth, while differing in their opinion of what the truth is. The result of their controversy will be, incidentally, that one view will be adopted and the other put aside, but the main result will be that the truth will be

established and God thereby served. This is a fine lesson, and one
which ought to be taken to heart by every church that has persecuted heretics.

Controversy which is not for the name of heaven is where there
is merely rebellion against authority, and in that case the authority
is vindicated by the defeat of those who rebelled. This also is
true, but not if the rebellion be itself undertaken as a service of
God. The two cases are illustrated by the examples of (a) the con-
troversies of Hillel and Shammai, end (b) the revolt of Korah and
his followers against Moses. The two famous teachers, or rather
the two 'houses' of their disciples, were sharply opposed; but both
were sincere in desiring to establish the truth, as it was finely
said «the words of both are the words of the living God", (j. Ber. 3ᵇ).

The illustrative examples may be editorial additions by the compiler. The
thought contained in the general statement has a close parallel in the speech
ascribed to R. Gamliel I in the N. T. Acts V. 38—39 "If this counsel or this
"work be of men it will be overthrown; but if it is of God ye will not be
"able to overthrow them; lest haply ye be found even to be fighting against
"God." Was R. Gamliel perhaps the author of the axiom in this verse of
Aboth?

The passage is found in A. R. N.ᴬ XL, and (ᴮ) XLVI.

21. כָּל־הַמְזַכֶּה אֶת־הָרַבִּים אֵין חֵטְא בָּא עַל יָדוֹ, וְכָל־הַמַּחֲטִיא אֶת־
הָרַבִּים אֵין מַסְפִּיקִין בְּיָדוֹ לַעֲשׂוֹת תְּשׁוּבָה, מֹשֶׁה זָכָה וְזִכָּה אֶת־הָרַבִּים
זְכוּת הָרַבִּים תָּלוּי בּוֹ שֶׁנֶּאֱמַר צִדְקַת יְיָ עָשָׂה וּמִשְׁפָּטָיו עִם יִשְׂרָאֵל
יָרָבְעָם בֶּן־נְבָט חָטָא וְהֶחֱטִיא אֶת־הָרַבִּים חֵטְא הָרַבִּים תָּלוּי בּוֹ שֶׁנֶּאֱמַר
עַל חַטֹּאות יָרָבְעָם אֲשֶׁר חָטָא וַאֲשֶׁר הֶחֱטִיא אֶת־יִשְׂרָאֵל:

21. על ידו M. לידו; ישראל . . . ירבעם. A.M. om.

21. Every one who makes the many virtuous, sin comes not by
his means. And every one who makes the many to sin, they give
him not the chance to repent. Moses was virtuous and made the
many virtuous, and the virtue of the many is ascribed to him, as
it is said (Dent. XXXIII. 21): — 'He executed the righteousness of
the Lord and his judgment with Israel.' Jeroboam the son of Nebat
sinned and caused the many to sin; the sin of the many is ascribed
to him, as it is said (1. Kings XIV. 16): — The sin of Jeroboam who
sinned and made Israel to sin.'

21. The lesson here taught may be called a doctrine of imputed righteousness; and though it is not on the lines of strict justice it is not open to the same objection as that which rightly condemns the orthodox Christian doctrine on the same subject. Instead of the righteousness of the one hiding and covering up the sin of the many, who remain sinners in spite of it, the righteousness of the many which they have learned from the one acts as a defence to him so that his sin if he have any may not be reckoned against him. There is a fine chivalry in the Jewish doctrine which is conspicuously absent from the Christian doctrine. Where it fails is in the fact that if the one who taught the many did nevertheless himself sin afterwards, nothing but his own repentance would suffice to make him righteous again. Everyone, before the divine justice, is answerable for his own sins.

The converse is based on the same idea of solidarity between the one and the many. If the one have led the many into sin, then the sins which they commit rise up in judgment against him; he may repent of his own sins, he cannot repent of theirs, "they give him not the opportunity to repent". Here again the doctrine is not wholly in accordance with divine justice, or rather the divine forgiveness. For if a sinner repents he is forgiven and is no longer a sinner, even though they whom he has led into sin continue in sin. But forgiveness to such a one would not undo what he had done; and, just because he had himself come to see the evil of his own sin, he would feel the torture and the shame of the sins which he had led others to commit, which he was now powerless to prevent and on which his own repentance had no effect. The Christian doctrine, being framed for a special theological purpose, does not include this converse aspect. That remains as a solemn lesson which Jewish teachers alone have had the moral insight to discern and the wisdom to teach.

Here again the illustrative examples of Moses and Jeroboam may be editorial. The thought would be made more clear if there had been given an example of one who made many righteous and afterwards fell into sin. There was one notable instance of such in Elisha b. Abujah (see above, IV. 25). He had been at one time a respected and accepted teacher, as is shown by the fact that his words are included in Aboth with no mark of disapprobation. He therefore, by teaching Torah, did as much as any Rabbi to "make the many righteous". It is notorious that he afterwards became an apostate, of whom his fellowmen would not speak by his name, referring to him as "Aher", "another". He was not shielded from condemnation nor accounted righteous for the sake of the righteousness of those whom he had

once led in the ways of Torah. And though it is said that he was urged to
repent but declared that he could not, it is not said that he had led the
many to sin, so that it would be their sins which kept him from repentance.
The lesson of the present passage is broadly true, so far as it goes; but
a deeper lesson is taught by the love of R. Meir for his old teacher even
after his apostasy, and the lonely remorse of the man who knew he had
fallen.

The commentators do not touch upon these aspects of the lesson; they
point out how unfair it would be if, on the one hand, a man who had made
many righteous should for his subsequent sin be banished to Gehinnom while
his followers were enjoying the bliss of Gan Eden, or on the other, if one
who had led many into sin should himself be in heaven through his own
repentance, while those whom he had led into sin were in torment in hell.
It may be that the whole line of thought in this passage started from the
statement about Jeroboam (I Kings XIV. 16) that he caused Israel to sin,
and that the general theory worked out was the result of reflecting upon the
implications of that statement.

The passage is found, though not verbatim, in A. R. N.^A XL, and (^B) XLV.

22. כָּל־מִי שֶׁיֶּשׁ־בּוֹ שְׁלֹשָׁה דְבָרִים הַלָּלוּ הוּא מִתַּלְמִידָיו שֶׁל אַבְרָהָם
אָבִינוּ, וּשְׁלֹשָׁה דְבָרִים אֲחֵרִים הוּא מִתַּלְמִידָיו שֶׁל בִּלְעָם הָרָשָׁע, עַיִן
טוֹבָה וְרוּחַ נְמוּכָה וְנֶפֶשׁ שְׁפָלָה תַּלְמִידָיו שֶׁל אַבְרָהָם אָבִינוּ, עַיִן רָעָה
וְרוּחַ גְּבוֹהָה וְנֶפֶשׁ רְחָבָה תַּלְמִידָיו שֶׁל בִּלְעָם הָרָשָׁע: מַה בֵּין תַּלְמִידָיו
שֶׁל אַבְרָהָם אָבִינוּ לְתַלְמִידָיו שֶׁל בִּלְעָם הָרָשָׁע תַּלְמִידָיו שֶׁל אַבְרָהָם
אָבִינוּ אוֹכְלִין בָּעוֹלָם הַזֶּה וְנוֹחֲלִין הָעוֹלָם הַבָּא שֶׁנֶּאֱמַר לְהַנְחִיל אֹהֲבַי | יֵשׁ
וְאוֹצְרוֹתֵיהֶם אֲמַלֵּא: תַּלְמִידָיו שֶׁל בִּלְעָם הָרָשָׁע יוֹרְשִׁין גֵּיהִנֹּם וְיוֹרְדִין
לִבְאֵר שָׁחַת שֶׁנֶּאֱמַר וְאַתָּה אֱלֹהִים תּוֹרִידֵם לִבְאֵר שָׁחַת אַנְשֵׁי דָמִים
וּמִרְמָה לֹא יֶחֱצוּ יְמֵיהֶם וַאֲנִי אֶבְטַח בָּךְ:

22. יורדין ... יורשין .M. om.; מה בין ... שנאמר .M. om.; אמלא ... בלעם הרשע
.M. transpose; שחת .M. omit.; שחת ... ואתה .M. om.

22. Every one in whom there are these three things is of the
disciples of Abraham our father. And *every one, in whom are*
three other things is of the disciples of Balaam the wicked. A
good eye, a lowly spirit and a humble mind *are the marks* of the
disciples of Abraham our father. An evil eye a haughty spirit
and a proud mind, are *the marks* of the disciples of Balaam the
wicked.

What is the difference between the disciples of Abraham our father and the disciples of Balaam the wicked? The disciples of Abraham our father eat in this world and inherit the world to come, as it is said (Prov. VIII. 21): — 'That I may cause them that love me to inherit substance, and I will fill their treasuries.' Disciples of Balaam the wicked inherit Gehinnom and go down to the pit of destruction, as it is said (Ps. LV. 24): — 'But thou O God wilt bring them down to the pit of destruction. Men of blood and deceit shall not live out half their days; but I will trust in Thee.'

22. The marks of the true and the false disciple; in each case three qualities are named as characteristic of the true disciple, called the disciple of Abraham, and their opposites as characteristic of the false disciple, called the disciple of Balaam. The three virtues are unselfishness, meekness and humility, the three opposites selfishness, haughtiness and pride. With these may be compared the discussion on the right way and the wrong by the disciples of R. Joḥanan b. Zaccai (see above II. 13. 14).

The passage would be an ordinary ethical lesson, if it were not for the mention of Balaam as the type of the false teacher. The reason is not obvious why he should be brought in as the antitype of Abraham. It is true that a good deal of attention was paid to him in the Midrash, so that he became a stock example of a tempter and deceiver of Israel, and it may be that the present passage, along with another in the Mishnah (Sanh. X. 2), represent an early stage in the process. In my "Christianity in Talmud and Midrash" p. 69 I expressed the opinion "that wherever Balaam is mentioned "there is a sort of undercurrent of reference to Jesus, and that much more "is told of Balaam than would have been told if he and not Jesus had really "been the person thought of". I should now modify that opinion to the extent of saying that Balaam became an object of haggadic study on his own account, as having been a peculiarly dangerous enemy to Israel; and that only occasionally did it occur to some teacher (as in b. Gitt. 56ᵇ. 57ᵃ) to draw a quite explicit comparison, from this point of view, between Balaam and Jesus. I do not now think that every mention of Balaam contains a covert reference to Jesus. In the present passage nothing more may be meant than to teach that selfishness pride and haughtiness are the specially un-Jewish vices, such as to mark the holders of them as disciples of Balaam, one of the arch-enemies of Israel. It is hardly likely that in a work so unpolemical as Aboth, a piece of rather violent polemic would have been included. The first half of the passage is found in A. R. N.ᴮ XLV, with proof-texts to illustrate each of the three virtues and vices respectively. The second half may be a later expansion. The whole is found in Yalkut on Ps. LV, § 774. A comparison of the texts (see Taylor) shows that there was considerable variation in the concluding verses of Aboth, of which ch. V is really the end. It does not

seem possible to determine the exact form of the original conclusion of
Aboth.

The two clauses which describe the contrast between the disciples of
Abraham and those of Balaam do not form an exact opposition. The former
are said to 'eat', i. e. to enjoy prosperity, in the present world and to inherit the world to come. The latter are said to inherit Gehinnom, but nothing
is said of their portion in this world. The two statements would seem to be
rather deductions from Scripture than conclusions from history.

23· יְהוּדָה בֶּן־תֵּימָא אוֹמֵר הֱוֵי עַז כַּנָּמֵר וְקַל כַּנֶּשֶׁר רָץ כַּצְּבִי וְגִבּוֹר
כָּאֲרִי לַעֲשׂוֹת רְצוֹן אָבִיךְ שֶׁבַּשָּׁמָיִם: הוּא הָיָה אוֹמֵר עַז פָּנִים לְגֵיהִנֹּם וּבוֹשׁ
פָּנִים לְגַן עֵדֶן: יְהִי רָצוֹן מִלְּפָנֶיךָ יְיָ אֱלֹהֵינוּ וֵאלֹהֵי אֲבוֹתֵינוּ שֶׁיִּבָּנֶה בֵּית
הַמִּקְדָּשׁ בִּמְהֵרָה בְיָמֵינוּ וְתֵן חֶלְקֵנוּ בְּתוֹרָתֶךָ:

23. After שבשמים, M. arranges the vv. thus:—

שמואל הקטן וגו' (as in IV. 24) הוא היה אומר בן חמש וגו' ר' יהודה הנשיא היה אומר
עז פנים.

All the rest of the chapter is omitted in M. which has the following ending found
also in D., and in Maḥzor Vitry:

עז פנים ר' אליעזר או' ממזר ר' יהושע או' בן הנדה ר' עקיבא או' ממזר ובן הנדה ועל כלם
אליהו כותב והקב"ה חותם אני לו למי שפוסל את זרעו ופוגם את משפחתו ונושא אשה שאינה
הגנת לו אליהו כופתו והקב"ה פוסל וכל הפוסל פסול ואינו מדבר בשבחו לעולם ואו' שמואל
במדמו פוסל סוף אדם למות וסוף בחמ' לשחיטה וזהכל למיתה עומדין. ר' אבא או' אשרי
מי שגדל בתורה ועמלו בתורה ועושה נחת רוח ליוצרו גדל בשם טוב ונפטר בשם טוב מן
העולם ועליו א' שלמה בחכמתו טוב שם משמן טוב ויום המות מיום הולדו. למוד תורה
הרבה כדי שיתנו לך שכר הרבה ודע מתן שכרן של צדיק לעתיד לבא. סליק פירקא.

23. **Jehudah ben Tema** said: Be bold as a leopard and light as
an eagle and swift as a gazelle and strong as a lion to do the
will of the father which is in Heaven.

He used to say: The boldfaced man is for Gehinnom and the
shamefaced man is for the Garden of Eden. May it be thy will.
O Lord our God and the God of our fathers that the Temple may
be built speedily in our days. And grant our portion *to be* in thy
Torah.

23. A return to the personal sayings ascribed to known teachers.
The lesson is simply one of entire and willing devotion to the
service of God, expressed in four vigorous comparisons.

R. Jehudah b. Tema is occasionally mentioned in the Rabbinical literature,
but there is hardly any evidence by which to determine the chronology of
his life. R. Joḥanan b. Dahabai speaks in his name (b. Ḥag. 2ᵃ), but the date
of R. Joh. b. D. is also uncertain.

The saying of R. Jehudah b. Tema probably ends with the words "Father in heaven", and this may have been the original conclusion of Aboth. The doxology "May it be thy will &c. "would hardly have been placed where it is except by one who regarded the preceding sentence as the end of Aboth.

The clause beginning "He used to say" cannot with certainty be ascribed to R. Jehudah b. Tema. The Munich MS and other texts ascribe it to R. Jehudah ha-Nasi, possibly the grandson of Rabbi. From here onwards there is no agreement among texts and commentators as to what, if anything, belonged to the original Aboth, and what was added later. The variations can be seen in Taylor, with the exception of the reading of the Munich MS which will be dealt with below. I keep for the present to the text and translation which I have adopted.

24. הוּא הָיָה אוֹמֵר בֶּן־חָמֵשׁ שָׁנִים לַמִּקְרָא בֶּן־עֶשֶׂר שָׁנִים לַמִּשְׁנָה בֶּן־
שְׁלֹשׁ עֶשְׂרֵה לַמִּצְוֹת בֶּן־חָמֵשׁ עֶשְׂרֵה לַגְּמָרָא בֶּן־שְׁמוֹנֶה עֶשְׂרֵה לַחֻפָּה
בֶּן־עֶשְׂרִים לִרְדּוֹף בֶּן־שְׁלֹשִׁים לַכֹּחַ בֶּן־אַרְבָּעִים לַבִּינָה בֶּן־חֲמִשִּׁים לְעֵצָה
בֶּן־שִׁשִּׁים לִזְקְנָה בֶּן־שִׁבְעִים לְשֵׂיבָה בֶּן־שְׁמוֹנִים לַגְּבוּרָה בֶּן־תִּשְׁעִים
לָשׁוּחַ בֶּן־מֵאָה כְּאִלּוּ מֵת וְעָבַר וּבָטֵל מִן הָעוֹלָם:

24. He used to say: At five years old *one is ready* for the scripture, at ten years for the Mishnah, at thirteen for the commandments, at fifteen for Talmud, at eighteen for marriage, at twenty for pursuit *of righteousness*, at thirty for full strength, at forty for discernment, at fifty for counsel, at sixty for old age, at seventy for grey hairs, at eighty for 'labour and sorrow' (Ps. XC. 10), at ninety for decrepitude, at one hundred he is as though he were dead, and had passed away and faded from the world.

24. The several stages of life, a favourite theme of all moralists. Here they are stages in the life which is based on Torah. Fourteen stages are distinguished, which fall into three groups. The first group comprises all the preparation for the real task of life; in this period the training begins with the study of scripture, to be followed by Mishnah and Talmud, thus covering the entire field of Torah on its theoretical side. This period includes also the assumption of moral responsibility involved in becoming 'bar mitzvah'. It also includes marriage. The man has now completed his training, and is ready at twenty to begin on the real task of his life. This period last for fifty years, from twenty to seventy. The third period is one of decline and senile decay, and ends with death. The terms in which the several stages are described are all clear with the

exception of that for age twenty. The word means pursuit, and there is nothing to show what is the object pursued. Following the lead of Rashi, who has an excellent note on the passage, I take the pursuit to mean the pursuit of the real object in life, that for which all the previous training and equipment were acquired. This object is the practical fulfilment of the Torah, the doing of all the mitzvoth with the most perfect devotion of heart and will, the giving of all the personal force he can to that service of God for which Torah is the guide. Fifty years of the best of a man's life are what he can give; after that period is over his real work is done, and he fades away.

Many of the texts ascribe this passage to Samuel the small, (see above IV. 24). As it stands in the present text it would naturally be ascribed to R. Jehudah b. Tema since it begins "He used to say". But where a name is given to the author of this saying, that name is always Samuel the small. If the choice of name was merely capricious there would be a variety of names in the several texts. Plainly therefore there was some reason for connecting this passage with Samuel. Either he said it or it was said of him. The former appears to me to be less probable than the latter. If Samuel according to the usual opinion died in very early manhood, he would hardly be interested in moralising on extreme old age. If, as I hold, he died in extreme old age, he would scarcely be in a condition do to so when he had fallen into senile decay. But one who had seen Samuel in old age, when his memory was gone (b. Ber. 28[b]) and knew how his fame had extended through all Israel, (j. Sanh. 18[c]) might very well describe the stages of his life in the way here presented.

I should be inclined to add this passage to those given above (IV. 24) as tending to confirm the view that Samuel lived to a very great age.

The passage does not occur in ARN.

25. בֶּן־בַּג בַּג אוֹמֵר הֲפָךְ בַּה וַהֲפָךְ בַּה דְּכֹלָּא בַּה וּבַהּ תֶּחֱזֵי וְסִיב וּבְלֵה בַּהּ וּמִנַּהּ לָא תָזוּעַ שֶׁאֵין לְךָ מִדָּה טוֹבָה הֵימֶנָּה:

25. Ben Bag Bag said:—Turn it and turn it for all is in it and look in it and grow grey and old in it, and turn not away from it, for there is no better rule for thee than it.

25. A brief eulogy of Torah. It is an inexhaustible treasure that can satisfy every aspiration of the devout soul that seeks and serves God.

Ben Bag Bag is said to have been a disciple of Hillel. His name was Johanan (b. Kidd. 10[b]), and, the epithet denotes that he was either a proselyte

himself or the son of proselytes. Ben BG-BG might mean, as some explain it, 'Ben Ben-Ger and Bath-Ger', i. e. that his father and mother had
been proselytes. Or it might mean that he had become 'a son of Abraham
and Sarah', i. e. a proselyte himself. In this case the explanation turns on the
numerical values of ב״ג which together equal five. This is also the numerical
value of ה, and that letter (or its value) was added to the name of Abram
to make it Abraham and taken from the name of Sarai to make it Sarah.
In any case the epithet was a mere nickname, a kind of pious witticism.
The latter explanation is virtually that given in Tos. Hag. 9ᵇ; it suggests
that Ben Bag-Bag was the same man as Ben He He in the next verse; for
ב״ג is the same in value as ה, and if the latter were spelled according to
its name it would be הא. Thus בן הא הא = בן בג בג. Ben He He is also
said to have been contemporary with Hillel.

בֶּן הֵא הֵא אוֹמֵר לְפוּם צַעֲרָא אַגְרָא: 26.

26. Ben He He said According to the labour is the reward.

The Munich MS has a different ending to this chapter. After
nº 23ᵃ "... Father in Heaven" it continues "Samuel the small said"
&c. as in IV. 24. Then, as in v. 24 "He used to say: at five years
old" &c. down to "faded from the world". Then as follows:

Kallah I.
26*. R. Jehudah the Prince said: The bold faced man is for
Gehinnom, and the shame faced for the Garden of Eden. The bold
faced man. R. Eliezer said he is a bastard; R. Jehoshua said he
is the son of a 'niddah'; R. Akiba said he is a bastard and son of
a 'niddah'. And concerning all of them Elijah writes and the Holy
One, blessed be He seals, Woe to him who 'disqualifies' his off-
spring, degrades his family and marries a wife who is not suited
Kidd. 70ᵃ
to him. Elijah binds him and the Holy One blessed be He lashes
him. And everyone who 'disqualifies' is himself 'disqualified', and
never speaks a good word. Samuel said He accuses others of his
own defect.

Man is destined to death, and the beast to slaughter; and all
await death.

Ber. 17ᵃ
ר' יוחנן
R. Abba said: Happy is he who has grown up in Torah, and
whose labour is in Torah, and who makes quietness of mind for
his maker. He grows up with a good name, and he departs from
the world with a good name, and of him Solomon said in his
wisdom (Ecc. VII. 1):—'A good name is better than precious oint-
ment, and the day of death than the day of birth.

Learn much Torah, so that they may give thee much reward, ⎫
and know that the giving of the reward of the righteous is in the ⎬ Ab. II. 21
time to come. ⎭

26. A last echo of one of the prevailing notes in Aboth. It was
added here, along with the preceding words of the same teacher,
presumably in order to make a more hopeful and auspicious conclusion to Aboth than the mournful end of v. 24.

For Ben He He see the preceding verse.

The Munich MS, as will be seem from the translation, and the critical
notes, gives a wholly different ending to this chapter. This version is found
also in the Maḥzor Vitry but only as an appendix after the real conclusion
of Aboth, which ends with ch. V. Duran gives part of it, and includes it in
Aboth. It is a cento of passages to be found elsewhere, viz.:—Kallah I,
b. Kidd. 70ª, b. Ber. 17ª, and Ab. II. 21. The inclusion of the last shows
that it is later than the original Aboth. There is no obvious connexion of
thought between the several clauses. The first part is an expansion of the
thought implied in the statement that the bold faced or impudent man is
destined for Gehinnom. The explanation is sought in the presumption of a
tainted birth, and that is followed by a denunciation of such as disregard
the precepts of Torah in relation to marriage.

Then follows an allusion to death as the destiny of all. The gloom is
then relieved by one of the most beautiful passages in the Talmudic
literature, so far as I have read in it, a passage which applies in its essence
to every true saint whether Jewish or Christian. Doubtless every reader can
recall some one whom he has known, who "made quietness of mind for his
maker"[1], who "grew up with a good name and departed from the world with
a good name".

The passage, and the treatise, end with R. Tarphon's words on the reward
of the righteous.

---

[1] This phrase is a literal translation of the Hebrew. I am assured that no more
is meant by it than "does what is acceptable to his maker". That is of course
what he does, and it is precisely by so doing that he "makes quietness of mind
for his maker". I cannot bring myself to let go what seems to me the fine ex
pression of an unusual thought.

פרק ששי CHAP. VI.

א. שָׁנוּ חֲכָמִים בִּלְשׁוֹן הַמִּשְׁנָה בָּרוּךְ שֶׁבָּחַר בָּהֶם וּבְמִשְׁנָתָם: רַבִּי מֵאִיר אוֹמֵר כָּל־הָעוֹסֵק בַּתּוֹרָה לִשְׁמָהּ זוֹכֶה לִדְבָרִים הַרְבֵּה וְלֹא עוֹד אֶלָּא שֶׁכָּל־הָעוֹלָם כֻּלּוֹ כְּדַי הוּא לוֹ, נִקְרָא רֵעַ אָהוּב אוֹהֵב אֶת־הַמָּקוֹם אוֹהֵב אֶת־הַבְּרִיּוֹת מְשַׂמֵּחַ אֶת־הַמָּקוֹם מְשַׂמֵּחַ אֶת־הַבְּרִיּוֹת וּמַלְבַּשְׁתּוֹ עֲנָוָה וְיִרְאָה וּמַכְשַׁרְתּוֹ לִהְיוֹת צַדִּיק חָסִיד יָשָׁר וְנֶאֱמָן וּמְרַחַקְתּוֹ מִן הַחֵטְא וּמְקָרַבְתּוֹ לִידֵי זְכוּת וְנֶהֱנִין מִמֶּנּוּ עֵצָה וְתוּשִׁיָּה בִּינָה וּגְבוּרָה שֶׁנֶּאֱמַר לִי עֵצָה וְתוּשִׁיָּה אֲנִי בִינָה לִי גְבוּרָה וְנוֹתֶנֶת לוֹ מַלְכוּת וּמֶמְשָׁלָה וְחִקּוּר דִּין וּמְגַלִּין לוֹ רָזֵי תוֹרָה וְנַעֲשֶׂה כְּמַעְיָן הַמִּתְגַּבֵּר וּכְנָהָר שֶׁאֵינוֹ פוֹסֵק וֶהֱוֵה צָנוּעַ וְאֶרֶךְ רוּחַ וּמוֹחֵל עַל עֶלְבּוֹנוֹ וּמְגַדַּלְתּוֹ וּמְרוֹמַמְתּוֹ עַל כָּל־הַמַּעֲשִׂים:

VI. 1. כמעין שאינו פוסק וכנהר שמתגבר M. כמעין וגו', M. שנו ... במשנתם. M. om.; וחולך. M. adds כולם מעשים.

1. The Wise have taught in the language of the Mishnah—blessed is he, who has made choice of them and their Mishnah,—R. Meir said: Everyone who is occupied with Torah for its own sake is worthy of many things; and not only so, but the whole world is his equivalent. He is called friend, beloved, one that loves God and that loves mankind, that makes glad both God and mankind. And it clothes him with humility and fear and fits him to be righteous pious upright and faithful. It keeps him far from sin and brings him near to virtue. Men are benefitted by him with counsel and sound knowledge discernment and strength, as it is said:— (Prov. VIII. 14):—'Counsel is mine and sound knowledge; I am discernment I have strength'. It gives to him sovereignty and dominion and the searching out of justice. They reveal to him secrets of Torah, and he is made like a spring that increases and like a river that does not cease. And *he will* be modest longsuffering and forgiving of insult; it makes him great and lifts him above all things.

It is universally recognised that this chapter, known as פרק ר' מאיר or פ' קנין תורה did not form part of the original Aboth. This is expressly said by several of the commentators, amongst them Rashi and Maimonides who most certainly knew what was the tradition on the subject. It was probably compiled in order to provide for the reading of Aboth on six successive Sabbaths, (see Introduction § 4, on the use of Pirkē Aboth).

It might have been omitted from the present work on the ground that it was not part of Aboth. But it has been for many centuries so closely associated with the original book, and is so much on the same lines, that it is fairly included in an attempt to interpret the meaning and value of the original work. To exclude it would be to deprive many readers of what is hardly if at all less precious than the words of the earlier chapters.

The heading of the chapter, "The Wise have taught &c." is a clear intimation that its contents did not form part of the original Aboth. They were not Mishnah, but they were taught as tradition in the language of the Mishnah, and they were taught by the Wise, by some of those same teachers who had given the Mishnah to Israel. They were therefore entitled to the same, or almost the same, veneration as that shown towards the Mishnah itself.

שנו חכמים is the Hebrew equivalent of the phrase תנו רבנן constantly used in the Gemara to denote a Baraitha, i. e. teaching not included in the Mishnah but forming part of the contemporaneous traditional matter from which the Mishnah was only a selection. From the fact that the term usual in the Gemara is not here employed we may conclude that those who compiled this chapter did not wish to claim for it equality with the Gemara in spite of its close kinship with the Mishnah; also, that the compilation was made at some period after the Gemara had been closed.

The commentators who deal with ch. VI understand by "he who has made choice &c." the man who has done so, meaning any student who ponders their words and their memory. This may be so; but it is conceivable that the blessing here pronounced was meant for the compiler of the chapter that followed, the man who had "chosen" the ancient teachers and their words which he recorded. It is also possible that "he who has made choice &c." refers to God, as having in some sense raised up the Mishnah teachers to fulfil a divine purpose. I took this view in my translation in the Oxford Apocrypha, because it had not occurred to me that the phrase meant anything else. I do not now withdraw that opinion; I merely leave it as one possible interpretation of the phrase in question. In any case it is merely a parenthesis. The main line of the sentence is:—"The Wise have taught ... that R. Meir said &c."

1. A recital of the blessings which attend the study of Torah, the virtues which it fosters in him who does so, the privileges which he enjoys. It may be called a description of the perfect

man in terms of Torah. The perfection described is, naturally, in
respect of ethical and religious qualities, and a philosopher would
pronounce it incomplete. But what is described is a very beautiful
and saintly type of character; and the Gentile would do well to
reflect that this type of character is produced by pure Pharisaism,
and could not be produced by anything else.

Although the passage begins with R. Meir said, it does not seem probable
that he said the whole of it; possibly it may be made up of a number of
sayings by him, but it hardly has the character of a connected utterance.
The grammatical construction changes several times in the course of these
few lines in a way which would not be necessary or desirable if one teacher
spoke it all continuously. The same features are presented in the long
passage v. 6; and it is conceivable that the one is the continuation of the
other, and that both represent some discussion, or what would in modern
times be called a symposium, in which several teachers contributed each
some remark on the subject of praise of Torah.

The phrase כָּל הָעוֹלָם כֻּלּוֹ כְּדַי הוּא לוֹ needs some explanation, on account of the word כְּדַי. Without it, the passage would be clear and intelligible,
'the whole world is his'. The Yemenite MS mentioned in the Introd. Br.
Mus. Or. 2390, in its version of this passage omits כְּדַי. But the versions in
Kallah R. and Tanna de Be Eliahu Zuta both have כְּדָאי; and the editor in
the latter passage comments on the phrase, explaining that it means that
the whole world was created on his account. The word can therefore hardly
be regarded as superfluous, and due merely to an error of translation from
an assumed Aramaic original, כְּדִילֵיהּ, as F. Perles ingeniously suggests in
a written communication to me.[1] Perles compares a phrase used by R. Meir
in Koh. R. V. 14, כְּלוֹמַר כָּל הָעוֹלָם כֻּלּוֹ שֶׁלִּי; but the likeness is only in the
words, for the phrase there is applied to a new-born infant and has no
bearing on the saint who studies Torah. I hold that כְּדַי must be retained
and read כְּדָאי. The meaning then is that the whole world (and not less
than the whole world, כֻּלּוֹ), is worthy of him, is his equal in spiritual value.
The translation in the Authorized Daily Prayer Book, (Singer) is "the whole
world is indebted to him", which may be true but is not implied in כְּדָאי
or כְּדַי. In Midr. Shemuel, ad loc., R. Ephraim is quoted as explaining the
phrase in the form וְלֹא עִיד אֶלָּא שְׁדִי לְעוֹלָם בּוֹ, which at least shows that
he found some difficulty in the word.

The remainder of the passage is simple and needs no comment.

2. אָמַר רַבִּי יְהוֹשֻׁעַ בֶּן־לֵוִי בְּכָל־יוֹם וָיוֹם בַּת קוֹל יוֹצֵאת מֵהַר חוֹרֵב
וּמַכְרֶזֶת וְאוֹמֶרֶת אוֹי לָהֶם לַבְּרִיּוֹת מֵעֶלְבּוֹנָהּ שֶׁל תּוֹרָה שֶׁכָּל מִי שֶׁאֵינוֹ
עוֹסֵק בַּתּוֹרָה נִקְרָא נָזוּף שֶׁנֶּאֱמַר נֶזֶם זָהָב בְּאַף חֲזִיר אִשָּׁה יָפָה וְסָרַת
טָעַם: וְאוֹמֵר וְהַלֻּחֹת מַעֲשֵׂה אֱלֹהִים הֵמָּה וְהַמִּכְתָּב מִכְתַּב אֱלֹהִים הוּא

---

[1] Perles' explanation has been published in R. E. J. 1921, p. 215.

חָרוּת עַל הַלֻּחֹת, אַל תִּקְרָא חָרוּת אֶלָּא חֵרוּת שֶׁאֵין לְךָ בֶּן־חוֹרִין אֶלָּא
מִי שֶׁעוֹסֵק בְּתַלְמוּד תּוֹרָה וְכָל־מִי שֶׁעוֹסֵק בְּתַלְמוּד תּוֹרָה הֲרֵי זֶה מִתְעַלֶּה
שֶׁנֶּאֱמַר וּמִמַּתָּנָה נַחֲלִיאֵל וּמִנַּחֲלִיאֵל בָּמוֹת:

2. חלמוד M. om. *bis*; אחת ... אוֹ דבור M. om.; קראו M. עשאו.

2. R. Jehoshua ben Levi said: Everyday a Bath Kol goes forth
from Mount Horeb, and proclaims and says 'Woe to mankind
because of their insulting the Torah; for everyone who is not
occupied with Torah is called reprobate, as it is said (Prov. XI. 22):
—'As a jewel of gold in the snout of a swine so is a fair woman
without sense'. And *Scripture* says (Exod. XXXII. 16):—'And the
tables were the work of God, and the writing writing of God graven
on the tables'. Read not haruth (graven) but heruth (freedom), for
none is your freeman but he who is occupied with the study of
Torah. And every one who is occupied in the study of Torah,
lo, he exalts himself, as it is said (Num. XXI. 19):—'And from
Mattanah to Nahaliel and from Nahaliel to Bamoth'.

2. A fanciful haggadah in which the central thought, the praise
of Torah, is almost hidden under a veil of word-play, of the kind
which delights the haggadist and is the despair of the Gentile
who does not see from the haggadic point of view. The lesson
really taught is that Torah, as the supreme revelation from God,
is wronged by the neglect and ignorance shown towards it by
mankind. Ignorance and neglect of what God has revealed are a
form of bondage; and he only is truly free who receives and studies
the divine gift. This alone exalts man to what he ought to be,
as a child of God. The teacher who taught that lesson did so as
a religious instructor not as a grammarian dealing with a text.
He knew well that the grammatical sense of the scripture which
he quoted was not what he drew forth from it, and the knowledge
did not trouble him. His purpose was to connect the lesson he
wished to teach with any hints which scripture might give, to
light up, by rays from that jewel of many facets, the truth he
meant to convey.

R. Jehoshua b. Levi, one of the most famous haggadists of the Talmud,
belonged to the period after the completion of the Mishnah. The chronology
of his life cannot be precisely determined. He was a disciple of Bar Kappara, but there is no evidence to show that he ever met Rabbi. An incident
in which he took part is related in j. Terum. 46ᵇ, and this is placed by Grätz
G. d. J. IV. 299, with much probability, in the reign of Zenobia (267—273,

C. E.). The most that can be said is that he was probably born at the end of the second or the beginning of the third century, C. E., and that he died about 275. C. E.

A brief survey of the passage may serve to remove some of its obscurities. There are parallels to it in Shem. R. XLI, Tanḥ. Ki Tissa 12, and Echah R. Pethihah 2. These show that the haggadic interpretation of נזוך and the whole of the last clause are later addition. The original saying was probably that a Bath Kol. proclaimed &c. down to 'reprobate', then "The tables were the work of God ... graven on the tables". This is ascribed to R. Jeh. b. Levi in the versions mentioned above, except Shem. R. where it is anonymous. Various interpretations of חרות are assigned in Shem. R. to R. Jehudah, R. Jeremiah and 'our Rabbis'. The interpretation of נזוך is probably haggadic embroidery by the compiler of the supplement to Aboth. The passage about Mattanah &c. is found in its haggadic portion in b. Erub. 54ᵃ. The Bath Kol. in Rabbinic usage was understood to be a sound conveying some intimation from heaven. It was less articulate than the word of the Lord which came to a prophet, and served for an age when there were no more any prophets. The Bath Kol. from Horeb, making daily proclamation, denotes the perpetual witness of the Torah given on Sinai (Horeb) denouncing the neglect shown to it by man. Every one showing such neglect is reprobate, נזוך the subject of the divine rebuke. The reason being that the Torah which he neglected was "the work of God".

The word נזוך does not occur in the Scripture, and some haggadist devised a certainly far-fetched connexion by linking it on to the text (Prov. XI. 22) נזם זהב באף חזיר with which it has nothing to do. He combined אף and נזם to make a sort of parallel to נזוך, and drew the conclusion that as a fair woman without sense is נזופה so a man without Torah is נזוך.

The interpretation of חרות depends on a change of vocalisation from חָרוּת to חֵרוּת, not because the original reading was open to doubt but in order to allow of a quite different application for the purpose of teaching a different lesson.

The last clause contains a piece of haggadah which seems to have originated with Rab, and to have been developed by later teachers, (see a very interesting passage in b. Erub. 54ᵃ). The maxim that every one who studies Torah exalts himself is merely intended to lead up to the interpretation of the text 'Mattanah ... Bamoth'. The three place-names are taken to suggest 1ˢᵗ that Torah was *given* (Mattanah) 2ⁿᵈ that God 'gives an inheritance' (Nahaliel) to the man who studies Torah, 3ʳᵈ that such inheritance is 'the *heights*' (Bamoth). The compiler of Aboth omitted the concluding words of the text, on which the Gemara in Erubin founds the lesson that if a man becomes proud and conceited he is led from the height to the valley, i. e. God humbles him.

The passage in Erubin contains the interpretation of חרות, but does not connect it with R. Jehoshua b. Levi.

3. הַלּוֹמֵד מֵחֲבֵירוֹ פֶּרֶק אֶחָד אוֹ הֲלָכָה אֶחָת אוֹ פָסוּק אֶחָד אוֹ דִּבּוּר
אֶחָד אוֹ אֲפִילוּ אוֹת אֶחָת צָרִיךְ לִנְהַג בּוֹ כָּבוֹד שֶׁכֵּן מָצִינוּ בְּדָוִד מֶלֶךְ יִשְׂרָאֵל
שֶׁלֹּא לָמַד מֵאֲחִיתֹפֶל אֶלָּא שְׁנֵי דְבָרִים בִּלְבָד קְרָאוֹ רַבּוֹ אַלּוּפוֹ וּמְיֻדָּעוֹ
שֶׁנֶּאֱמַר וְאַתָּה אֱנוֹשׁ כְּעֶרְכִּי אַלּוּפִי וּמְיֻדָּעִי: וַהֲלֹא דְבָרִים קַל וָחוֹמֶר וּמַה
דָּוִד מֶלֶךְ יִשְׂרָאֵל שֶׁלֹּא לָמַד מֵאֲחִיתֹפֶל אֶלָּא שְׁנֵי דְבָרִים בִּלְבָד קְרָאוֹ רַבּוֹ
אַלּוּפוֹ וּמְיֻדָּעוֹ הַלּוֹמֵד מֵחֲבֵרוֹ פֶּרֶק אֶחָד אוֹ הֲלָכָה אֶחָת אוֹ פָסוּק אֶחָד
אוֹ דִּבּוּר אֶחָד אוֹ אֲפִילוּ אוֹת אֶחָת עַל אַחַת כַּמָּה וְכַמָּה שֶׁצָּרִיךְ לִנְהַג
בּוֹ כָּבוֹד וְאֵין כָּבוֹד אֶלָּא תוֹרָה שֶׁנֶּאֱמַר כָּבוֹד חֲכָמִים יִנְחָלוּ, וּתְמִימִים
יִנְחֲלוּ טוֹב: וְאֵין טוֹב אֶלָּא תוֹרָה שֶׁנֶּאֱמַר כִּי לֶקַח טוֹב נָתַתִּי לָכֶם תּוֹרָתִי
אַל תַּעֲזֹבוּ:

3. או דבור אחד. ‎M. om.; ‎וכמה . . . על ‎M. om.; ‎לקח טוב. ‎M. add. ‎א"לי.

3. He who learns from his associate one chapter, one halachah,
one verse, one saying, or even one letter must show honour to
him; for thus we find in the case of David King of Israel that he
only learned two things from Ahitophel, but he called him his
master, his teacher his familiar friend. As it is said (Ps. LV. 13): —
'But thou, a man mine equal, my teacher, my familiar friend'. And
are not these things an argument *a fortiori?* If David King of
Israel who learned from Ahitophel only two things called him his
master his teacher his familiar friend, one who learns from his
associate one chapter one halachah one verse one saying even
one letter, by how much more is he bound to show honour to him.
And Honour only means Torah as it is said (Prov. III. 35): — 'The
wise shall inherit honour, and the perfect shall inherit good'. And
Good only means Torah, as it is said (Prov. XXVIII. 10): — 'And
I give you good doctrine; forsake not my Torah'.

3. On the duty of showing honour to any one who teaches
even the smallest portion of Torah. The general thought of the
passage is plain, the only difficulty arises in connexion with the
Scripture proof which is offered, (see the following paragraph). If
David showed honour to a subject who taught him, how much
more should the ordinary man show honour to one who will
teach him.

The difficulty of the logical sequence is solved by the brilliant conjecture
of Dr. J. H. Hertz, communicated to me in writing, and since published in
J. Q. R. new series. He suggests that ‎שני דברים should be read as one word

שנדברים. The difference in meaning would be that instead of saying that David learned only two things from Ahitophel the text says he did not learn (any thing) but they were merely conversing together. The logic of the argument is thus perfectly restored; if David honoured Ahitophel with whom he merely conversed, how much more should a man honour one who teaches him even the smallest portion of Torah. I adopt without hesitation Dr. Hertz' emendation. The use of נדברים in the assigned meaning is vouched for by Eze. XXXIII. 30, cp. Mal. III. 13. 16.[1] Dr. Hertz points out that the common reading is very old, because Raba (4th. cent. C. E.) gave an opinion as to what the two things were which David learned (Kallah R. VIII Gemara).

4. כָּךְ הִיא דַּרְכָּהּ שֶׁל תּוֹרָה פַּת בְּמֶלַח תֹּאכֵל וּמַיִם בִּמְשׂוּרָה תִּשְׁתֶּה וְעַל הָאָרֶץ תִּישָׁן וְחַיֵּי צַעַר תִּחְיֶה וּבַתּוֹרָה אַתָּה עָמֵל אִם אַתָּה עֹשֶׂה כֵּן אַשְׁרֶיךָ וְטוֹב לָךְ אַשְׁרֶיךָ בָּעוֹלָם הַזֶּה וְטוֹב לָךְ לָעוֹלָם הַבָּא:

4. אַחַת עמל M. om. אשריך (2nd) M. om.

4. This is the way of Torah: A morsel with salt shalt thou eat and water by measure shalt thou drink; and thou shalt lie upon the earth, and thou shalt live a life of hardship, and labour in the Torah. If thou doest thus (Ps. CXXVIII. 2) happy shalt thou be and it shall be well with thee. Happy in this world, and well with thee in the world to come.

4. The note of asceticism is not often heard in Talmudic literature, and seldom if ever so clearly as in this passage. The general attitude of Pharisaism towards indulgence in the good and enjoyable things of life was that of self-control rather than abstinence. The latter is characteristic of the Essenes rather than of the Pharisees, and was perhaps one reason why the former became a separate body from the latter. But, amongst men who took their religion so seriously as the Pharisees did, there must always have been the tendency to seek in asceticism the satisfaction of the passionate desire to serve God in the ways of the Torah with absolute and unsparing self-devotion. And examples are not wanting amongst the Tannaim and Amoraim of men who practised asceticism to a considerable extent. But the motive in these cases was desire to be free from hindrances in the way of study of Torah and service

---

[1] If it is objected, (Perles), that grammatically the phrase should be שהיו נירברים; the answer is that, as shown often in Aboth, אומר and היה אומר are used with no appreciable difference of meaning. חיו would therefore not be grammatically necessary.

of God, and seldom if ever the view that the body with its appetites and propensities was intrinsically evil. Jewish asceticism, so far as it existed at all, was fundamentally different from Christian asceticism, and any resemblance between them is only superficial. It is one of the grand foundations of Judaism in all its phases that the world as God made it is good, and all that he put there is to be regarded as from him.

On Jewish asceticism and ascetics see the articles in J. Enc. and especially Lazarus, Ethics of Judaism, § 246 fol.[1] It would be very interesting if it were possible to trace the origin of this passage to some older source whence the compiler of ch. VI of Aboth may have taken it. But I do not know of any evidence to connect it with any of the teachers of the Talmudic period, and even the compiler associated no name with it. The last clause, "happy shalt thou be &c." may be a reference to IV. 1, or merely an independent quotation of Ps. CXXVIII. 2, with the same interpretation as in the earlier passage.

5. אַל תְּבַקֵּשׁ גְּדֻלָּה לְעַצְמָךְ וְאַל תַּחֲמֹד כָּבוֹד יוֹתֵר מִלִּמּוּדֶךָ עֲשֵׂה וְאַל תִּתְאַוֶּה לְשֻׁלְחָנָם שֶׁל מְלָכִים שֶׁשֻּׁלְחָנְךָ גָּדוֹל מִשֻּׁלְחָנָם וְכִתְרְךָ גָּדוֹל מִכִּתְרָם וְנֶאֱמָן הוּא בַּעַל מְלַאכְתֶּךָ שֶׁיְּשַׁלֶּם לְךָ שְׂכַר פְּעֻלָּתֶךָ:

5. לעצמך M. om.   עשה M. om.

5. Seek not greatness for thyself, and crave not honour more than *is due to* thy learning; and desire not the table of kings, for thy table is greater than theirs and thy crown greater than theirs; and faithful is He, the master of thy work, to pay thee the reward of thy labour.

5. A lesson on unworldly ambition. The one goal of aspiration is the Torah, and no honour or glory or greatness is to be sought which is not dependent on Torah and the study of it. For greatness and honour which are so dependent it is right to seek, and the true hasid ought to seek it, because thereby he promotes the honour of Torah and not of himself. The Torah can give what the world can never give; its divine sustenance is better than what is spread on the tables of kings, and the crown it bestows upon its faithful servants is richer than any earthly crown. Service of Torah is service of God, and he is faithful to mark what his servants do, and to "render unto every man according to his work".

The readings show some variation. The Munich MS and some commentators omit לעצמך, which may have been added to guard against misunder-

---

[1] See also Büchler, Types of Jewish Palestinian Piety, 1922.

standing. Greatness may be sought, but not for oneself. The honour which may be sought is that only which comes from the learning of Torah; and it is not the honour given to a learned man as such, but the honour shown to the Torah of which he by his learning is the human exponent. The word עשה is also omitted by some authorities and the passage is intelligible without it. If it is read it should be taken with what follows not with what precedes it. In my translation in the Oxford Apocrypha I rendered the clause "perform more than thou hast learned"; but I no longer think that this is correct and I withdraw it. The construction in this case would be יותר מלימודך עשה which is harsh and forced. The last clause is a direct quotation from II. 19.

6. גְּדוֹלָה תוֹרָה יוֹתֵר מִן הַכְּהֻנָּה וּמִן הַמַּלְכוּת. שֶׁהַמַּלְכוּת נִקְנֵית בִּשְׁלֹשִׁים מַעֲלוֹת וְהַכְּהֻנָּה בְּעֶשְׂרִים וְאַרְבַּע. וְהַתּוֹרָה נִקְנֵית בְּאַרְבָּעִים וּשְׁמוֹנָה דְבָרִים. וְאֵלּוּ הֵן בְּתַלְמוּד בִּשְׁמִיעַת הָאֹזֶן בַּעֲרִיכַת שְׂפָתַיִם בְּבִינַת הַלֵּב בְּאֵימָה בְּיִרְאָה בַּעֲנָוָה בְּשִׂמְחָה בְּטָהֳרָה בְּשִׁמּוּשׁ חֲכָמִים בְּדִקְדּוּק חֲבֵרִים בְּפִלְפּוּל הַתַּלְמִידִים בְּיִשּׁוּב בְּמִקְרָא בְּמִשְׁנָה בְּמִעוּט סְחוֹרָה בְּמִעוּט דֶּרֶךְ אֶרֶץ בְּמִעוּט תַּעֲנוּג בְּמִעוּט שֵׁנָה בְּמִעוּט שִׂיחָה בְּמִעוּט שְׂחוֹק, בְּאֶרֶךְ אַפַּיִם בְּלֶב־טוֹב בֶּאֱמוּנַת חֲכָמִים בְּקַבָּלַת הַיִּסּוּרִין הַמַּכִּיר אֶת־מְקוֹמוֹ וְהַשָּׂמֵחַ בְּחֶלְקוֹ וְהָעוֹשֶׂה סְיָג לִדְבָרָיו וְאֵינוֹ מַחֲזִיק טוֹבָה לְעַצְמוֹ אָהוּב אוֹהֵב אֶת־הַמָּקוֹם אוֹהֵב אֶת־הַבְּרִיּוֹת אוֹהֵב אֶת־הַצְּדָקוֹת אוֹהֵב אֶת־הַמֵּישָׁרִים אוֹהֵב אֶת־הַתּוֹכָחוֹת וּמִתְרַחֵק מִן הַכָּבוֹד וְלֹא מֵגִיס לִבּוֹ בְּתַלְמוּדוֹ וְאֵינוֹ שָׂמֵחַ בְּהוֹרָאָה נוֹשֵׂא בְעוֹל עִם חֲבֵרוֹ וּמַכְרִיעוֹ לְכַף זְכוּת וּמַעֲמִידוֹ עַל הָאֱמֶת וּמַעֲמִידוֹ עַל הַשָּׁלוֹם וּמִתְיַשֵּׁב לִבּוֹ בְּתַלְמוּדוֹ שׁוֹאֵל וּמֵשִׁיב שׁוֹמֵעַ וּמוֹסִיף הַלּוֹמֵד עַל מְנָת לְלַמֵּד וְהַלּוֹמֵד עַל מְנָת לַעֲשׂוֹת הַמַּחְכִּים אֶת־רַבּוֹ וְהַמְכַוֵּן אֶת־שְׁמוּעָתוֹ וְהָאוֹמֵר דָּבָר בְּשֵׁם אוֹמְרוֹ הָא לָמַדְתָּ כָּל־הָאוֹמֵר דָּבָר בְּשֵׁם אוֹמְרוֹ מֵבִיא גְאֻלָּה לָעוֹלָם שֶׁנֶּאֱמַר וַתֹּאמֶר אֶסְתֵּר לַמֶּלֶךְ בְּשֵׁם מָרְדְּכָי:

---

6. בדבוק. M. בדקדוק; בשכלות הלב M. add. בינת הלב.

After תלמידים M. reads as follows:—
בישיבה במקרא בדרך ארץ בארך אפים
בלב טוב באמונת חכמים בקבלת יסורין ובמיעוט שינה במיעוט שיחה במיעוט תענוג במיעוט שחוק במיעוט סחורה במיעוט מלאכה במיעוט דרך ארץ המכיר וגו'.

After הברייות. M. reads החזוכחות; שמח. M. adds לבו; אהב את התוכחות.

ומתישב ... בתלמודי M. om. מעמידו (2nd) M. om.

6. Greater is Torah than priesthood or kingship. For kingship is acquired through thirty virtues and priesthood through twenty four, but Torah is acquired through forty eight. And these are they: — By study, by the listening of the ear, by the ordering of the lips, by the discernment of the heart, fear, dread, humility, cheerfulness, purity, attendance on the Wise, cleaving to associates, discussion with disciples, sedateness, Scripture, Mishnah; by little business, little intercourse with the world, little pleasure, little sleep, little conversation, little laughter. By long suffering, a good heart, faith in the Wise, acceptance of chastisements, *by being* one that knows his place and rejoices in his portion, that makes a fence for his words, and claims not merit for himself, that is beloved, that loves God and loves mankind, that loves justice, that loves right courses, that loves reproof, and keeps aloof from honour, and puffs not his heart up with learning, and delights not in giving decisions, that takes up the yoke with his associate and judges him with a leaning to merit; that establishes him upon truth, and upon peace and does not exalt his heart over his study, that asks and answers, that hears and adds thereto, that learns with a view to teaching, that learns with a view to acting, that makes his teacher wise, that defines accurately what he hears, that repeats a thing in the name of him who said it. So thou hast learned: He who repeats a thing in the name of him who said it brings deliverance to the world, as it is said (Esth. 11. 22): — And Esther spake to the king in the name of Mordecai.

6. In praise of Torah, as compared with priesthood or royalty. Its excellence is extolled by enumerating the qualities necessary for its acquisition, in other words the distinguishing marks of the true hasid. It is especially this passage which gives to the whole chapter its alternative title the chapter on the acquisition of Torah, ‏פ׳ קנין תורה‎.

It has been suggested above, p. 150, that this long passage may originally have been continuous with VI. 1, which it closely resembles in style. If that were so, there would be the more reason for calling the whole chapter by its title of the acquisition of Torah, as that is the explicit subject of the present passage and is implied in the earlier portion, v. 1. There is in both the same looseness or even absence of grammatical construction; and the impression made by the earlier portion is strengthened in the present passage, viz: — that each represents not the words of one teacher but the contributions of many, as if a company of teachers and disciples had joined in composing a sort of panegyric in praise of Torah. One might even suppose that when first the idea was started in some Babylonian school of com-

piling a sixth chapter to Aboth the beginning was made by such a symposium amongst the members of that school. This is only a conjecture for
which no proof can be offered, nor any evidence except internal probability;
but at least it serves to show how such a remarkable passage may have
originated. The alternative would be to suppose an original passage, by some
one teacher, extensively interpolated till its former shape had been entirely
lost. The reader must judge for himself, and in either case the substance
of the passage remains unaltered.

The number 'forty eight' applied to the excellences of Torah is not adhered to, for the number actually reached in the series is fifty one. Possibly
three have been interpolated, but there is nothing to show which they are.

The various texts show some variation in the order of the several clauses,
as is only likely when there is little or no logical connexion between them.
The ideas expressed are familiar from the earlier chapters of Aboth, and
need no detailed explanation. For a further study of this passage see my
Pharisaism pp. 327—330.

The last clause, "So, thou hast learned &c." is a reference to what is
taught in the Talmud. The maxim "He who repeats a word in the name
of him who said it &c.", is found in b. Meg. 15ᵃ, Hull 104ᵇ, and Nidd. 19ᵇ;
in each case the Scripture proof is the same (Est. II. 22), but in the first
passage it is ascribed to R. Hanina, in the second to R. Josē, while in the
third it would seem to be a current saying which R. Josē only quoted. The
importance of the maxim depends on the principle that he who has disclosed some portion of the meaning of Torah should be individually remembered, and not forgotten in a mere general tradition. This perhaps
underlies the formula found everywhere in the Rabbinical literature, 'Rabbi
A. said in the name of Rabbi B.' &c.

7. גְּדוֹלָה תּוֹרָה שֶׁהִיא נוֹתֶנֶת חַיִּים לְעוֹשֶׂיהָ בָּעוֹלָם הַזֶּה וּבָעוֹלָם הַבָּא
שֶׁנֶּאֱמַר כִּי חַיִּים הֵם לְמֹצְאֵיהֶם וּלְכָל־בְּשָׂרוֹ מַרְפֵּא: וְאוֹמֵר רְפְאוּת תְּהִי
לְשָׁרֶּךָ וְשִׁקּוּי לְעַצְמוֹתֶךָ: וְאוֹמֵר עֵץ חַיִּים הִיא לַמַּחֲזִיקִים בָּהּ וְתֹמְכֶיהָ
מְאֻשָּׁר: וְאוֹמֵר כִּי לִוְיַת חֵן הֵם לְרֹאשֶׁךָ וַעֲנָקִים לְגַרְגְּרֹתֶיךָ: וְאוֹמֵר תִּתֵּן
לְרֹאשְׁךָ לִוְיַת חֵן עֲטֶרֶת תִּפְאֶרֶת תְּמַגְּנֶךָ: וְאוֹמֵר כִּי בִי יִרְבּוּ יָמֶיךָ וְיוֹסִיפוּ
לְךָ שְׁנוֹת חַיִּים: וְאוֹמֵר אֹרֶךְ יָמִים בִּימִינָהּ בִּשְׂמֹאולָהּ עֹשֶׁר וְכָבוֹד: וְאוֹמֵר
כִּי אֹרֶךְ יָמִים וּשְׁנוֹת חַיִּים וְשָׁלוֹם יוֹסִיפוּ לָךְ:

7. After תמגנך M. adds שלום :תיבוחתיה וכל :נימם דרכי דר־ביה ויאו.
ויאומר . . . וכבוד M. om.

7. Great is Torah for it gives to those that practise it life in
this world and in the world to come, as it is said (Prov. IV. 22):

'For they are life to those that find them and health to all their flesh'. And *Scripture* says (Prov. III. 8): — 'It shall be health to thy navel and marrow to thy bones'. And it says (*ib.* III. 18): — 'She shall be a tree of life to those that lay hold on her and happy is every one that retaineth her'. And it says (*ib.* I. 9): — 'They are a chaplet of grace for thy head and chains about thy neck'. And it says (*ib.* IV. 9): — 'She shall give to thy head a chaplet of grace, a crown of beauty shall she deliver thee'. And it says (*ib.* IX. 11): — 'For by me thy days shall be multiplied and they shall increase to thee years of life'. And it says (*ib.* III. 16): — 'Length of days are in her right hand, and in her left riches and honour'. And it says (*ib.* III. 2): — 'For length of days and years of life and peace shall they add to thee'.

7. This is virtually a continuation of the preceding passage in so far as the subject is still the praise of Torah. But all after the first clause consists of Scripture texts taken from the book of Proverbs. What is there said of Wisdom is here applied to Torah. No comment seems necessary.

8. רַבִּי שִׁמְעוֹן בֶּן־יְהוּדָה מִשּׁוּם רַבִּי שִׁמְעוֹן בֶּן־יוֹחַאי אוֹמֵר הַנּוֹי
וְהַכֹּחַ וְהָעוֹשֶׁר וְהַכָּבוֹד וְהַחָכְמָה וְהַזִּקְנָה וְהַשֵּׂיבָה וְהַבָּנִים נָאֶה לַצַּדִּיקִים
וְנָאֶה לָעוֹלָם שֶׁנֶּאֱמַר עֲטֶרֶת תִּפְאֶרֶת שֵׂיבָה בְּדֶרֶךְ צְדָקָה תִּמָּצֵא: וְאוֹמֵר
תִּפְאֶרֶת בַּחוּרִים כֹּחָם וַהֲדַר זְקֵנִים שֵׂיבָה: וְאוֹמֵר עֲטֶרֶת זְקֵנִים בְּנֵי
בָנִים וְתִפְאֶרֶת בָּנִים אֲבוֹתָם: וְאוֹמֵר וְחָפְרָה הַלְּבָנָה וּבוֹשָׁה הַחַמָּה כִּי
מָלַךְ יְיָ צְבָאוֹת בְּהַר צִיּוֹן וּבִירוּשָׁלַיִם וְנֶגֶד זְקֵנָיו כָּבוֹד: רַבִּי שִׁמְעוֹן בֶּן
מְנַסְיָא אוֹמֵר אֵלּוּ שֶׁבַע מִדּוֹת שֶׁשָּׁנוּ חֲכָמִים לַצַּדִּיקִים כֻּלָּם נִתְקַיְמוּ בְּרַבִּי
וּבְבָנָיו:

8. לצדיקים M. adds להם נאה: after תמצא the clauses in M. are transposed thus: "אומר עטרת זקנים וגו' ואומר תפארת בחורים כחם וגו' ואומר וחפרה הלבנה ובושה וגו'.

8. R. Simeon ben Jehudah said, in the name of R. Simeon ben Johai, Beauty and strength, riches, honour, wisdom, old age, grey hair and children are comely for the righteous and comely for the world as it is said (Prov. XVI. 31): — 'The hoary head is a crown of glory, it shall be found in the way of righteousness. And it says (*ib.* XX. 29): — 'The glory of young men is their strength and the beauty of old men is the hoary head'. And it says (*ib.* XVII. 6): — The crown of the old men are children's children, and

the ornament of children are the fathers'. And it says (Isa XXIV. 23):— 'Then the moon shall be confounded and the sun ashamed, for the Lord of Hosts shall reign in Mount Zion and in Jerusalem and before his ancients gloriously'.

R. Simeon ben Menasia said: These seven graces which the Wise have ascribed to the righteous were all fulfilled in Rabbi and in his sons.

8. An enumeration of seven (eight) possessions which are the outward adornments of the righteous. The contrast is remarkable between the teaching of this passage and the austere asceticism of v. 4. It would be hard for any righteous man to meet both sets of conditions, and perhaps the intention of including them both in this chapter is to teach that many can be righteous and all ought to be, but that few are called upon to be 'hasid'.

The passage is found in T. Sanh. XI. 8, and in a somewhat shorter form j. Sanh. XI. 4. In the former, the real author is R. Simeon, who is R. Simeon b. Johai, and whose words are reported by R. Simeon b. Jehudah. In the latter the saying is ascribed to R. Simeon b. Menasia, the same who in our passage applies the saying to Rabbi and his sons. It would seem that the compiler of the chapter in Aboth preferred the version in the Tosephta to that in the Palestinian Talmud, and there seems no reason to reject his opinion. R. Simeon b. Jehudah is known as the reporter of sayings by R. Simeon b. Johai and was presumably his disciple. R. Simeon b. Menasia may have been another disciple, and was evidently a devoted admirer of Rabbi. His remark is one of the few illustrations to be found in Aboth of the personal relations of the Rabbis with one another.

The difference between this passage and the style of the original Aboth is seen in the abundance of proof-texts, though these are alluded to in Tosephta and Jerushalmi.

The last proof-text, Isa XXIV. 23, is peculiar to Aboth, and its bearing on the subject in hand is not clear. Possibly the connecting link is the mention of 'elders', and the meaning may be that the crowning glory of elders is that they shall stand in the presence of the Lord when in the Messianic age he shall reign in Zion. But this is certainly far-fetched.

9. אָמַר רַבִּי יוֹסֵי בֶּן קִסְמָא פַּעַם אֶחָת הָיִיתִי מְהַלֵּךְ בַּדֶּרֶךְ וּפָגַע בִּי אָדָם אֶחָד וְנָתַן־לִי שָׁלוֹם וְהֶחֱזַרְתִּי לוֹ שָׁלוֹם אָמַר־לִי רַבִּי מֵאֵיזֶה מָקוֹם אַתָּה אָמַרְתִּי לוֹ מֵעִיר גְּדוֹלָה שֶׁל חֲכָמִים וְשֶׁל סוֹפְרִים אָנִי אָמַר לִי רַבִּי רְצוֹנְךָ שֶׁתָּדוּר עִמָּנוּ בִּמְקוֹמֵנוּ וַאֲנִי אֶתֵּן לְךָ אֶלֶף אֲלָפִים דִּינְרֵי זָהָב וַאֲבָנִים טוֹבוֹת וּמַרְגָּלִיּוֹת אָמַרְתִּי לוֹ אִם אַתָּה נוֹתֵן לִי כָּל־כֶּסֶף וְזָהָב וַאֲבָנִים

טוֹבוֹת וּמַרְגָּלִיּוֹת שֶׁבָּעוֹלָם אֵינֵי דָר אֶלָּא בִּמְקוֹם תּוֹרָה וְכֵן כָּתוּב בְּסֵפֶר
תְּהִלִּים עַל יְדֵי דָוִד מֶלֶךְ יִשְׂרָאֵל טוֹב לִי תוֹרַת פִּיךָ מֵאַלְפֵי זָהָב וָכָסֶף:
וְלֹא עוֹד שֶׁבִּשְׁעַת פְּטִירָתוֹ שֶׁל אָדָם אֵין מְלַוִּין לוֹ לְאָדָם לֹא כֶסֶף וְלֹא
זָהָב וְלֹא אֲבָנִים טוֹבוֹת וּמַרְגָּלִיּוֹת אֶלָּא תוֹרָה וּמַעֲשִׂים טוֹבִים בִּלְבָד
שֶׁנֶּאֱמַר בְּהִתְהַלֶּכְךָ תַּנְחֶה אוֹתָךְ בְּשָׁכְבְּךָ תִּשְׁמֹר עָלֶיךָ וַהֲקִיצוֹתָ הִיא
תְשִׂיחֶךָ: בְּהִתְהַלֶּכְךָ תַּנְחֶה אוֹתָךְ בָּעוֹלָם הַזֶּה בְּשָׁכְבְּךָ תִּשְׁמֹר עָלֶיךָ בַּקֶּבֶר
וַהֲקִיצוֹתָ הִיא תְשִׂיחֶךָ לָעוֹלָם הַבָּא. וְאוֹמֵר לִי הַכֶּסֶף וְלִי הַזָּהָב נְאֻם
יְיָ צְבָאוֹת:

9. עמנו .M ;אצלנו; מרגליות . . . ואבנים twice M. om.
שנ׳ .M adds ;מצירנו ב .M כתוב; ישראל . . . על ידי.
א לי מפני מה אמרת לי כך. אמרתי לו לפי reads .M .ולא עוד . . . של אדם
שכשהאדם נפטר מן העולם וגו׳.
ואומר לי . . . הצבאות .M. omit.

9. R. Jose ben Kisma said: Once I was walking by the way
and there met me a man, and he greeted me and I greeted him
again. He said to me Rabbi whence comest thou? I said to him
From a great city of wise men and scribes am I. He said to me
Rabbi, if it please thee to dwell with us in our place I will give
thee a thousand thousand gold 'dinars' and precious stones and
pearls. I said to him If thou wert giving me all the silver and
gold and precious stones and pearls that are in the world I would
not dwell save in a place of Torah; and thus it is written in the
Book of Psalms, by the hand of David King of Israel, (Ps. CXIX. 72):—
'The Torah of thy mouth is better unto me than thousands of gold
and silver'. And not only so, but in the hour of a man's death
it is neither silver nor gold nor precious stones nor pearls which
accompany him but Torah and good works only, as it is said
(Prov. VI. 22):— 'When thou walkest it shall lead thee; when thou
liest down it shall watch over thee, and when thou wakest it shall
talk with thee'. 'When thou walkest it shall lead thee' — in this
world. 'When thou liest down it shall watch over thee' — in the
grave. 'When thou wakest it shall talk with thee', — in the world
to come. And it says (Hagg. II. 8):— "The silver is Mine and the
gold is Mine, saith the Lord of Hosts".

9. This passage is in form a personal reminiscence by a well
known teacher; but the substance of it is the praise of Torah, as
throughout this chapter, and it passes from the form of anecdote

to the more usual one of homily supported by proof-texts. The especial point of the reported saying of the Rabbi is the incomparable worth of the Torah; and probably only the earlier part of the passage is due to him, the later clauses with the proof-texts being added by the compiler.

R. Josē b. Kisma was a contemporary and friend of R. Ḥananjah b. Teradion, (III. 3 above), and what is much more remarkable was in high favour with the Roman officials in Cæsarea (Philippi) where he lived and died (b. A. Zar. 18ᵃ). The Hadrianic persecution had already begun before his death, but apparently he died a natural death unmolested, and it is said that his funeral was attended by the "great ones of Rome". There are no data by which to determine the length of his life. If the anecdote be historical, and not a homiletic invention, the incident must have taken place some time before the Bar Cocheba war, since afterwards there was no safe dwelling place for wise men and Scribes. Probably Jabneh is denoted by the 'great city'; if not great in size, it was the home and centre of all that was greatest in Jewish life in the period between the fall of Jerusalem and the last war.

10. חֲמִשָּׁה קִנְיָנִים קָנָה הַקָּדוֹשׁ בָּרוּךְ הוּא בְּעוֹלָמוֹ וְאֵלּוּ הֵן תּוֹרָה
קִנְיָן אֶחָד שָׁמַיִם וָאָרֶץ קִנְיָן אֶחָד אַבְרָהָם קִנְיָן אֶחָד יִשְׂרָאֵל קִנְיָן אֶחָד
בֵּית הַמִּקְדָּשׁ קִנְיָן אֶחָד: תּוֹרָה מִנַּיִן דִּכְתִיב יְיָ קָנָנִי רֵאשִׁית דַּרְכּוֹ קֶדֶם
מִפְעָלָיו מֵאָז: שָׁמַיִם וָאָרֶץ מִנַּיִן דִּכְתִיב כֹּה אָמַר יְיָ הַשָּׁמַיִם כִּסְאִי וְהָאָרֶץ
הֲדֹם רַגְלָי אֵי־זֶה בַיִת אֲשֶׁר תִּבְנוּ לִי וְאֵי־זֶה מָקוֹם מְנוּחָתִי: וְאוֹמֵר מָה
רַבּוּ מַעֲשֶׂיךָ יְיָ כֻּלָּם בְּחָכְמָה עָשִׂיתָ מָלְאָה הָאָרֶץ קִנְיָנֶךָ: אַבְרָהָם מִנַּיִן
דִּכְתִיב וַיְבָרְכֵהוּ וַיֹּאמַר בָּרוּךְ אַבְרָם לְאֵל עֶלְיוֹן קֹנֵה שָׁמַיִם וָאָרֶץ: יִשְׂרָאֵל
מִנַּיִן דִּכְתִיב עַד יַעֲבֹר עַמְּךָ יְיָ עַד יַעֲבֹר עַם זוּ קָנִיתָ: וְאוֹמֵר לִקְדוֹשִׁים
אֲשֶׁר בָּאָרֶץ הֵמָּה וְאַדִּירֵי כָּל־חֶפְצִי־בָם: בֵּית הַמִּקְדָּשׁ מִנַּיִן דִּכְתִיב
מָכוֹן לְשִׁבְתְּךָ פָּעַלְתָּ יְיָ מִקְדָּשׁ אֲדֹנָי כּוֹנְנוּ יָדֶיךָ: וְאוֹמֵר וַיְבִיאֵם אֶל גְּבוּל
קָדְשׁוֹ הַר זֶה קָנְתָה יְמִינוֹ:

10. Five possessions hath the Holy One, blessed be He, acquired in His World, and these are they:— Torah is one posses-

sion, heaven and earth is one possession, Abraham is one possession, Israel is one possession, the house of the Sanctuary is one
possession. Whence *is this concerning* Torah? As it is written (Prov.
VIII. 22): — 'The Lord possessed me in the beginning of His way,
before His works of old'. Whence *concerning* heaven and earth?
As it is written (Isa LXVI. 1): — Thus saith the Lord, the heavens
are My throne and the earth is My footstool. What manner of
house will ye build for Me and what place is My rest'? And it
says (Ps. CIV. 24): — 'How manifold are Thy works, O Lord, in
wisdom hast Thou made them all, the earth is full of Thy possessions'. Whence *concerning* Abraham? As it is written (Gen. XIV.
19):—'And He blessed him and said Blessed be Abraham of God
Most High, possessor of heaven and earth'. Whence *concerning*
Israel? As it is written (Exod. XV. 16): — 'Till Thy people pass
over, O Lord, till this people pass over which Thou hast possessed'.
And it says (Ps. XVI. 3): — 'As for the saints that are in the earth,
they are the excellent ones in whom is all My delight'. Whence
concerning the House of the Sanctuary? As it is written (Exod.
XV. 17): — 'The place O Lord which Thou hast made to dwell
in, the Sanctuary O Lord which Thy hands have prepared'. And
it says (Ps. LXXVIII. 54): — 'And He brought them to the border
of his Sanctuary, this mountain which His right hand hath possessed'.

10. A numerical series somewhat after the manner of those in
ch. V, all turning upon the thought that God in some special
manner possessed, or acquired, or founded or declared himself the
lord of, certain things or institutions or persons. All things were
created by him, but the five here mentioned he claimed especially
as his own. The first is Torah, and this probably led the compiler to include the whole passage in this chapter, with which it
has not otherwise any special connexion.

This passage is an expansion of older material. The same thought is
found in Siphrē II, § 311, where the 'things' are three, — Torah, Israel and
the Sanctuary; also in Mechilta Beshall. p. 43[a, b] where 'heaven and earth'
are added to the list. In b. Pes. 87[b] the same four are mentioned, in a
haggadic exposition by R. Johanan, but apparently as an interpolation. The
original series was probably suggested by a comparison of the texts which
mentioned קנין, or קנה, in connexion with God. The addition of Abraham
was presumably due to the compiler of this chapter, and is not quite in
keeping with the other four. For the proof-text quoted in support does not
say that God 'possessed' Abraham, but invokes upon him the blessing of
God who is the possessor of heaven and earth.

יא. כֹּל מַה שֶּׁבָּרָא הַקָּדוֹשׁ בָּרוּךְ הוּא בְּעוֹלָמוֹ לֹא בְרָאוֹ אֶלָּא לִכְבוֹדוֹ
שֶׁנֶּאֱמַר כֹּל הַנִּקְרָא בִשְׁמִי וְלִכְבוֹדִי בְּרָאתִיו יְצַרְתִּיו אַף עֲשִׂיתִיו: וְאוֹמֵר ‎|‎ יְיָ
יִמְלֹךְ לְעֹלָם וָעֶד:

רַבִּי חֲנַנְיָא בֶּן עֲקַשְׁיָא אוֹמֵר רָצָה הַקָּדוֹשׁ בָּרוּךְ הוּא לְזַכּוֹת אֶת יִשְׂרָאֵל לְפִיכָךְ
הִרְבָּה לָהֶם תּוֹרָה וּמִצְוֹת שֶׁנֶּאֱמַר יְיָ חָפֵץ לְמַעַן צִדְקוֹ יַגְדִּיל תּוֹרָה וְיַאְדִּיר:

11. לא בראו ... כל מה M. וכולם לא בראם.
M. om. ... ואומר יי ... ועד
In place of חנניא וגו' ר' M. has בן בג בג או' as in v. 25, but not בן הא הא.

11. All which the Holy One, blessed be He, created in His
world He created not except for His glory as it is said (Isa
XLIII. 7): — 'Every thing that is called by my name, and that I
have created for my glory, I have formed it, yea I have made it'.
And it says (Exod. XV. 18): — 'The Lord shall reign for ever and
ever'.

R. Hanania ben Akashia said 'It pleased the Holy One Blessed
be He, to make Israel able to aquire merit. Therefore He multiplied to them Torah and precepts, as it is said (Isa XLII. 21): —
'It pleased the Lord, for his righteousness sake to magnify the
Torah and make it honourable'.

11. Following on the thought of the preceding passage the present
one utters the thought that all creation shows forth the glory of
the Creator, and was formed for that purpose. The Creator is the
Eternal, Sovereign Lord of all. This is as it were a doxology to close
the chapter, and was probably the original ending. For liturgical
purpose a verse was added on containing a saying by R. Hanania
b. Akashia, a teacher of unknown date, expressing what is the
central thought of Pharisaism, that God gave to Israel Torah and
precepts in order to enable his people to acquire merit, by giving
them the opportunity of abundant service and perfect obedience.
This verse does not belong to Aboth, even to the last chapter. In
the prayer books it is repeated at the end of each chapter, just as
the verse "All Israel have a portion in the world to come" is prefixed to each chapter.

CHRONOLOGICAL TABLE

of the Teachers named in Pirkē Aboth.

The dates assigned are based on the evidence given in the commentary under the several names.
All the dates are of the common era (C. E.) except those marked B. C.

NAME	ABOTH	APPROXIMATE DATE
ABTALION.	I. 10. 11.	. . . 50 B. C. . . .
AKABIAH b. Mahalalel.	III. 1.	contemporary with Hillel.
AKIBA b. Joseph.	III. 17.18.19. 20.	50?—134.
ANTIGONOS of Socho.	I. 3.	. . . 250? B. C.
AZAI, Simeon b.	IV. 2.	. . . 138.
BAG-BAG, b.	V. 25.	contemporary with Hillel.
DOSA b. Harchinas.	III. 14.	10?—90?
DOSTHAI b. Jannai.	III. 10.	end of 2nd—beginning of 3rd century.
ELEAZAR b. Arach.	II. 10. 19.	. . . 80 . . .
— b. Azariah.	III. 21.	70?—before 135.
— Hisma.	III. 23.	. . . 96 . . .
— ha-Kappar.	IV. 28.	end of 2nd century.
— ha-Modi'i.	III. 15.	. . . 80—135.
— b. Shammua.	IV. 15.	115?—190?
— of Bartotha.	III. 8.	circa 100.
ELIEZER b. Horkenos.	II. 10. 15.	40?—117.
— b. Jacob.	IV. 13.	. . . 135 . . .
ELISHA b. Abujah.	IV. 25.	80?—150?
GAMLIEL I.	I. 16.	. . . before 68.
— b. Rabbi.	II. 2.	circa 200.
HALAPHTA b. Dosa.	III. 7.	. . . 135 . . .
HANANIAH b. Teradion.	III. 3.	. . . —135.
HANINA b. Dosa.	III. 11.	. . . 65—80 . . .
— b. Hachinai.	III. 5.	80?—135.
— deputy of the Priests.	III. 2.	20?—70 . . .
HE-HE, b.	V. 26.	contemporary with Hillel.
HILLEL.	I. 12.13.14. II. 5. 6. 7. 8. (IV. 7).	end of last century B. C.
ISHMAEL (b. Elisha)·	III. 16.	60?—140?
— b. Johanan b. Berokah.	IV. 6.	. . . 140 . . .
— b. Josē.	IV. 9.	135?—210?
JACOB.	III. 9.	. . . 120 . . .
JANNAI.	IV. 19.	middle of 2nd century.

NAME	ABOTH	APPROXIMATE DATE
JEHOSHUA b. Hananiah.	II. 10. 16.	50—before 135.
— b. Perahiah.	I. 6.	end of 2ⁿᵈ century B. C.
JEHUDAH (b. Illai).	IV. 16.	100?—180.
— b. Tabbai.	I. 8.	beginning of last century B C.
— b. Tema.	V. 23.	date unknown.
JOHANAN b. Berokah.	IV. 5.	. . . 80—135.
— ha-Sandelar.	IV. 14.	. . . 120—140 . . .
— b. Zaccai.	II.9.10.11.12.13.	1?—80?
JONATHAN.	IV. 11.	. . . 138 . . .
JOSE (b. Halaphta).	IV. 8.	97?—180?
— ha-Cohen.	II. 10. 17.	. . . 80 . . .
— b. Jehudah.	IV. 26.	. . . 160 . . .
— b. Joezer.	I. 4.	. . . 162 B. C. . . .
— b. Johanan.	I. 4.	. . . 162 B. C. . . .
LEVITAS. of Jabneh.	IV. 4.	date unknown.
MATTITHIA b. Harash	IV. 20.	120
MEIR.	IV. 12. VI. 1.	110?—175?
NEHORAI.	IV. 18.	. . . 117—140 . . .
NEHUNIAH b. ha-Kanah.	III. 6.	. . . 30?—90 . . .
NITTAI ha-Arbeli.	I. 6.	end of 2ⁿᵈ century B. C.
RABBI (Jehudah ha-Kadosh, ha-Nasi).	II. 1. IV. 27.	135—219.
SAMUEL ha Katan, (the Small)	IV. 24.	10? B. C.—80.
SHAMMAI.	I. 12. 15.	end of last century B. C.
SHEMAIAH.	I. 10. 11.	. . . 50 B. C. . . .
SIMEON	I. 17.	date unknown
SIMEON b. Eleazar.	IV. 23.	140?—215.
— b. Gamliel (I).	I. 18.	10? B. C.—66.
— b. Johai.	III. 4. IV. 17.	100?—160.
— b. Nathaniel.	II. 10. 18.	50?—80 . . .
— b. Shetah.	I. 8.	beginning of last century B. C.
— the Just.	I. 2.	. . . 270 B. C.
TARPHON.	II. 20.	46?—117.
ZADOK.	IV. 7.	. . . 30—90 . . .
ZOMA, (Simeon) b.	IV. 1.	end of first century.

INDICES

GENERAL SUBJECTS.

INDEX OF NAMES.

RABBINICAL PASSAGES CITED.

OLD TESTAMENT PASSAGES.

Lam. III. 28.	66.	Joel II. 13.	59.
Isa. X. 5.	65.	Amos IX. 6.	71.
XXIV. 23.	160.		
XXVIII. 8.	68.	Hagg. II. 8.	161.
XLII. 21.	164.		
XLIII. 7.	164.	Zech. VII. 12.	130.
LX. 21.	19.	VIII. 16.	37. 38.
LXVI. 1.	163.		
Jer. XVII. 1.	130.	Mal. II. 6.	32.
6. 8.	92.	III. 16.	42. 66. 71. 154.
Ezek. III. 9.	130.	Ecclus. VII. 17.	99 .
XVI. 49.	134.	XXXVIII. 24.	47.
XXXIII. 30.	154.		
XLI. 22.	68.	1 Macc. VII. 16.	25.